Where to wა

Switzerland

Marco Sacchi, Peter Rüegg, Jacques Laesser

Translated by Michael Wilson

Supported by Schweizer Vogelschutz SVS – BirdLife Switzerland

BirdLife®
INTERNATIONAL
SVS – BirdLife Switzerland

Christopher Helm
A & C Black · London

© 1999 Marco Sacchi, Peter Rüegg, and Jaques Laesser

Christopher Helm (Publishers) Ltd, a subsidiary of
A & C Black (Publishers) Ltd, 35 Bedford Row, London WC1R 4JH

0-7136-5183-0

A CIP catalogue record for this book
is available from the British Library

First published in Switzerland in 1998 as *Vögel beobachten in der Schweiz*
by Ott Verlag, Thun

Printed and bound in Great Britain by The Cromwell Press, Trowbridge

CONTENTS

Contents

FOREWORD

The marvellous variety of birds, their size, shape and plumage coloration fascinates both lay people and experienced ornithologists. No other vertebrate group is as easy to observe as birds, most of which are active during the daytime. The phenomenon of bird migration fills us with astonishment and a sense of awe. It is not surprising therefore that birdwatching or, in current jargon, birding, continues to increase in popularity. However, this very same wave of enthusiasm also has hidden dangers for the few sites which have remained more or less unspoilt. In Switzerland, the majority of the most attractive and most-visited birdwatching sites are situated in the protected areas of the Central Plateau. So why a book which sets out to introduce the reader to these very same places? Are yet more people to be encouraged to make the pilgrimage to these protected areas? Can the reserves cope with the increase in visitor numbers? We, the authors, are aware that a book like this gives rise to controversy. The much-discussed conflict about the role of reserves is something with which we were also much preoccupied: must people be completely excluded from nature reserves or should measures be taken to enable them to visit these natural oases? Both sides of the argument need to be considered: certain sites would be destroyed by an increase in the number of visitors, while others lend themselves well to showing people some of the wonders of the natural world. Unfortunately, in Switzerland, we are still in the very early stages of learning how properly to manage visitors, and yet, if you want to win over future generations for nature conservation, then you have to show clearly what will be lost if nothing is done to protect and conserve wildlife and wildlife habitats. Popularizing birdwatching according to the motto 'What I know, I protect' is one tool to be used to that end. We are, of course, guided by the following rules:

• Birdwatchers are not to be directed to the most sensitive areas. No information is given on the location of grouse leks or the nesting-places of endangered species.
• Recommendations are made with the aim of channelling the stream of visitors and guiding people through the sites without creating problems (for example, only on existing paths and tracks, sites where the management of visitors is really exemplary).
• Special mention is made of the use of public transport to get to the sites dealt with.

This is the first book of its kind for Switzerland and that means there is a chance of bringing about important changes. The problems are known, yet visitor management at the sites has not been improved. Most of the places still have no hides or other facilities which would allow visitors to watch the birds without disturbing them. With the help of the specific and detailed information presented in the book, this situation can be improved and without the need to wag a threatening finger at visitors and to spoil the enjoyment they derive from observing nature.

ACKNOWLEDGEMENTS

We should like to thank especially our sponsors, who made possible the publication of this book. For generous financial support, we thank:

- Leica Camera AG, Nidau
- Migros Kulturprozent
- Finance Department of the canton of Zürich, Fund for Charitable Purposes
- Finance Department of the canton of Lucerne
- Building Works Department of the canton of Aargau
- Governing Council of the canton of Schwyz, Lottery Fund
- Lottery Fund of Police and Military Department, the canton of Bern

We should like to thank several ornithologists who have assisted us with the project and shown so much understanding, interest and patience. Our special thanks go to Stefan Wassmer for his many valuable suggestions and for the detailed information he supplied. Also to Bertrand Posse from whose profound knowledge of Western Switzerland we derived so much benefit. His critical checking of parts of the manuscript was most helpful to us. The support of Werner Müller from Schweizer Vogelschutz SVS—BirdLife Switzerland was decisive in getting the book published. Hans Schmid of Vogelwarte Sempach (The Swiss Institute of Ornithology) gave us valuable advice and active support. We were able to draw on his rich fund of experience and his detailed knowledge to write several of the site accounts. We also extend our thanks to Walter Wettstein for his energetic support in the field and for critically checking individual chapters in the book.

We owe a particular debt of gratitude to those ornithologists who provided us with the kind of detailed information which was indispensable to the writing of individual site accounts and are especially grateful to the following for being so open and generous in this particular role: Adrian Aebischer, Michel Baudraz, Pierre Charvoz, Flurin Filli, Anatole Gerber, Adrian Jordi, Christoph Katzenmaier, Matthias Kestenholz, Peter Knaus, Roberto Lardelli, Peter Lustenberger, Lionel Maumary, Mathis Müller, Bertrand Posse, Benoît Renevey, Bruno Schelbert, Hans Schmid, Stéphane Theytaz, Christoph Vogel, Bernard Volet, Stefan Wassmer, Martin Weggler, André Weiss and Laurent Willenegger.

Various people have given us energetic support during the project and have contributed to this site-guide in a variety of ways. We offer our thanks to all of them here: Laudo Albrecht, Eric Altorfer, Christine Andrey, Olivier Biber, Jean-Daniel Blant, Hugues Dupuich, Christa Glauser, Laurent Gogniat, Jérôme Gremaud, Alessia Guggisberg, Adrian Jordi, Michel Juillard, Fabien Klötzli, Valère Martin, Christian Monnerat, Rachel Muheim, Bertrand Posse, Verena Schatanek, Manuel Schweizer, Bernard Volet, Martina Walser and Beat Wartmann.

Translator's acknowledgements

I am most grateful to Marco Sacchi for his patience and good humour and for the detailed explanations he sent in response to my many queries. I should also like to thank Professor Christopher Perrins, Director of the Edward Grey Institute, Oxford University and Linda Birch of the EGI's Alexander Library for continuing kindness and support, as well as Stella Brecknell (Hope Library, Oxford University), Melanie Heath (BirdLife International), Brian Hillcoat and Dorothy Vincent, for helping me by providing information on a variety of topics.

Michael Wilson

INTRODUCTION

Where birds occur is influenced by several different factors. Topographical or climatic conditions can determine the distribution of a species just as much as can the presence of a particular plant community. The following sections give a survey of the most important prevailing conditions which influence to a considerable extent the composition of Switzerland's bird fauna.

Geography

Switzerland is a land-locked country with a total surface area of a little over 41,000 square km. The shortest distances to the North Sea measure around 500 km, to the Mediterranean 155 km. In the west, the country borders on France, in the north, on Germany. Its eastern neighbours are Austria and Liechtenstein. In the south, Switzerland shares a common border with Italy.

There are three large geographical regions formed by the main topographical units: the Jura mountains, the Central Plateau (*Mittelland* in German) and the Alps. These extend as more or less parallel belts from southwest to northeast, from Geneva (Genève, Genf) as far as Lake Constance (*Bodensee* in German).

*Being a land of so many different landscape types, Switzerland has a correspondingly rich and diverse range of bird species
(Photo: Schweizer Vogelschutz SVS, Zürich)*

The Jura is a range of low mountains, which were folded upwards from Jurassic and Cretaceous rock strata at roughly the same time as the Alps. Two strikingly different forms are distinguished: the Chain or Folded Jura (*Kettenjura*) and the Tabular Jura (*Tafeljura*). The first of these follows the western border of Switzerland in several parallel chains and then bends round in a more easterly direction. The highest point is the Crêt de la Neige (1723 m) on the French side near Geneva. The easternmost outlier of the Chain Jura, the Lägern, lies just within the canton of Zürich. Joined to the northeast Chain Jura in the north is the Tabular Jura which is composed of more or less fractured massifs of unfolded Jurassic rocks. This formation extends from the cantons of Basel and Aargau to Schaffhausen (Randen), where it reaches its highest point (926 m).

Between the Alps and the Jura lies the Central Plateau. This is narrow where it begins near Geneva, but finally extends as a band some 40 to 50 km wide between Lake Geneva (Lac Léman, Genfersee) and Lake Constance. The lower-lying drainage channel or gully of the Plateau, which follows the Jura, drops gradually from southwest to northeast. The Plateau is mostly undulating hill country, which also has some almost alpine massifs (Napf, Tössbergland). The highest elevation, at around 1400 m, lies in the Napf region, while the lowest point, the so-called Wassertor ('Watergate') near Brugg (Aargau), is at around 350 m. From Lake Bienne (Lac de Bienne, Bielersee) onwards, it is drained by the Aare catchment, most of the rivers of the Central Plateau being tributaries of that river. Typical ice-age relicts are the numerous lakes. Large parts of the Plateau are now densely populated and practically nothing remains of the original vegetation, much of the land being intensively farmed.

The Alps cover approximately 60 percent of Switzerland and are thus the country's main landscape feature. They have a significant influence on climate and hydrography in other parts of the country. The deep west-to-east furrow of the Rhône and Rhine valleys divides the Alps clearly into a northern and a southern part. The Northern Alps comprise the Vaud, Fribourg, Bernese, Central Swiss, Glarus and St Gallen Alps, while the Southern Alps are made up of the Valais, Ticino and part of the Grisons Alps. A further part of the Grisons Alps belongs to the Eastern Alps which, in addition, are less high than the western mountains. While the highest peaks of the Western Alps attain heights of over 4600 m, those in the east barely reach 4000 m. Man has been able to make far less impact on the wild regions of the Alps than in other parts of Switzerland, so that the original vegetation has survived largely intact.

The Swiss climate

The great contrasts in landscape, with the highest Alpine peaks on the one side and typical plains in the Central Plateau on the other, have shaped the climate of Switzerland. Conditions often change abruptly within a very small area. However, the strongest influence on the country is exerted, as would be expected from the geographical latitude and the short distance separating Switzerland from the Atlantic, by the **oceanic climate**. A balanced temperature pattern without extreme highs and lows and balanced precipitation levels, with an average of 1000–2000 mm during the year—this is how you would briefly describe the typical climate of the Central Plateau as it manifests itself in the area between Lake Geneva and Lake Constance. Areas lying in the rain shadow of an obstacle such as a mountain or chain of hills will, however, receive far less precipitation (for example, the Lake Geneva basin, the Randen near Schaffhausen). On the northern fringe of the Alps, the precipitation increases and even amounts to over 2000 mm. The air cools by an average of 0.6°C for every hundred metres of altitude.

The so-called **insubrian climate** on the south side of the Alps already has some features characteristic of the Mediterranean climate. Temperatures are generally milder and the sun shines more frequently than on the north side. Despite this, warm and humid Mediterranean air brings astonishingly large amounts of precipitation to Ticino, most of this falling as downpours in violent summer thunderstorms. In winter, on the other hand, quite long periods of dry weather occur.

The Engadine and Valais are among the driest regions in Switzerland. These valleys lie in the rain shadow of high mountains which largely hold back the precipitation. Annual rainfall is between 600 and 800 mm. The sky thus more often remains cloudless than in other regions. High insolation during the day and the fact that heat is lost by radiation under clear skies at night encourages marked daily and seasonal temperature fluctuations. This **continental** climate is also the reason why the tree-line comes to lie far higher up than in the Northern Alps. These dry valleys are among the richest parts of Switzerland, in respect of both their wildlife and their plants.

Vegetation

In Switzerland, a range of different plant communities has developed, the particular character of each depending on type of land management, climate, soil and altitude. As these communities in turn influence the distribution of the country's birds, they will be briefly described below.

The **colline zone** comprises the lowest levels up to 600 m in the Jura and the Central Plateau, up to 700 m in the Central Alps and up to 800 m on their southern slopes. The characteristic forests are mixed broadleaf and these are of importance for a wide range of bird species. With over 50 breeding species, the typical oak-hornbeam forests of this zone are among the most species-rich habitats in Switzerland. However, beech dominates over other tree species and often forms pure stands. Above the colline zone lies the **montane zone**, which reaches up to 1200 m in the Jura and on the northern edge of the Alps, up to 1400 m in the Central Alps and to 1700 m in the south. Numerous forest communities of beech and beech mixed with spruce dominate the zone. Above this, in the **subalpine zone**, Norway spruce forms almost pure stands up to the tree-line. At this limit, which lies at just 1800 m in the Northern and at 1900 m in the Southern Alps, the forest gradually breaks up and, after a transition zone ('krummholz zone'), gives way to alpine grassland. In many places, the tree-line is now lower than it was formerly. The development of hay meadows and pasture for grazing cattle as well as the exploitation of the forest for building materials and fuel have driven the forest downhill by around 100 to 200 m. Dwarf-shrub communities still mark the original extent of the wooded area. In the central Alpine valleys, with their 'forest-friendly' climate, Arolla pine and larch form continuous tracts of forest above the spruce belt. This **supra-subalpine zone** reaches up to altitudes of 2400 m. The woods are often of pure larch as man selectively felled the Arolla pine in order to improve the grazing and to acquire building timber.

Just about one-third of the land surface of Switzerland lies in the **alpine zone** above 1800 m. Alpine short-grass communities and scree often form a colourful mosaic. With increasing altitude, the unbroken turf cover gradually becomes sparse, with just a few patches of vegetation and then only isolated remnants. The uppermost, **nivale zone** is almost devoid of vegetation and only mosses and lichens thrive, apart from a few higher plants in places with a favourable micro-climate (south-facing slopes).

Originally, more or less the entire land surface of Switzerland was covered by woodland. The only treeless areas were lakes, shallow lake-margins subject to silting-up and successive invasion by vegetation, peatbogs or mires, special dry localities (short, steppe-type grassland) or clearings caused by natural elements such as storms and gales. The impact of ungulates like the red deer and, before its extinction, the aurochs, possibly gave rise to savanna-like, open wooded steppes. However, it was man who initiated large-scale forest clearance, laid out fields and kept economically-useful animals. Earlier generations thus unwittingly created space for many different species of birds which were originally unknown in Switzerland or occurred there in only small numbers. Many now critically-endangered and valuable habitats owe their existence to the fact that they have been managed extensively. Unimproved mesobromion meadows and fenland where sedge, etc. is cut for litter would become overgrown again if regular mowing did not prevent scrub and trees from appearing. Belts of orchards were planted around settlements which eventually satisfied the demand for various types of fruit. All of these different landscape elements contribute to the creation of a rich and diverse bird fauna which is now regarded as typical.

Transport

One of the factors determining the choice of sites described in this book was the question of accessibility by public transport and it therefore makes sense to give special emphasis to this environmentally-friendly and stress-free form of travel in a guide of this kind. There follows a short summary of the most important methods of transport:

Train: the Swiss rail network measures over 5000 km; even some of the smaller towns and villages often have a rail link. Alongside the Schweizerische Bundesbahn or SBB for short (Swiss Federal Railways), there are 65 private rail companies, some of them operating on narrow-gauge tracks. The largest is the Rhätische Bahn in the canton of Graubünden (the Grisons).

Postbus: the network of the 660 state-run postbus services, which follow postal routes, measures over 8000 km. In the mountains and in various thinly-populated areas, the postbus is a reliable form of transport.

In addition, there are about 650 mostly privately-run **cable cars** and **rack (cogwheel) railways** as well as numerous shipping lines.

Together, these forms of transport constitute the densest and most efficient public transport system in the world. Connections are in most cases well-coordinated and waiting times are not excessive. Postbuses, most private rail companies and some cable cars and rack railways operate a shared fares policy with Swiss Federal Railways (SBB).

Swiss residents can travel cheaper by purchasing a one-day travel card, a half-fare card or a general season ticket. For visitors from abroad, there are different kinds of flat-rate tickets, such as the Swiss

Pass, the Swiss Flexi Pass, the Swiss Card, the STS Family Card or the special Half-Fare Travel Card valid for one month.

Bicycles can be hired at almost every rail station in Switzerland. The larger stations usually have quite a large number of bicycles available for hire. In the case of smaller stations and during holiday times, we recommend that you make a booking for your particular destination several days in advance. It is, of course, possible to hand in your bike at station ticket-offices or load it onto the train yourself. The second alternative is very much to be recommended for day trips.

Nature and bird conservation in Switzerland

In the second half of the 20th century, the essential conditions for life of many species of birds have deteriorated alarmingly. Some formerly widespread or even common species are already extinct or verging on extinction. Contributory factors include the intensification and mechanization of agriculture, almost unlimited building activity (above all, an expansion of the road network), and the razzmatazz associated with the recreation business and tourism which is increasingly overstepping all bounds, so that not even the remotest regions are safe from invasion. The inevitable consequence of this is the fact that almost half of all Switzerland's breeding birds are now on the Red List. Species such as Hoopoe and Little Owl, formerly so widely distributed, are in danger of becoming extinct. Snipe and Great Grey Shrike have largely disappeared as breeding birds. A number of different institutions, organizations, government departments and research institutes are working to protect and conserve birds and their habitats. The Schweizer Vogelschutz SVS—BirdLife Switzerland (Swiss Association for the Protection of Birds) is the national association of local-community (i.e. commune) nature conservation clubs which are joined together in cantonal associations and, at the same time, it is the BirdLife Partner for Switzerland. Other societies, active in different regions of the country, are the Ala (Schweizerische Gesellschaft für Vogelkunde und Vogelschutz, German-speaking Switzerland), Ficedula (Società pro avifauna della Svizzera italiana; Southern Switzerland) and Nos Oiseaux (Société romande pour l'étude et la protection des oiseaux; Western Switzerland). Both Ala and Ficedula are members of the SVS. The Schweizerische Vogelwarte in Sempach is the foremost ornithological research institute in Switzerland (for addresses, see p. 181). Other large organizations concerned with nature conservation such as Pro Natura and WWF Switzerland also invest considerable sums of money in order to secure the future of valuable wildlife sites and to introduce extensive forms of land-use throughout the countryside. Although much has been achieved, conditions for birds in Switzerland continue to deteriorate. Responsible and committed birdwatchers ought therefore to lend their support to the efforts of the organizations listed (see p. 181), whether that be by becoming a member, making a donation, or actively working for conservation.

Equipment for birders

The most important item is binoculars. Pay attention to the light-gathering power and the sharpness of the image, especially around the edges. Someone just starting out in birding can begin with a cheaper pair, but most will change to one of the top models later, for example, a Leica glass or one from one of the other leading makers of optical equipment.

At most sites, it's worth taking a telescope with you. The comments made about binoculars (see above) also apply to scopes. A stable tripod is absolutely essential.

From the large number of field and identification guides available, we especially recommend that by Svensson *et al*—*Collins Birds of Britain and Europe*, published by HarperCollins. Waterproof clothing, sturdy and comfortable footwear and protection against the sun, i.e. sunscreen, sun-glasses and a hat, are important for most birding trips. Especially when you are going into the mountains, we recommend that you take with you, as a supplement to the maps in this book, a relevant area map in the excellent Landeskarte der Schweiz (henceforth **LdS**) series 1:25,000 (ideal for walkers, birders, etc.) or 1:50,000.

Good optical equipment makes birdwatching so much easier
(Photo: Leica Camera)

Birdwatchers' code of conduct

Watching wild birds in their natural habitat is a very special experience which gives great pleasure to an increasing number of people. However, birdwatching must not be allowed to become a threat to wildlife and plants. Bad behaviour by a few individuals can cause a lot of disturbance and, in addition, damage the reputation of the well-behaved majority of bird enthusiasts. We feel it appropriate, therefore, to set out here something akin to a little book of etiquette—a bird-watchers' code of conduct:

- The welfare of birds comes first, regardless of whether you are watching birds purely for pleasure or studying them scientifically.

- Keep disturbance to a minimum! Do not try to get close to birds. Keep to public paths.
- It goes without saying that birdwatchers must abide by laws concerned with the protection of wildlife and the environment at all times. Do not cause damage to farmland.
- Never attempt to photograph birds at the nest.
- Do not use tape-lures.
- Show special care and consideration for endangered species.
- Being environmentally-aware, birdwatchers do without the car whenever possible, using public transport or walking instead.
- When abroad, make sure that your attitude and behaviour with regard to the conservation of nature and the environment are exemplary.

The selection of sites and itineraries in this book was deliberately made in such a way that disturbance (in particular of rare and endangered species) is reduced to a minimum. None the less, we are aware that it is just these rare species that hold a special attraction for birdwatchers. We appeal to the sense of responsibility of each and every individual to heed the message that these and other species need protecting so that other people, including future generations, can enjoy them as well. Each chapter gives information on the protection of the site or of particular species.

Western Switzerland
1 Vallée de Joux
2 Rade de Genève
3 Préverenges
4 Les Grangettes
5 Rochers de Naye/Col de Jaman
6 Col de Cou/Bretolet
7 Chavornay
8 Champ-Pittet
9 Yverdon–Thielle
10 Mont Sagne
11 Chaseral
12 Clos-du-Doubs
13 Vingelzberg
14 Fanel and Chablais de Cudrefin
15 Auried at Kleinbösingen
16 Marais de la Grône
17 Leuk
18 Aletsch

Central Switzerland
19 Hahnenmoos Pass
20 Gurnigel-Wasserscheide
21 Wauwilermoos
22 Reuss Delta
23 Nuolener Ried

Northern Switzerland
24 Ulmethöchi
25 Klingnauer Stausee
26 Flachsee Unterlunkhofen
27 Pfäffikersee and Robenhuserriet
28 Neeracher Ried
29 Niderholz
30 Kaltbrunner Riet
31 Stein am Rhein
32 Ermatingen Basin
33 Romanshorn–Kreuzlingen

Eastern Switzerland
34 Rhine Valley, St Gallen
35 Obertoggenburg
36 Flims
37 Vals
38 Schanfigg
39 Ramosch
40 The Swiss National Park
41 Maloja and Upper Engadine

Southern Switzerland
42 Val Piora/Lago Ritom
43 Maggia Delta
44 Bolle di Magadino
45 Monte Generoso

Outline map of Switzerland showing sites described

All the sites dealt with in the book are shown on the map with a dot and numbered in sequence from west to east. The numbers correspond to those of the chapters. The division of the country into the large regions of Western, Northern, Central, Southern and Eastern Switzerland is designed to help readers to find their way around more quickly. The border between the francophone West and German-speaking Central and Northern Switzerland follows the linguistic boundary. For practical reasons, the canton of Valais has been included in Western Switzerland.

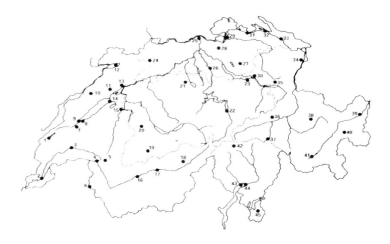

Selection of sites

The guide aims to give the reader an overview of all the typical habitats and their birdlife, from the Central Plateau up to the high Alps. Included in the selection are:

- Marsh and fenland sites which are especially attractive to migrants and therefore have a wide range of species.
- Wintering sites on rivers or lakes.
- Forests (oak, Norway spruce) with the typical faunal elements of Switzerland.
- Migration watch points on Alpine passes.
- Sites in the mountains with the corresponding bird fauna.

Arrangement of the site accounts

Each chapter begins with an at-a-glance summary of basic information (canton, height above sea level, grid reference, etc.) on the site in question. The first section is a general description of the site. For most places, we have attempted to show a sensible route from which all the important species, all those typical of the area, can be observed. Particularly good observation points along the recommended route are marked with numbers on the maps and explained in more detail in the text. You can, of course, see plenty of interest at many other places between the numbered points, but no details are given for those. The species lists, divided according to season—winter, spring, breeding season and autumn— are an essential part of the text. The same species are often to be seen on both spring and autumn migration. Such species are normally listed only once (usually under 'Spring') and listing them again under 'Autumn' would have been unnecessary. The autumn list in such cases includes only species which occur exclusively or more commonly in that season. Species listed can normally be seen at the time of year stated. If there is nothing special to see in a particular period, the corresponding section was omitted. The section entitled 'Access' contains information of how to get there using public transport, but the information provided has been kept general and visitors will need to confirm exact departure times by checking timetables for themselves. In order to make it easier to check train connections in the official timetable, the corresponding line numbers have been added in brackets (for example, 201 = the Vallorbe–Le Brassus line). Similarly, the section on accommodation was made as general as possible in order to save space. The heading 'Useful tips' points out special circumstances, while 'Nearby sites' indicates which other interesting birdwatching sites might be visited in the surrounding area.

Key to the maps
The recommended route is shown in red; numbers indicate (some of) the best places to stop and look for birds along the route, these being also dealt with in the text.

———————	recommended route
– – – – – – –	access route; not described in detail
①Q	observation point described in text
P	car-parking
❶	visitor centre

GLOSSARY

Insects

Odonata

      Common hawker *Aeshna juncea*
      Azure hawker *A. caerulea*
      White-faced dragonfly *Leucorrhinia dubia*
      Alpine emerald *Somatochlora alpestris*
      Cordulegaster bidentatus (no English name)

Lepidoptera

      Lesser purple emperor *Apatura ilia*
      Great banded grayling *Brintesia circe*
      Alcon blue *Maculinea alcon*
      Scarce large blue *M. teleius*

Orthoptera

      Swiss gold grasshopper *Chrysochraon keisti*
      Saddle-backed bush-cricket *Ephippiger ephippiger vitium*
      Marsh-cricket *Pteronemobius heydeni*

Coleoptera

      Cockchafer or maybug *Melolontha melolontha*

Dictyoptera

      Praying mantis *Mantis religiosa*

Amphibians and reptiles

Alpine salamander *Salamandra atra*
Alpine newt *Triturus alpestris*
Viviparous lizard *Lacerta vivipara*
Grass frog *Rana temporaria*
Tree frog *Hyla arborea*
Natterjack toad *Bufo calamita*
Aesculapian snake *Elaphe longissima*
Asp viper *Vipera aspis*
Grass snake *Natrix natrix*

Fishes

Bream *Abramis brama*
Carp *Carassius carassius*

Mammals

Aurochs *Bos primigenius*
Beaver *Castor fiber*
Chamois *Rupicapra rupicapra*
Red deer *Cervus elaphus*
Roe deer *Capreolus capreolus*
Red fox *Vulpes vulpes*

Brown hare *Lepus europaeus*
Mountain (Alpine) hare *L. timidus*
Ibex *Capra ibex*
Wild pig *Sus scrofa*
Stoat *Mustela erminea*

Trees

Green alder *Alnus viridis*
Grey alder *A. incana*
Common ash *Fraxinus excelsior*
Common beech *Fagus sylvatica*
Birch *Betula*
Sweet (Spanish) chestnut *Castanea sativa*
Silver fir *Abies alba*
Hornbeam *Carpinus betulus*
European larch *Larix decidua*
Lime *Tilia*
Maple *Acer*
Oak *Quercus*, including
Downy oak *Q. pubescens*
Arolla pine *Pinus cembra*
Swiss mountain pine *P. mugo*
Plane *Platanus*
Poplar *Populus*
Norway spruce *Picea abies*
Willow *Salix*, including
White willow *S. alba*

Other plants

Alpine aster *Aster alpinus*
Bilberry *Vaccinium*
Broom *Cytisus scoparius*
Cowbane *Cicuta virosa*
Lake Constance forget-me-not *Myosotis rehsteineri*
Black false helleborine *Veratrum nigrum*
Yellow flag-iris *Iris pseudacorus*
Siberian iris *I. sibirica*
Mistletoe *Viscum album*
Common reed *Phragmites*
Reedmace *Typha*
Rush *Juncus*
Sedge *Carex*

1 VALLÉE DE JOUX

Canton:	Vaud
Grid reference:	506/161
Height a.s.l.:	1020 m
Start:	Solliat/Golisse rail station
Finish:	Chez-le-Maître station (or Solliat/Golisse station)
Itinerary:	La Golisse–L'Arcadie–end of lake–Sentier village–Sagne du Campe–Orbe Bridge–Chez-le-Maître (–Derrière la Côte–La Golisse)
Duration:	allow half a day to 1 day; distance c.6 km (c.9 km including return walk to La Golisse)
Best time:	interesting all year; (apart from winter, when lake freezes over from mid-December)
Status:	wetland of national importance; IBA
Map:	LdS 1:25,000; sheet 1221 (Le Sentier)
Equipment:	walking boots, telescope

The special attraction of the Vallée de Joux compared with the rest of the Jura is the lake (Lac de Joux). Many birds are not especially drawn to the pebble beach, but the southwest corner, where the Orbe flows out of the lake, provides a surprisingly varied array of habitats for many breeding birds and passage migrants. Within a relatively small area, there is a sedge (Macro *Carex*) fen, patches of valley bog, wet meadows, a narrow reedbed fringing the shore and sandbanks uncovered at low water. The site's unspoilt character make it particularly delightful. Not far from the lake there are still extensive hay meadows where many species that have otherwise almost vanished from the Central Plateau still breed successfully. The remnants of raised bogs also add to the charm of the Vallée de Joux.

Recommended routes

From Solliat/Golisse rail station, follow the road which crosses the railway northeast of there. After c.200 m, you reach the lake at L'Arcadie (1). First chance to see waterbirds. From there, change to the footpath which branches off sharply from the road and runs south along the lakeshore (2). In the rows of trees, bushes and in the small wood, you will find typical species of this habitat such as Tree Pipit, Willow Warbler and Redpoll. Follow the path which runs parallel to the shore for c.1 km until you come to a fork. Here take the small path which peters out after c.150 m in a marsh by the mouth of the Orbe (3). This is the best place to observe the migrant gulls and terns that feed and rest here as well as breeding birds of the reedbed. Afterwards, you have to follow the same path back to where it joins the other one and then go straight ahead to the road where you turn first left and, after c.300 m, right again. Follow this path for c.1 km, past the waste-water treatment works and as far as the junction with the road, where you turn sharp left and follow the Orbe upstream for c.700 m. Turn left onto the road and take the right fork after c.80 m, then right again after a further c.200 m, and cross Sagne du Campe (4). The wet meadows have breeding Quail and Whinchats, but to have a chance of hearing the rare Corncrake, you'll have to go out at night. By the last houses at the end of Le Campier village, take the path that leads straight across the plain to Chez-le-Maître. You can get to the station by following the road for c.300 m to the right after the railway crossing. Make your return journey from

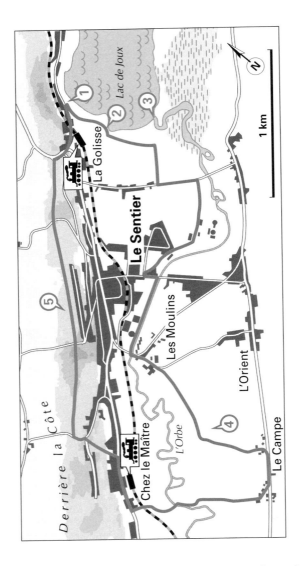

there or complete the circuit by walking back to the starting point in La Golisse (*c*.3 km). After 200 m on the road, turn off left on to a footpath and follow it for *c*.300 m up to the road. Continue for *c*.50 m along the road, then immediately turn off right again back onto the footpath. This lovely path (5) will take you through mixed broadleaf woodland, meadows and grazing land. On the left-hand side, there are still remnants of raised bogs. Your reward for this quite long walk will be Kestrel, Tree Pipit, Whinchat, Redstart, Ring Ouzel and various other thrushes, Siskin, and Crossbill or Yellowhammer. The path ends by a road 300 m from La Golisse station, where you started out.

Calendar

Wide range of different habitat types which are especially attractive to bird species of wet meadows, fen and bog; various waterbirds.

Winter: The lake may be frozen over from mid-December; up to that point, you can see Great Crested and Black-necked Grebes, Pochard and Tufted Duck and Black-headed Gull. Slightly less common: Gadwall, Teal, Pintail, Red-crested Pochard, Scaup and Goldeneye, Goosander; Kingfisher and various passerines are not uncommon.

Spring: Cormorant, Teal, Pintail, Garganey, Shoveler and Red-crested Pochard, Lapwing, Little Ringed Plover, various waders (*Calidris, Tringa*), Snipe, Black-headed Gull, Common and Black Terns.

Breeding season: Little, Great Crested and (in some years) Black-necked Grebes, Grey Heron, Mallard and Tufted Duck, Black and Red Kites, Honey Buzzard, Kestrel and Peregrine, Corncrake (rare), Black-headed and (only summering) Yellow-legged Gulls, Long-eared Owl, Skylark, Tree and Meadow Pipits, Grey Wagtail, Redstart, Whinchat, Ring Ouzel and various other thrushes, Marsh and Reed Warblers, Garden Warbler and Blackcap, Willow Warbler, Spotted Flycatcher, Siskin and Redpoll, Crossbill, Scarlet Rosefinch (recent arrival), Yellowhammer and Reed Bunting.

Autumn: Wigeon and Pochard; occasionally Shelduck, Marsh Harrier or various gulls and terns.

Useful tips

The meadows are mowed around mid-June. After that, many meadow birds vanish and the site becomes much less attractive.

Access

There is a regular train service to the Vallée de Joux on the Vallorbe–Le Day–Le Brassus line (201). From Lausanne, take the train for Vallorbe (200) as far as the Le Day halt (just before the terminus). Coming from Yverdon, you have to change at Cossonay for the Lausanne–Cossonay–Le Day–Vallorbe line (210). Trains on the Vallorbe–Le Brassus line stop in Solliat/Golisse and in Chez-le-Maître, but also at Sentier, Le Brassus and at several other stations along the northern shore of the lake.

Accommodation

The Le Rocheray campsite (tel: 021/845 51 74) is situated in Le Sentier, 1.5 km from La Golisse. Le Sentier also has two hotels. Further information from: Office du tourisme de la Vallée de Joux, Centre sportif, 1347 Le Sentier (tel: 021/845 62 57).

Site protection

Meadowland breeders such as Whinchats, Skylarks, etc. are suffering because the trend in modern agriculture is for grass to be cut earlier and earlier. Drainage and the application of fertilizers are an additional burden on the vegetation. There is pressure on the Lac de Joux waterside from the sheer number of visitors. Important conservation measures include deciding on a time for grass-cutting which favours meadowland breeding birds and educating the local population. Please keep strictly to the footpaths to avoid damaging the vegetation when you are walking through sensitive areas such as reedbeds, sedge fen, flat and raised bogs. Walking in the hay meadows is forbidden and the farmers are often more than willing to emphasize personally that such a ban exists. Out of respect for them and for the flora and fauna of this habitat, ornithologists should make sure that their behaviour here is exemplary and beyond reproach.

Disabled access

The length of the route described makes it unsuitable for visitors with walking impairments. Most of the paths are suitable for wheelchairs, however, and some observation points are easily accessible; nevertheless, some of the most interesting places are not suitable (e.g. numbers 3 and 5).

Nearby sites

Risoux Wood on the north slope and above the Vallée de Joux has all the characteristic birds of the Jura forests. In this extensive woodland composed of beech, Norway spruce and silver fir, there are grouse species, Woodcock, Pygmy and Tengmalm's Owls, though it's a matter of luck whether you will see any of these shy and elusive species. More likely to be found are Black Woodpecker, Willow, Crested and Coal Tits, also Siskin and Crossbill. Warning—it's easy to get lost in this wood!

Meadow Pipit (drawing by J. Laesser)

2 RADE DE GENÈVE

Canton:	Geneva
Grid reference:	501/118
Height a.s.l.:	370 m
Start:	Genève-Plage
Finish:	Botanic Garden
Itinerary:	Genève-Plage–Quai Gustave-Ador (–Parc des Eaux Vives)–harbour–Perle du Lac–Botanic Garden
Duration:	allow 1 hr to half a day; distance *c.*5 km
Best time:	autumn (at migration time) and winter (for winter visitors)
Status:	Ramsar site; reserve for waterbirds and and migrants of national and international importance; IBA
Map:	LdS 1:25,000; sheet 1301 (Geneva) or street map of Geneva (free from Tourist Information Office at rail station)
Equipment:	telescope, warm clothes

Anyone not so familiar with the ornithological scene in and around Geneva (Genève, Genf) will be surprised to learn that the city is an outstanding staging and wintering site for many waterbirds. Wedged between the Jura Mountains and the Alps, Lake Geneva (Lac Léman, Genfersee) narrows to form a funnel shape at Geneva. The end of the lake and particularly the harbour (la Rade) with its concentrations of waterfowl during the autumn migration period is an ideal place to watch birds. The remarkable variety of staging waterbirds and others passing through offer a small measure of consolation for the complete destruction of all the natural lakeside habitats. However, as you might expect, it is only the undemanding and adaptable species that manage to survive in the artificial habitat created.

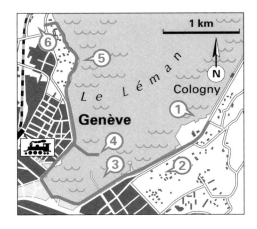

Recommended routes

For an early-morning walk, the recommendation is to begin at the beach (Genève-Plage) (1). This is the way to make the best use of the light conditions in the morning. From this vantage point, you can scan a great expanse of the lake for waterbirds and here you will find the first ducks, including sawbills.

If you walk along the Quai Gustave-Ador, it is perhaps worth a short detour into the Parc des Eaux-Vives (2) where there are occasionally interesting passerines at migration time.

The harbour proper is located between the two harbour walls which jut out into the lake (3). This is the area where you will find a large proportion of the diving and dabbling ducks, Coot, grebes and gulls. Duck hybrids are regularly encountered and provide an opportunity to make a closer study of this phenomenon and thus to learn a lot about the diagnostic features of ducks in general. On the other side of the lake, you can get a good view from the Pâquis Pier (4) as this extends a long way into the lake. This is a really excellent place for observing birds as they arrive from the north or pass through in the autumn migration period. Experience has taught regular observers that this is a watchpoint with great potential, though there is considerable variation from day to day in the number and variety of birds seen. None the less, the number of different wader and gull species recorded is certainly impressive. Migrant passerines are regularly found in the plane trees on the pier. If you follow the lakeside promenade, you will reach Perle du Lac (5) from where you get a good view of the lake and the staging or wintering waterbirds. You can continue along the shore promenade for another couple of hundred metres, but will soon reach the Botanic Garden (6) via an underpass. Despite the presence of migrant passerines, the garden has actually more to offer the visitor whose main interest is plants.

Calendar

Convenient observation point for watching a large number of staging and wintering waterbirds on a flyway of national importance. The main attractions are the autumn migration and winter visitors.

Winter: Red-throated and Black-throated Divers, Little, Great Crested, Red-necked and Black-necked Grebes, Cormorant, Pochard, Tufted Duck, Red-crested Pochard, Goldeneye, Eider and Velvet Scoter, Red-breasted Merganser and Goosander, Black-headed, Yellow-legged and Common Gulls; less commonly seen are Slavonian Grebe, Scaup, Ferruginous Duck, Common Scoter and Long-tailed Duck, Smew, Lesser Black-backed and Mediterranean Gulls. In addition, occasional observations of exotic escapes (mainly ducks).

Spring: Slightly less interesting than autumn migration, but unexpected species (waders, gulls) are possible at any time: Little Gull, Black Tern, Whiskered Tern (more regular than in autumn), passerines.

Breeding season: Goosander, Black Kite, Yellow-legged Gull (present, but not always breeding), passerines in the parks and gardens.

Autumn: Marsh Harrier, Osprey, Hobby, Common Sandpiper, Dunlin, Little Ringed and Ringed Plovers are all regular; also Sanderling, Little Stint, Curlew, Whimbrel, Spotted Redshank, Redshank, Greenshank, Wood Sandpiper and Turnstone. Skuas (mostly juveniles) are regular from the end of August to October. Lesser Black-backed, Little and Mediterranean Gulls, Common Tern, Caspian Tern (regular from end of August to September), Black Tern. Among the passerines, many hirundines, Yellow and Grey Wagtails, Wheatears, *Sylvia* and

Phylloscopus warblers (can also be found in the Botanic Garden or in the Parc des Eaux-Vives). From September, Black-necked Grebe, various ducks, Yellow-legged and Common Gulls.

Useful tips
In autumn, the Pâquis Pier is a favourite meeting-place for observers from the region. At weekends (especially in September), you will often find yourself in the company of fellow birders.

Access
You can get to the beach (Genève-Plage) from the main rail station (Cornavin) with a No.6 bus (marked Malagnou) or a No.9 (Petit Bel-Air), both of which stop at Eaux-Vives. From there, take a No.2 bus to the terminus which is Genève-Plage. For the Botanic Garden, take a No.4 bus to Voirets or a No.44 and get off at Palettes. For just a short visit or if you want to birdwatch from the Pâquis Pier, alight at Rue du Mont-Blanc, then go left for about 500 m along the Quai du Mont-Blanc to reach the pier. During the bathing season, there is an entry fee. Try to use public transport if at all possible; car parking is limited.

Accommodation
There are plenty of hotels in Geneva offering rooms with a wide range of prices. The youth hostel is in a very convenient location: Rue Rotschild 28–30 (tel: 022/732 62 60). For further information, contact the Office du Tourisme de Genève, World Trade Center, Route de l'Aéroport, CP 596, 1215 Geneva 15 (tel: 022/929 70 00).

Site protection
The Ramsar site lies in the centre of Geneva, at the point where the Rhône leaves the lake. Restrictions have been placed on boat traffic and water-sports activities to avoid disturbing the waterbirds.

Disabled access
The area is actually very suitable for visitors with walking impairments, but it is an advantage to use public transport (wherever possible) as it's difficult to find convenient parking places. All the paths are wheelchair-accessible.

Nearby sites
The reedbed fringing the lake at Pointe-à-la-Bise occasionally holds interesting migrants such as Penduline Tit, Great Reed Warbler, etc. Birds recorded breeding include Great Crested Grebe, Water Rail, Reed Warbler and Reed Bunting. Entry to this area is strictly prohibited, but you can get to it from the main rail station in Geneva (Cornavin) by bus No.8 as far as 'Rive'; change there to the Hermance bus E and alight at La Bise. Follow the campsite signs in the direction of the lake. The best time to visit the area is early morning or on workdays. Use regional trains on the Geneva–Nyon line to reach further interesting places on the right (northwest) shore of the lake such as Le Reposoir, Le Vengeron, Creux-de-Genthod, Versoix-le-Bourg, Coppet, etc. Other vantage points worth mentioning on the left (southeast) shore include Ruth, la Pointe à la Bise, Bellerive, Bellerive Point, Anières and Hermance and these can all be reached with the Hermance bus.

The Rhône above the Verbois barrage is a well-known site for various species of waterbirds (staging passage migrants, winter visitors). Common Terns nest on specially-constructed rafts near the dam. The area below the power station is extremely interesting in the breeding season. There is nowhere else in Switzerland where Turtle Dove, Nightingale, Melodious Warbler and Willow Warbler occur at higher densities.

3 PRÉVERENGES

Canton:	Vaud
Grid reference:	530/151
Height a.s.l.:	370 m
Start:	'Venoge' bus-stop
Finish:	'Morges, St.Louis' bus-stop
Itinerary:	4–5 km; Venoge–reedbeds of Saint-Sulpice and mouth of the Venoge– along Préverenges beach–Morges
Duration:	allow half a day
Best time:	April–May and winter
Status:	small reedbed nature reserve
Map:	LdS 1:25,000; sheet 1242 (Morges)
Equipment:	telescope

Both at a regional (Romandie or French-speaking Western Switzerland) and national level, you regularly see the name Préverenges in ornithological reports, especially under the headings 'Waders' and 'Gulls'. The site owes this to its favoured location on a migration route which, in spring, runs along the northern edge of Lake Geneva (Lac Léman, Genfersee) and this is, of course, well known to many observers. Ornithologists are able to make frequent visits to the site because it is easily accessible from Lausanne. If you can spend a morning here at the right time of year, you are likely to be rewarded with some unusual sightings.

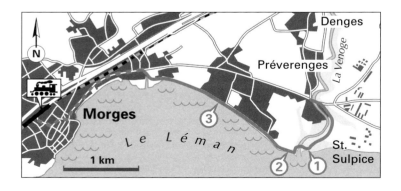

Recommended routes

From the bus-stop, proceed along the left bank of the Venoge. Near the mouth of the river, there is a small reedbed (1) on the left bank. This nature reserve had to be fenced off in order to stop people going into the reeds. At certain times, Water Rail, Spotted Crake, Reed Warbler, Penduline Tit and Reed Bunting can be observed in the reeds. In winter, a beaver is regularly seen by the mouth of the river.

You can get to point (2) by crossing the bridge over the Venoge. This place, immediately adjacent to the river mouth, is superb for watching waterbirds and waders on the lake or on the lakeshore. Waders favour the sandbanks, which are uncovered in the spring (especially low water level in leap years), for resting and feeding. In addition, many gulls and terns pass through: Little and Mediterranean Gulls as well as rarer gull species, Common, Whiskered, White-winged Black and Black Terns, less frequently skuas. Divers, grebes and numerous ducks are regular on the lake in winter. You can continue along the shore towards Morges (3). There are further interesting areas extending as far as Bief Harbour near Morges where you can go back onto the main road and the bus-stop is just a couple of hundred metres to the right.

Calendar

Important staging and passage site in spring for various species of waders, gulls and terns.

Winter: Red-throated Diver, less commonly Black-throated and Great Northern Divers; all the grebes, various ducks, including Long-tailed Duck.

Spring: Night Heron, Osprey, Spotted Crake, Oystercatcher, Black-winged Stilt, Avocet (occasionally), Little Ringed, Ringed, Kentish and Grey Plovers, all the passage *Calidris* and *Tringa* species; Ruff, Black-tailed and Bar-tailed Godwits, Whimbrel; Mediterranean and Little Gulls, Common, Whiskered, Black and White-winged Black Terns, Swift and Alpine Swift, Hoopoe, various hirundines, Bluethroat, Penduline Tit, Reed Bunting, Ortolan Bunting.

Breeding season: Goosander, Water Rail, Lesser Spotted Woodpecker, Reed Warbler.

Autumn: Only moderately interesting: occasionally plovers, Little Stint, Dunlin and Common Tern (a few individuals).

Access

From Lausanne: métro-ouest (TSOL) as far as 'Bourdonnette' (102), then change to the Venoge–St Sulpice bus and get out at 'Venoge' (102.10). The bus-stop by Bief Harbour is 'Morges, St.Louis'. To get back to Lausanne, take the bus to 'Ecublens, EPFL' and change to the métro-ouest. Morges rail station is about 1.5 km from Port du Bief. First walk along the lakeshore, then turn right into the town when you are level with the church. The narrow lakeside road is a pedestrian walkway and closed to motor vehicles. Direct train service to Lausanne (150).

Accommodation

Hôtel Pré-Fleuri in Saint-Sulpice, Hôtel de la Plage in Préverenges. More possibilities in Morges and Lausanne.

For information, contact: Ass. des Intérêts de la Région Morgienne ADIREM; Office de tourisme, Place du casino 1, Case postale, 1110 Morges (tel: 021/801 32 33) or Office du tourisme & des congrès, Av. de Rhodanie 2, Case postale 49, 1000 Lausanne (tel: 021/613 73 21).

Useful tips

As almost everywhere, the best time for birdwatching is the early morning, but the midday period can also be interesting as the gulls, terns and waders often form large gatherings at this time and waders passing through are attracted by this activity phase.

As at Les Grangettes (Site 4), conditions in the spring of leap years are especially attractive. The water level is lowered artificially and large expanses of mud are exposed.

Site protection

Despite the great importance of this site, dredging operations still continue in the mouth of the Venoge and that prevents the formation of a natural delta. Numerous walkers with dogs and people on mountain-bikes disturb the resting migrants. Special information displays have been put up to explain the problems to the public. At the present time, various proposals are under consideration to improve the site for wildlife. For example, sandbanks are to be created along a stretch of about 200 m and these will be out of bounds to passers-by. The perimeter is being marked with posts and large boulders which serve as resting-places for the birds. Shrubs are to be planted on the lakeshore and there is to be a raft for terns to nest on.

Disabled access

The lakeside from Préverenges to the mouth of the Venoge is wheelchair-accessible and very suitable for other visitors with walking impairments.

4 LES GRANGETTES

Canton:	Vaud
Grid reference:	558/138
Height a.s.l.:	370 m
Start:	Villeneuve rail station
Finish:	Bouveret (or Villeneuve) rail station
Itinerary:	Villeneuve quay–Saviez plain–lakeshore–Grand Canal embankment– farmland near Noville (or cross over Grand Canal and Rhône–Bouveret)
Duration:	allow half a day to 1 day; distance 7–8 km
Best time:	all year (especially interesting in spring)
Status:	Ramsar site; nature reserve; reserve for waterbirds and migrants of national and international importance; IBA
Map:	LdS 1:25,000; sheet 1143 (Montreux)
Equipment:	telescope

A huge delta has formed where the Rhône enters the extreme eastern part of Lake Geneva (Lac Léman, Genfersee) and this is now known as 'Les Grangettes'. Despite the considerable impact on the site from agriculture, water-sports enthusiasts, anglers and walkers, Les Grangettes has retained at least some of its original character up to the present day. Typical elements of the landscape include reedbeds, marshland, riverine forest and ox-bow lakes along the River Rhône. Nevertheless, man's activities have definitely left their mark, with artificial water bodies, drainage channels, campsites, also spruce and poplar plantations all spoiling the natural landscape. The combination of various habitat types attracts a large number of different bird species. Wedged as it is between the Savoie, Vaud and Valais Alps, Les Grangettes is an outstanding site for observing bird migration: no fewer than 265 species have been recorded here; people who are keen on reptiles and amphibians will also be richly rewarded as there are 17 species of these at the site—impressive evidence of its species richness.

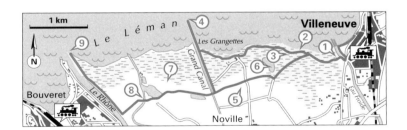

Recommended routes

From Villeneuve station, walk west along the lakeside promenade of the little town. Straight away, you will find the first waterbirds. You then come to the canal 'Eau Froide'; follow this upstream for a short distance. Cross the canal at the earliest opportunity and continue towards the lake so that you come out onto the Les Saviez plain. Opposite the old waste-water treatment works, there is a commune rubbish tip (1).

This is a very good vantage point for views over the reeds and the bay. The breakwaters or groynes are visible in the lake—huge boulders

29

*Extensive reedbeds and various other alluvial habitats
are typical features of Les Grangettes (photo: M. Sacchi)*

designed to protect the reedbed behind them from erosion.
Cormorants, Grey Herons, terns and gulls regularly perch on the blocks
and Mediterranean Gulls, Caspian Terns and other unusual visitors are
occasionally found among the flocks in spring. Interesting migrants
such as *Sylvia* warblers and other passerines occur in the surrounding
bushes. After around 500 m, a small path branches off right and this
takes you through the wood directly behind the reedbed. You then
cross a narrow drainage ditch after walking a further *c*.200 m in the
same direction; about 50 metres further along the canal in the direction
of the lake will bring you to the shore (2). Please keep to the path here
so as not to disturb the wildlife.

After a short distance on the path through the wood, you come to a
second, slightly wider ditch (3) which supports very rare aquatic plants,
spiders and snails. Continue along this path to the Grand Canal. From
the canal embankment (4), you can see much of the upper part of Lake
Geneva. A telescope will enable you to scan the lakeshore from
Bouveret right across to Villeneuve. This is an ideal place from which to
observe diving and dabbling ducks, grebes and passing migrants such
as terns or waders. When the water is low in the spring, sandbanks
appear directly in front of, and east of, the campsite and these often
have waders resting on them. On the canal, apart from the innumerable
small boats, there are Little Grebes, Goosander and Moorhens. To get to
the nearest rail station, there are two alternatives. The return to
Villeneuve is by a more inland route (5), where you may find migrant
passerines on the arable and other fields. If you go the short distance to
the small La Mure pond (6), watch out for the fascinating Aesculapian

snakes (there is quite a large population in the area). Reed Warblers nest in the reeds at the pond and their loud song is a characteristic feature of the breeding season. If you decide to head for Bouveret station, you will pass a newly-created shallow pond (7). Close to the right-hand side of the path there is a small mound composed of the spoil from the excavation and this is a good place from which to view the pond which occasionally attracts various herons and egrets. There are also many different kinds of dragonflies and damsel flies; the total number recorded at Les Grangettes is 33 species. A bit further on, you reach an old arm (ox-bow lake) of the Rhône (8) part of which has been destroyed by harbour installations. There are plenty of opportunities to observe birds of open-country habitats along this route: regular visitors during the migration period include pipits, Yellow Wagtail, Wheatear, Whinchat, also many finch species. If you want to venture as far as the mouth of the Rhône (9), there's a detour to be taken into account, but the reward may be sightings of waterbirds.

Calendar

Important wetland at the upper end of Lake Geneva with quite large reedbeds, various other alluvial habitats and open water. Waterbird site with many species of ducks, waders and gulls. Important stopover site for migrating passerines.

Winter: Great Crested, Little and Black-necked Grebes, Cormorant, various dabbling and diving ducks, Eider and Goldeneye, Goosander, Yellow-legged and Common Gulls, Kingfisher. Scarcer species: Red-throated and Black-throated Divers, Red-necked and Slavonian Grebes, Bittern, Ferruginous Duck, Scaup, Long-tailed Duck, Common and Velvet Scoters, Smew and Red-breasted Merganser.

Spring: Various herons and egrets, Teal, Garganey and Shoveler, Eider (summering since 1988), Black Kite; numerous waders such as plovers, *Calidris* and *Tringa* species, etc.; Mediterranean, Little and Lesser Black-backed Gulls, Common Tern and sometimes other tern species; pipits, Yellow Wagtail, Whinchat, Wheatear, Penduline Tit, Ortolan Bunting.

Breeding season: Great Crested Grebe, Tufted Duck, Goosander, Black Kite, Common Tern (on artificial nesting rafts), Lesser Spotted Woodpecker, Marsh and Reed Warblers, Great Reed and Savi's Warblers (both rare), Golden Oriole, Reed Bunting.

Autumn: Less good than in spring: Great White Egret (rare), various ducks, Dunlin, Snipe, Common Sandpiper, Black Tern, Little Gull. Less commonly, species such as Little Ringed and Ringed Plovers, Sanderling, Little Stint and Curlew Sandpiper, Turnstone or skuas.

Useful tips

In leap years, the spring water level in Lake Geneva is artificially lowered more than usual. Huge areas of mudflats provide ideal conditions for waders. Other species also benefit: herons and egrets, gulls, terns, pipits and wagtails.

Access

Unfortunately, fast trains do not stop at Villeneuve. From Lausanne, it's best to take a fast train to Montreux (100) and to change there to a regional service (100.1); the journey time to Villeneuve is c.7–8 minutes. If you are coming from Valais, change trains at Aigle and from there it is only a 9-minute journey to Villeneuve. There is only an irregular bus service to Bouveret on the 'Tonkin' line St Gingolph–Monthey–Saint-Maurice (100.2).

Accommodation

There are various campsites in the environs of Les Grangettes and a youth hostel in Montreux-Territet (tel: 021/963 49 34). In addition, the Villeneuve and Montreux area has a large number of hotels in different price categories.

More information from: 'Société de développement & du tourisme', Grand' rue 10, 1844 Villeneuve (tel: 021/960 22 86), the Montreux Tourist Information Office, CP, 1820 Montreux (tel: 021/962 84 84), or from the 'Société de développement' in 1897 Le Bouveret (tel: 024/481 51 21).

Site protection

Les Grangettes has a great appeal for walkers, those seeking recreation and for ornithologists. This all results in a huge impact on the nature reserve from the sheer numbers of visitors. Not even the remotest corners are safe from visitors and this inevitably means serious disturbance to the wildlife. Gravel extraction in the lake just off Les Grangettes and the canalization of the Rhône impede the natural dynamic of the river. The shoreline is also very much under threat from the action of the waves and erosion is eating away more and more land. If anti-erosion measures and wetland management are expanded, the future for Les Grangettes could look good. Since 1990, Les Grangettes has been recognized as a wetland of international importance (Ramsar Convention, reserve for waterbirds and migrants of international importance). This could accelerate the measures outlined above. Incidentally, the Fondation des Grangettes, which is responsible for overseeing management of the site and also aims to educate people more effectively, was founded in the same year. With these measures to manage visitors, the conservationists hope to be able to relieve at least some of the uncontrolled recreational pressure on the site so that it can continue to provide favourable conditions for a wide range of animal and plant species.

Disabled access

In general, this site is easily accessible to visitors with walking impairments, but there are some paths which are covered with woodchips and thus not so easily negotiated in a wheelchair.

Nearby sites

Wallcreepers occasionally overwinter on the walls of the Château de Chillon (Chillon Castle) between Villeneuve and Montreux.

An interesting site for observing raptor migration—N.B. in spring—lies near **Thollon** on the French side of Lake Geneva and this can be reached from St Gingolph (Valais) via Lugrin (France). In Thollon, head north to the hamlet of Le Hucel (Leucel; grid reference 543/138).

There is a tall telecommunications mast below the little village and the foot of this mast is the best place from which to watch for migrants. Species passing through between February and May include Black Stork, Honey Buzzard, Goshawk, Sparrowhawk, Red and Black Kites and, more rarely, even Short-toed and Booted Eagles and Osprey.

For Rochers de Naye and Col de Jaman, see Site 5.

Penduline Tit (drawing by J. Laesser)

5 ROCHERS DE NAYE/COL DE JAMAN

Canton:	Vaud (Fribourg)
Grid reference:	562/140
Height a.s.l.:	up to 2040 m
Start:	Les Echets halt
Finish:	Villeneuve rail station
Itinerary:	Les Echets–Creux de la Sierge–Les Dentaux–Rochers de Naye–Col de Chaude–Vallon de la Tinière–Villeneuve station
Duration:	allow 1 day; distance *c*.15 km
Best time:	for breeding birds: June–July for migrants: August–October
Status:	nature reserve; IBA
Map:	LdS 1:25,000; sheet 1264 (Montreux)
Equipment:	walking boots, map 1:25,000, picnic lunch, warm clothing

Owing to its rich variety of Pre-Alpine habitats, the area around Rochers de Naye supports an extremely diverse avifauna. The special topographical position of the Col de Jaman makes it an excellent site from which to observe the impressive autumn bird migration. Channelled by the Saane valley, the migrants are more or less forced to cross the Col de Jaman at the top of the pass and they then continue their journey along the northern shore of Lake Geneva (Lac Léman, Genfersee). Scientists at the Col de Jaman ringing station have been studying the phenomenon of bird migration for a number of years.

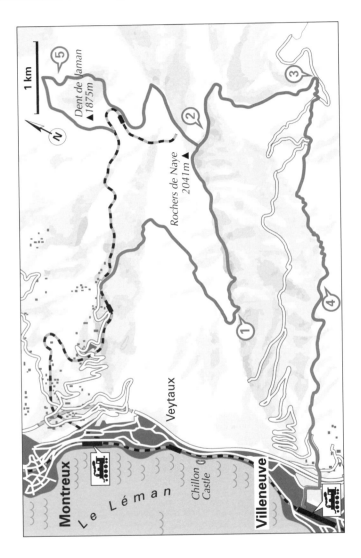

Recommended routes

From Les Echets halt, follow the road which crosses the railway lines in the direction of Raveyre. The road soon becomes a farm track and, after about 3.5 km, you reach the ridge (1) at Creux de la Sierge. Walking along the ridge in the direction of Rochers de Naye, you may reasonably hope to see some of the more elusive forest species: Hazel Grouse, Pygmy Owl and Three-toed Woodpecker all occur there. Rochers de Naye (2) is the highest point of the ridge. The summit region (with Alpine garden) is the terminus of the rack railway and has well-developed tourist facilities. Apart from the fantastic view of Lake Geneva, don't forget the Alpine Accentors and Alpine Choughs which are regularly present at the site. The walk continues in the direction of Col de Chaude (3) via Plan d'Areine. There is a good chance of seeing Black Grouse and Rock Thrush on this stretch. For the descent to Villeneuve, follow the path through the Vallon de la Tinière (4). In the valley bottom (Black Woodpecker), the path leads along a stream of the same name (Dipper). To reach the Col de Jaman (5) via Dent de Jaman takes about an hour on foot (3–4 km). The pass is well situated for observing the autumn bird migration. Most spectacular is the passage of large numbers of migrants in October when finches are especially numerous. However, raptors do not occur in large numbers at this time. The ringers put up an impressive array of mistnets each autumn to catch migrant birds (and bats) which are then ringed, weighed and measured, etc.

Calendar

The site has many typical woodland species, also those characteristic of the Pre-Alpine summit region. Good site for observing autumn migration (August to October).

Breeding season: Golden Eagle, Kestrel, Hazel Grouse, Ptarmigan, Black Grouse and Rock Partridge, Pygmy Owl, Black and Three-toed Woodpeckers, Water Pipit, Alpine Accentor, Whinchat, Rock Thrush, Wallcreeper, Citril Finch, Redpoll.

Autumn: Woodpigeon, Tree, Meadow and Water Pipits, Yellow Wagtail, Skylark and Woodlark, House Martin and Swallow, Whinchat, Wheatear, Black Redstart and Redstart, Ring Ouzel, Fieldfare, Song and Mistle Thrushes, Willow Warbler, Chiffchaff and various other *Phylloscopus* and *Sylvia* warblers (particularly at the ringing station); Pied Flycatcher, tits, Nutcracker, finches.

Useful tips

Both visitors and helpers are always welcome at the Col de Jaman ringing station. Further information on site or from Georges Gilliéron, Crausaz 97, 1814 La Tour-de-Peilz (tel: 021/944 23 35).

Access

From Montreux, there is a rack railway up to Rochers de Naye (121) with stops at Caux and Jaman. It's a good half-hour (1.2 km) on foot from Jaman stop to the Col de Jaman ringing station. The private railway is expensive: in 1998, a single to Caux cost 12 Swiss francs, to Jaman Sfr28 and to Rochers de Naye Sfr34.

An alternative is to travel with the MOB (Montreux-Oberland Bernois). Les Avants station is on the Montreux–Zweisimmen line (120) and it's a walk of about 2 hours from there up to the Col de Jaman; from Les Cases halt, it will take you only about 1.5 hours.

Regional trains serving Villeneuve run regularly between Lausanne or Vevey and Aigle.

Accommodation
On the Col de Jaman, it is possible to stay in the huts of the Swiss Alpine Club (SAC; information from Charly Neyroud, 1803 Chardonne (tel: 021/922 68 19)) and those of the Ski Club (contact Frau Engler, Rives-Bleue 129, 1897 Le Bouveret (tel: 024/481 47 19)). Montreux and Villeneuve (see Site 4, Les Grangettes) also have plenty of hotels and other types of accommodation available. For further information, contact: Office des Congrès & du Tourisme, CP, 1820 Montreux (tel: 021/962 84 84).

Site protection
At weekends in fine weather, the site attracts quite large numbers of visitors. Please keep to the existing pathways in order not to increase disturbance to especially sensitive species.

Disabled access
Hiking trails not suitable for wheelchairs are not necessarily suitable for other visitors with walking impairments either. It is possible to get close to the ringing station by car on the Vaud side of the Col de Jaman, but the last hundred metres have to be covered on foot and the slope is relatively steep.

Nearby sites
The pastures, rocks and scree below Rochers de Naye and Dent de Jaman are very interesting. The same is true of the track which runs north of the Col de Jaman along Les Verraux in the direction of Col de Pierra Perchia.

6 COL DE COU/COL DE BRETOLET

Canton:	Valais (on the border with France)
Grid reference:	550/110
Height a.s.l.:	1920 m
Start:	arrival by train: Champéry; arrival by car: Barme
Finish:	ditto
Itinerary:	Champéry–Barme–La Berthe–and return
Duration:	1 day; allow at least a couple of hours on La Berthe. Stretch from Champéry to La Berthe c.11 km (c.4.5 hrs). Stretch from Barme to La Berthe c.5 km (c.1.5 hrs)
Best time:	August to October
Status:	migratory bird reserve of national importance
Map:	LdS 1:25,000; sheet 1304 (Val d'Illiez)
Equipment:	mountain boots, telescope, picnic lunch (no restaurant on the way)

The relief of the Alpine chain forces the migrating birds to use particular routes. This leads to concentrations of migrant flocks in places such as valleys and low passes, as the birds want to avoid flying over high barriers. The configuration of the Val d'Illiez corresponds to the main flight direction taken by the migrating birds, namely southwest. The

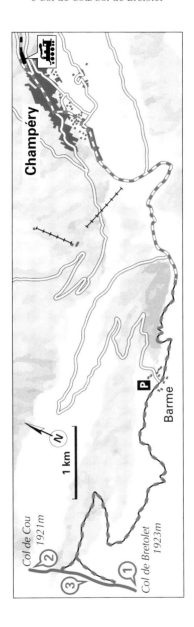

southern limit of the valley is marked by the Dents du Midi and migrants have to overfly the Col de Cou/Bretolet.

Ornithologists from the French-speaking part of Switzerland first began to take an interest in the autumn migration in this part of the Alps in the 1950s and, since that time, the Col de Cou/Bretolet has played an important role in migration studies. The initiative originally came from the Nos Oiseaux Youth Group and the pass has since gained a good reputation as an Alpine research station. The Swiss Ornithological Institute (Vogelwarte Sempach) began its ringing programme in 1958, when it also built some accommodation at the pass. The main focus of interest is on ringing and the scientific analysis of the data collected.

Recommended routes

From the car park in Barme, take the path which leads up the slope on the right-hand side of the mountain stream. After an ascent of some 3 km, you reach the floor of the cauldron-like valley, 500 m below the Col de Bretolet. You can climb up directly to the top of the pass from there, or take the easier route on to the Berroi-Ridge. When you are level with the chalet, continue along the ridge to the left in the direction of La Berthe. After about 1 km, the track divides, the left fork leading to the Col de Bretolet (1), the right fork to the Col de Cou (2).

The best place for observing the migrants is the small summit of La Berthe (3), between the Col de Bretolet and the Col de Cou. The two passes lie some 800 m apart, but are connected by a path leading along the ridge. The Col de Cou, in particular, attracts numbers of ornithologists at weekends in September. You can get superb views of raptors in flight from this spot. Ringing is carried out every autumn at Col de Bretolet, with an impressive barrier of nets being erected along the ridge. Visitors are asked not to go near the nets. Ringing assistants regularly check the nets and remove the trapped birds which are then ringed (see 'Useful tips').

Calendar

Impressive observations of heavy autumn raptor passage and many migrating passerines. A westerly wind is the best for observing passerine migration.

Breeding season: Golden Eagle, Peregrine, Black Grouse, Water Pipit, Wheatear, Rock Thrush (rare), Lesser Whitethroat, Wallcreeper (breeds in the general area; occasionally flys over the pass), Nutcracker, Alpine Chough, Citril Finch and Redpoll.

Autumn: The main attraction is the impressive migration from August to October: Cormorant, Black Stork (rare but regular), Honey Buzzard, Black and Red Kites, Marsh and sometimes Hen and Montagu's Harriers, Goshawk, Sparrowhawk, Buzzard, Osprey, Kestrel, Merlin, Hobby, occasionally Lammergeier; Golden Eagle and Peregrine both breed locally; Tengmalm's Owl (breeds further down; especially immatures occasionally fly over the pass); Woodlark and Skylark, various hirundines, Tree, Meadow and Water Pipits, Yellow, Grey and White Wagtails, Ring Ouzel, Fieldfare, Song and Mistle Thrushes; in invasion years, very large numbers of tits. Impressive finch migration in October: Chaffinch, Brambling and Goldfinch, Serin, Siskin, Linnet, Redpoll, Hawfinch, etc.

Useful tips

The Swiss Ornithological Institute at Sempach, which runs the Col de Bretolet ringing station, regularly needs volunteer assistants from August to October to help with the ringing. Minimum stay one week to be arranged in advance. For further information and to apply, contact the Institute at Sempach (for address, see p. 181). Only experienced ringers may assist with the actual ringing.

The Col de Bretolet in the Western Alps (photo: P. Rüegg)

Access

Champéry station is the terminus of the Val d'Illiez line (AOMC): Aigle–Monthey–Champéry (126). Aigle station is served by fast trains running between Lausanne and Valais (100). From Champéry, follow the signposts to Barme; from there, the route is as described above under 'Recommended routes'.

If you are coming from Lausanne by car, leave the motorway at the St Triphon exit; if you are driving from Valais, take the Bix exit. From Monthey, take the Val d'Illiez road as far as Champéry; from there, as far as Creuses and Barme on the road leading to the campsite.

Accommodation
In Barme: Cantine de Barme (tel: 024/479 11 63) or Cantine des Dents Blanches (tel: 024/479 12 12).

In Champéry: various hotels or the Gran Paradis campsite (tel: 024/479 14 44); for further information, contact Office du Tourisme (tel: 024/479 20 20).

Site protection
Please keep to the existing paths.

Disabled access
Both the Col de Cou and the Col de Bretolet are unsuitable for disabled visitors.

7 CHAVORNAY

Canton:	Vaud
Height a.s.l.:	440 m
Grid reference:	533/174
Start:	Chavornay rail station
Finish:	Chavornay rail station
Itinerary:	Chavornay station–observation platform–along the ponds–Chavornay station
Duration:	3–4 km; allow 2–4 hours
Best time:	throughout year; mainly autumn
Map:	LdS 1:25,000; sheet 1203 (Yverdon)
Status:	nature reserve
Equipment:	telescope, possibly wellington boots (part of the route is through vegetation)

Small wetlands in the cleared and cultivated land of the Central Plateau act like oases. In the heart of the Orbe Plain, hidden from view between the motorway and intensively-cultivated fields, the Creux-de-Terre at Chavornay are one such green island. The vegetation is composed of beds of common reed and reedmace, thorn and alder scrub, as well as poplars and willow, some standing in water. Grassland and arable fields dissected by drainage ditches and canals lie adjacent to the site. Covering only 38 ha, this isolated pocket of wilderness is not very inviting for long nature walks. The great attraction is the concentration of large numbers of many different species. Around 240 species have been recorded, 80 of which have bred. The Creux-de-Terre keep on turning up the kind of surprise records which have become the hallmark of the ornithological history of Romandie (French-speaking Western Switzerland).

Recommended routes
To reach the site, head north from the rail station, cross the cantonal highway and you come to a farm track. The latter branches off to the right after about 150 m and then runs north parallel to the railway line

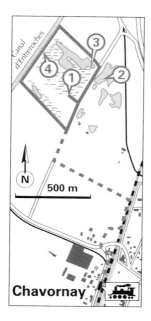

for several hundred metres. Take the next turn left. Part of the track then runs along the edge of a small wood and, at the end of this wood (after several hundred metres), you turn right. 400 m further on, a path to the left will take you to the screened observation platform (1) which affords good views over the most important parts of the shallow 'Pré-Bélisson' pond.

This is a good place for observing various waders, ducks and herons. Having returned to the path on which you came, continue in the same direction as before. 'Pré-Bélisson' is on your left, the pond 'Pré Bernard' (2) on your right. 'Pré Bernard' also has an interesting aquatic fauna and should be checked carefully. The way continues round the main pond after a sharp turn to the left. Shortly after this crossways, a small promontory (3) extends into the lake and more birds may be spotted from there. The species are more or less the same as those likely to be seen from the hide. Continue on the same path round the pond and turn left again when you reach the 'Entreroches' canal (4). Dabbling ducks, Green and Wood Sandpipers or migrant passerines can sometimes be seen here. Take the next turn left, heading away from the canal, and return to the hide for another look or head back to the rail station.

Calendar

Important stopover for waterbirds, waders and passerines in the Orbe Plain which has otherwise been cleared and is now intensively cultivated. Almost all the wader species occurring in Switzerland can be seen here.

Winter: Cormorant, Bittern, Great White Egret (irregular) and Grey

Heron, geese (rare), various ducks, Merlin, Peregrine, Water Rail, Meadow and Water Pipits, Grey Wagtail, Great Grey Shrike.

Spring (March–May): Water level higher than in autumn. Cormorant, all the dabbling ducks, Red-crested Pochard, Tufted Duck, Goldeneye, Goosander, Black Kite, Marsh and Hen Harriers, Osprey; Water Rail and Spotted Crake, waders (small numbers), Turtle Dove, Cuckoo, Hoopoe, Wryneck, pipits, Yellow Wagtail, Nightingale, Bluethroat, Whinchat and Stonechat, Redwing, Grasshopper and Savi's Warblers, Sedge Warbler, Aquatic Warbler (very rare), Reed Warbler, *Sylvia* and *Phylloscopus* warblers, flycatchers, Penduline Tit, Red-backed Shrike, Yellowhammer, Ortolan Bunting, Reed Bunting.

Breeding season: Little and Great Crested Grebes, Little Bittern, Night Heron (breeding only suspected), Tufted Duck, Water Rail and Moorhen, Turtle Dove, Cuckoo, Nightingale, Marsh, Reed and Great Reed Warblers, Whitethroat and Garden Warbler, Long-tailed Tit, Yellowhammer, Reed and Corn Buntings.

Autumn (August–October): The water level is lowered in the late summer. Similar to spring, but following species commoner: Great White Egret, Black Stork, ducks, Honey Buzzard, Spotted Crake, Little and Baillon's Crakes (both rare), plovers, Lapwing, Little and Temminck's Stints, Curlew Sandpiper and Dunlin, Ruff, Jack Snipe, Snipe, Curlew, Whimbrel (rare), all *Tringa* species, hirundines, pipits, Wheatear.

Access
The nearest rail station is Chavornay on the Yverdon–Lausanne line (210). Regional trains run hourly. Bicycles can be hired in Yverdon and from there it is about a 15-km ride.

Accommodation
There is no accommodation near the site. Orbe, 6 km from the Creux-de-Terre, has a campsite (tel: 024/441 38 57). If you don't want to camp, stay in Yverdon which has enough hotels and a youth hostel (see Site 9, Yverdon). Information can be obtained from the Office de tourisme, c/o Gare d'Orbe, 1350 Orbe (tel: 024/441 31 15).

Site protection
The most interesting parts of the site are protected and this ensures that the wildlife has areas where it is free of disturbance. Without regular management, the site would be invaded by scrub.

Nearby sites
On the stretch between Yverdon and Chavornay, it is well worth stopping at Ependes. Where the bridge crosses the Thielle between Ependes and Mathod, you can occasionally see Wigeon, various *Tringa* species, pipits, Yellow Wagtails and hirundines. Even the open cultivated area around the reserve is still used as a stopover by many passerines. The birds do not concentrate in particular places, but rainwater pools which form on the ploughed fields in autumn attract waders, raptors, larks, pipits and buntings and are worth checking for unusual species.
  The treeless peak of Le Suchet (1558 m) lies 12 km to the west of

Yverdon. Apart from the beautiful view, the summit region offers another chance of seeing Dotterel which stop off here on migration (mainly between 20 August and mid-September). Please avoid disturbing them.

Disabled access
The site is not wheelchair-accessible and not especially suitable for other visitors with walking impairments.

8 CHAMP-PITTET

Canton:	Vaud
Grid reference:	540/181
Height a.s.l.:	430 m
Start:	Yverdon rail station
Finish:	Champ-Pittet
Itinerary:	Yverdon station–campsite 'Iris'–shore path–Field of the Standing Stones–Champ-Pittet
Duration:	allow 3 hrs to 1 day; distance $c.7$ km on above route; $c.5$ km on more direct route through Yverdon
Best time:	interesting throughout the year (but ponds often frozen over in winter)
Status:	nature reserve, reserve for waterbirds and migrants of national and international importance; IBA
Map:	LdS 1:25,000; sheet 1203 (Yverdon)
Equipment:	possibly telescope

Champ-Pittet is situated near Yverdon on the southeastern shore of Lake Neuchâtel (Lac de Neuchâtel, Neuenburgersee). It comprises the southern end of the Grande Cariçaie, which is the largest wetland in Switzerland. The name derives from *Carex*, the Latin word for sedge,

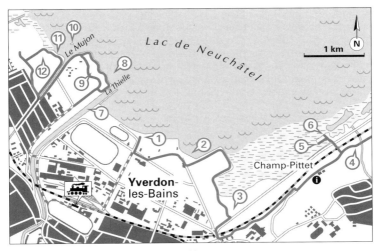

which is the dominant plant of the site. Following measures to control the flow of water originating in the Jura Mountains with the aim of preventing flooding, lowering the level of Lake Neuchâtel and draining marshes for agriculture, this site, still tiny compared with the huge area of wetlands lost, was formed in 1869. It is now a unique refuge for many rare and interesting wetland species. Here you will find all the various stages of silting-up and successive invasion by vegetation, from carr woodland through reedbed ('reedswamp') to floating-plant zone.

Recommended routes

Turn left out of Yverdon rail station, heading east. After the town park, follow the first canal left down to the lake. On the lakeshore (1), you have the first opportunity to watch ducks, gulls, terns and waders (if water level low). A slight detour to the mouth of the Thielle often produces further interesting observations (see Site 9).

Having passed to the right of the 'Iris' campsite, cross the small canal (Le Buron) and there is once again a good view out over the lake from the beach there (2). It's worth checking the shrubs and trees along the beach promenade as these often hold many passerine migrants in the early morning. Slightly further off, the view opens on to the extensive reedbeds of the Grande Cariçaie. The first Savi's Warblers are heard in song, a hunting Marsh Harrier may be quartering the reeds. However, this is just a taste of the reedbed birds which can be seen later from the observation tower.

After the small copse (Lesser Spotted Woodpecker, Golden Oriole), you come to the field with Neolithic menhirs or standing stones at Clendy (3), a site used by a Stone-Age cult. Go back along the road here for a short distance and cross the railway at the first level crossing. From there, follow the signposted route (first turn left after crossing the railway line) and, after about 10 minutes, you will reach Pro Natura's Champ-Pittet Nature Conservation Visitor Centre ('i'). The 'Château' is the starting-point for nature trails leading into the woodland (4) and into the reeds. Species to be expected in the wood include various woodpeckers and both *Phylloscopus* and *Sylvia* warblers as well as Golden Oriole and Nightingale.

To get to the observation tower (5), follow the path marked 'sentier marais'. From here, you have a view over the wide reedbed, the pools and the lake. Illustrated display boards show which bird species are regular. This is an ideal spot to see Little Bitterns in the breeding season. The Kingfisher does not breed at the site, but is seen there occasionally. Further along the nature trail, there's an observation platform (6) in the reeds, near the tower. Displaying Great Crested Grebes are an impressive sight in the courtship and breeding season.

Calendar

Largest reedbed in Switzerland. Many reedbed species can be seen well from the observation tower at Champ-Pittet. Also birds of carr woodland (along the path marked 'sentier forestier') and many waterbirds during migration.

Winter: Only few species in the reeds; also, the pools are usually frozen over. Bittern and Grey Heron are regular, Smew occasional; Goshawk, Water Rail. Open-water species (see Site 9, Yverdon–Thielle).

Spring and Autumn: The Grande Cariçaie is an important staging site for thousands of migrants. Night Heron, Purple Heron (mainly in spring), Teal, Garganey and various other ducks, Black Kite, Marsh Harrier, Osprey, Hobby, Water Rail, Spotted Crake, Snipe and occasionally other waders, skuas (chiefly September to early October), Black Tern, Whiskered Tern (mainly in spring), Grasshopper and Savi's Warblers, Sedge Warbler, Aquatic Warbler (very rare), Reed Warbler, *Phylloscopus* and *Sylvia* warblers, Bearded and Penduline Tits, Reed Bunting.

Breeding season: Little and Great Crested Grebes, Little Bittern and Grey Heron, Red-crested Pochard, Black Kite, Marsh Harrier (not breeding, but occasionally observed), Water Rail, Moorhen, Lesser Spotted Woodpecker, Nightingale, Savi's, Reed, Great Reed, Garden and Willow Warblers, Spotted Flycatcher, Bearded Tit (irregular), Golden Oriole, Reed Bunting.

Useful tips

The reedbed parcels mowed in rotation are attractive places for many passerines (e.g. larks, pipits, wagtails, Bluethroat) and waders during migration. You can look into these areas from the observation tower and from various places along the nature trail. A telescope is certainly an advantage for checking this habitat. The Grande Cariçaie still has a large population of grass snakes and there is probably no other place in Switzerland where you can watch these fascinating creatures so easily. In May and June, it is also possible to observe carp and bream from the tower as they spawn or perform their courtship rituals at the water surface by the edge of the reeds.

The Conservation Visitor Centre is an attraction in itself, with a wide range of activities and amenities on offer: changing exhibitions, multimedia presentations, nature trails, an environmental laboratory, solar-powered boats, guided tours and various kinds of excursions. The Centre is open from March to November and entry is free for Pro Natura members. Further information from: Nature Conservation Visitor Centre Champ-Pittet, 1400 Yverdon-les-Bains (tel: 024/426 93 41).

Access

Yverdon is on the line for fast trains Geneva–Yverdon–Bienne (210). From Yverdon station, either on foot (see itinerary above) or by bus (No. 1 CESSNOV) to Pré du Châtaigner (request stop only!). Getting there by bicycle is also recommended (bike-hire at Yverdon station). Follow the signs to Yvonand and you will come to the Yverdon-Yvonand cantonal highway. From the standing stones, use the cycle path parallel to the road. After about 1 km, you reach the underpass where you can leave your bike and from there it's only a two-minute walk to the observation tower (left) or to the Visitor Centre at Champ-Pittet (right).

From Yverdon, drivers should take the Yvonand road. From the roundabout with the 'obelisk', follow the signs to 'Champ-Pittet'. Parking 100 m from the Visitor Centre.

Accommodation

See Site 9, Yverdon–Thielle.

Site protection

The impact of large numbers of people seeking recreation is one of the main causes of disturbance along the entire shoreline of Lake Neuchâtel: The Nature Conservation Centre at Champ-Pittet makes it possible for those with an interest in natural history to explore this extraordinary site while causing the minimum of disturbance. The nature conservation organization Pro Natura is doing valuable work here to educate the public, pointing out the crucial importance of nature conservation and generally making people more aware of environmental issues. All visitors can make a contribution to the conservation of the site by keeping to the existing paths. There is a serious threat from erosion of the lakeshore, with some 5000 m² of the protected area being lost to this annually. Comprehensive protection measures are planned.

Disabled access

The Nature Conservation Centre and paths around Champ-Pittet are wheelchair-accessible and suitable for other visitors with walking impairments. There are also special disabled parking places at the Centre. Wheelchair-users will need help to negotiate the steep ramps in the two underpasses. Only the observation tower is likely to be inaccessible as a steep flight of steps has to be climbed up to the viewing platform.

Nearby sites

The end of the lake around the mouth of the Thielle is interesting above all during the autumn migration period (see Site 9).

Lying above the village of Onnens (10 km northeast of Yverdon) is the 'Chassagne', the only habitat of its kind in the entire region: this is a large expanse of dry, unimproved mesobromion meadowland with scattered bushes, hedges and clumps of trees. The site has long been known to botanists and entomologists, but also has something to offer those interested in birds: Wryneck, Woodlark (irregular breeder), Stonechat, Red-backed Shrike, Yellowhammer.

Bearded Tit (drawing by J. Laesser)

9 YVERDON–THIELLE

Canton:	Vaud
Grid reference:	539/181
Height a.s.l.:	430 m
Start:	Yverdon rail station
Finish:	Yverdon rail station
Itinerary:	Yverdon station–Thielle–Remblais–Bois des Vernes–Yverdon station
Duration:	allow 1 hr to half a day; distance c.3 km (c.4–5 km to Grandson)
Best time:	interesting throughout the year (but very large numbers of visitors in July and August)
Status:	reserve for waterbirds and migrants of national and international importance; IBA
Map:	LdS 1:25,000; sheet 1183 (Grandson) or street plan of Yverdon
Equipment:	telescope

The ends of lakes are highly interesting places for migrating birds, but—and this is the case at Yverdon—towns and housing estates tend to be situated there too. Fortunately, the otherwise incompatible habitat requirements of humans and migrant birds can be reconciled at Yverdon. The green belt between Lake Neuchâtel (Lac de Neuchâtel, Neuenburgersee) and the town as well as those sections of the lakeshore, parts of which have still not been built on or otherwise altered, make the area around the Thielle river mouth attractive for many bird species. While the site was famous up until the 1970s mainly for the many different species of waders which stopped off there to feed and rest in large numbers, interest now focuses on divers, ducks, gulls, terns and passerines. Waders are also still recorded there, but their numbers are much reduced since the large, low-lying mudbanks, previously exposed only at very low water, have been covered over.

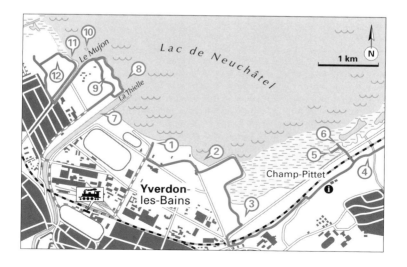

47

Recommended routes

From Yverdon station, turn right and follow the road parallel to the rail-way line (see map for Site 8). After 200 m, you come to the Thielle; turn off right, go under the rail bridge and on to the next bridge. Cross the canal there and walk along it on the opposite side towards Lake Neuchâtel: Birds to be seen in winter on the canal (7) include Little, Great Crested and Black-necked Grebes, various diving ducks, sawbills, Black-headed and Common Gulls. There is always the chance of a rari-ty, especially among the ducks, but in the case of unusual species, it is not easy to distinguish betwen genuine wild vagrants and possible escapes from captivity.

From the lakeshore (8), it is worth scanning the water surface and the embankment for winter visitors such as Red-throated and Black-throat-ed Divers, Red-necked and Black-necked Grebes, Common and Velvet Scoters, Goldeneye and Eider. There are also likely to be parties of Red-crested Pochard, Pochard, Tufted Duck and Goosander close to the shore. During migration, it's worth turning your attention to the gulls and terns. There's always a good chance of Little Gulls and Black Terns. Skuas occasionally turn up in autumn especially (chiefly September to early October).

On early autumn mornings, particularly in bad weather, the bushes and trees planted on the former spoil heap (9) often hold many inter-esting passerines: Redstart, *Sylvia* and *Phylloscopus* warblers, flycatch-ers, thrushes, etc. Slightly further along the lake, you will see a small arti-ficial island (10). This is surrounded by posts and, at low water, small sandbanks. Gulls and terns favour the posts as perches, while the sand-banks are used by waders. Outside the breeding season, various dab-bling ducks are found in this bay: Wigeon, Gadwall, Mallard, Pintail, Shoveler, also occasionally Shelduck, Teal, Garganey and Red-crested Pochard as well as Smew and Red-breasted Merganser. Apart from ducks and a few waders, this part of the lake attracts mainly gulls, Grey Herons and Cormorants. From here, you have a view over the edge of Les Vernes (12), a poplar plantation which takes on more and more the character of a riverine wood or swamp-forest the closer you get to the lakeshore. Waders and herons (occasionally, Night Heron or Great White Egret) occur on the unaltered section of the shoreline (11). The odd migrant raptor (e.g. Osprey) may fly over. From this point, there are two alternatives.

The first will take you behind the playground (which you previously passed on your left) along a path leading through the small wood (9). Passerine migrants tend to be numerous in the bushes and trees. The path ends by the Thielle river and, from there, you can use the same route back. The second, somewhat longer alternative takes you for about 250 m upstream along the little canal (Le Mujon) as far as the wooden bridge. On the other canal bank, you can head towards the lake again, where there is a choice of following the hiking trail (left straight after the bridge) to Grandson or of exploring the wood of Les Vernes on one of its many paths. There's an interesting path right behind the lakeshore. In the breeding season, you can expect to find Nightingale, Golden Oriole and Lesser Spotted Woodpecker in the wood, while there will be Reed Warblers and Reed Buntings in the reedbed. Waxwings feeding on mistletoe berries are often found in the wood in invasion years. The range of passerines likely to be encoun-tered in the autumn is similar to that for the small wood on the other side of the canal. This is the place where Spoonbills and Little Egrets wintered for the first time in Switzerland (winter 1994–1995). If on your return walk you cross the wooden bridge again and then go straight on, you will come directly to the youth hostel by the Thielle. The lakeshore on the other side of the river is very interesting for waterbirds and can be combined with a visit to Champ-Pittet (see Site 8).

Calendar
At migration times and in winter, various ducks, gulls and terns. Occasionally, waders, skuas and a variety of passerines. In summer, birds typical of wetlands, including riverine woods or swamp-forest.

Winter: Divers (especially Black-throated), Little, Great Crested, Black-necked and occasionally Red-necked Grebes, Cormorant, Grey Heron, Shelduck, Wigeon, Mallard, Gadwall, Pintail, Shoveler, Teal, Red-crested Pochard, Pochard, Tufted Duck, Eider, Velvet Scoter and sometimes Common Scoter, Goosander, less commonly Smew and Red-breasted Merganser, Goshawk, Sparrowhawk, Buzzard, Black-headed, Common and Yellow-legged Gulls.

Spring: Spring migration is much less conspicuous than the autumn passage, but you can still see some good birds: Black Kite, Marsh Harrier, Osprey and Common Tern.

Breeding season: Goosander, Black Kite, Yellow-legged Gull (occasionally summers, not breeding), Common Tern (not breeding), Lesser Spotted Woodpecker, Nightingale, Reed Warbler, Golden Oriole, Reed Bunting.

Autumn: The most interesting time: Great Crested Grebe, Cormorant, Grey Heron, occasionally Little Egret and Great White Egret; Shelduck and other ducks; rarely geese or Crane; Goshawk, Sparrowhawk, Buzzard, waders such as Common Sandpiper, various *Tringa* and *Calidris* species; Whimbrel and Curlew; skuas, Mediterranean and Little Gulls, Black Tern, many staging passerines.

Useful tips
For anyone who travels regularly by train between Basel and Lausanne or on the Geneva–Zürich–Romanshorn line, it's worth stopping off briefly at Yverdon. A couple of hours are often enough to find interesting birds. Particularly good times are when migrants are held up by the weather (e.g. heavy rainfall). The end of the lake and the little wood behind the shore are good places for such observations.

Access
From Yverdon rail station, it is 1 km along the Thielle river to the lake (for itinerary, see above). Yverdon is situated on the Neuchâtel–Lausanne and Neuchâtel–Geneva lines (210). There are also regular connections (252) between Yverdon and Fribourg.

Accommodation
The youth hostel (closed between 1 January and mid-March) is situated centrally on the Thielle river (tel: 024/425 12 33).
Campsite 'Les Iris' on the other side of the Thielle (tel: 024/425 10 89).

Campsite 'Pécos' in Grandson (tel: 024/445 49 69).

Both campsites are open from the beginning of April to the end of September. For further information, contact: Office du tourisme et du thermalisme, Place Pestalozzi, 1400 Yverdon (tel: 024/423 62 90).

Site protection

The recreational pressure on this region is a cause for concern, especially in the summer. Bathers and the massive amount of boat traffic cause huge disruption to species that need undisturbed conditions (for example, waders, Great Crested Grebes with young, reedbed nesters). Hitherto, only little regard has been given to the status of the site as a reserve for waterbirds and migrants of international importance. The sensitive areas need the kind of protection which they already have on paper, but which has yet to be implemented.

Disabled access

The short distances to be covered and well-built paths make the site an attractive one for visitors with walking impairments. Only the narrow paths created by walkers in the small wood (9) and in the Bois des Vernes (12) cannot be negotiated in a wheelchair.

10 MONT SAGNE

Canton:	Neuchâtel
Grid reference:	555/215
Height a.s.l.:	1190 m
Observation site:	pastureland northwest of Mont Sagne
Duration:	allow at least a couple of hours
Best time:	autumn (August to early November)
Status:	no special protection status
Map:	LdS 1:25,000; sheet 1144 (Val-de-Ruz)
Equipment:	telescope, folding chair, warm clothes towards end of season

Mont Sagne is situated about 2 km from La Chaux-de-Fonds. The hill is not very high, but lies at an angle to the main bird migration route. It is an especially popular site with ornithologists during the autumn migration period. The relief of the Jura mountains favours the creation of upcurrents, which are known to be used by many raptors. Together with other migrants, these cross Mont Sagne on a broad front.

Observation points

A good spot for observing the bird migration is at the foot of a solitary old maple tree (1). From there, you can take in the Pouillerel Ridge, the neighbouring part of France, Mont-Cornu, the Freiberge mountains, the Vallon de St-Imier, the Chasseral and its ridge right across to the Col de la Vue-des-Alpes. Several hours should be spent here.

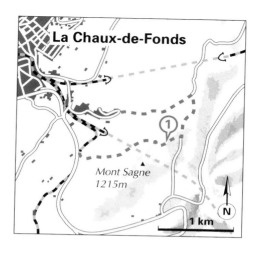

Calendar

Observation of raptors and passerines on autumn migration.

Breeding season: Black, Green and Great Spotted Woodpeckers, Tree Pipit, various thrushes, Nutcracker, etc.

Autumn: Cormorant, Black Stork, occasionally Grey Heron or White Stork; Honey Buzzard, Red and (less frequently) Black Kites, Buzzard, Goshawk (rare), Sparrowhawk, Marsh and Hen Harriers; less commonly Montagu's Harrier and Golden Eagle; Kestrel, Peregrine and Hobby, Merlin, Red-footed Falcon (rare); occasionally gulls; Stock Dove and Woodpigeon, Swift and sometimes Alpine Swift; hirundines, Skylark and Woodlark, Tree, Meadow and Water Pipits, Yellow Wagtail, thrushes, Jackdaw, Rook, various finches.

Useful tips

Not all raptors observed in the migration period are necessarily migrants. In order to distinguish betwen migrants and local residents, it is important to watch the birds carefully and to study their behaviour. A migrating raptor will typically ascend in a thermal, then glide for a distance in a southwesterly direction without losing much height, before using the next thermal to spiral up again, and so on. Several raptors will often migrate together and you will occasionally see different species using the same thermal 'carousel'. If there are no or only weak thermal upcurrents, the birds will use flapping flight and migrate in a direct line. Bouts of active flapping flight will then be followed by a short gliding phase. For some species such as buzzards, Osprey, Sparrowhawk and falcons, this kind of flight is typical.

Raptors that aren't migrating will also use these thermals, but will then, unlike the migrants, not head off southwest, but fly off in any direction. They may suddenly change direction or plunge headlong— manoeuvres not generally seen from migrating raptors.

The Red Kites often confuse observers on Mont Sagne. Watch carefully when several of these raptors are using the same thermal; some may be residents, others true migrants. Some residents are inquisitive, others tend to behave aggressively towards migrating birds.

Access

From La Chaux-de-Fonds by the La Sagne and Les Ponts-de-Martel train (222) as far as Reymond halt (request stop only). Then follow the track towards Prés de Suze, Vue-des-Alpes. At the fork after about 200 m, carry straight on into the wood. Go through the wood, across the clearing and along the left-hand edge of the wood until, after a further c.300 m, the track again leads through a wood. Finally, cross the pasture to the conspicuous lone maple.

A bus will take you from La Chaux-de-Fonds to the outskirts of Le Cerisier. This bus operates only irregularly on Saturdays and not at all on Sundays. From the terminus, you begin the ascent. After crossing some level ground, turn right and keep climbing for another 500 m until you reach the gate on your right. Continue through the gate to the solitary maple tree.

For car drivers, there is room for only two or three vehicles near the gate. An alternative would be to park in Boinod by the restaurant on the road to Vue-des-Alpes.

Accommodation

Campsite Bois-du-Convent in La Chaux-de-Fonds about 2.5 km from Mont Sagne (tel: 032/931 25 55). Youth hostel on the rue du Doubs 34, 2300 La Chaux-de-Fonds (tel: 032/968 43 15). Various hotels in La Chaux-de-Fonds. Further information from: Tourisme neuchâtelois-Montagnes, Espacité 1, 2300 La Chaux-de-Fonds (tel: 032/919 62 97).

Site protection

There is no threat to the migrating birds.

Disabled access

The site is not wheelchair-accessible and not entirely suitable for other visitors with walking impairments either. From the gate described above, about 100 m have to be covered on foot up across a sloping field.

Nearby sites

In the valley of La Sagne and Les Ponts, you will find, alongside extensive tracts of agricultural land, one of the largest raised bogs in Switzerland (Bois des Lattes). Birds to be seen here include various raptors, Quail, Corncrake (rare); Snipe and Green Sandpiper along the Le Bied stream; both Tree and Meadow Pipits breed; Water Pipit, Yellow Wagtail, Whinchat, Wheatear, Marsh and Willow Warblers, Redpoll, etc. The most varied habitats are on the Les Ponts-de-Martel side which can be reached by train from La Chaux-de-Fonds.

The Mont Racine-Tête ridge has typical species of the Jura summit zone such as Skylark and Woodlark, Tree and Meadow Pipits, Wheatear, Ring Ouzel, Nutcracker and Citril Finch.

11 CHASSERAL

Canton:	Bern and Neuchâtel
Grid reference:	570/220
Height a.s.l.:	up to 1600 m
Start:	Villeret
Finish:	Nods
Itinerary:	Villeret–Combe Grède–Petit Chasseral–Chasseral (summit)–southern slope–Nods
Duration:	allow 1 day; distance *c*.18 km
Best time:	from end of March to October
Status:	Combe Grède: nature reserve
Map:	LdS 1:25,000; sheet 1125 (Chasseral)
Equipment:	walking boots, map 1:25,000

The Chasseral (1607 m) is one of the Jura summits whose plant communities recall those of the Alps; treeless, short-grass pastures, rock ledges, etc. In the fauna too, there are many parallels. For example, the breeding birds include Water Pipit, Wheatear, Ring Ouzel and Citril Finch; all these are species otherwise found only in the Alps. On one side, the Chasseral's long ridge towers conspicuously above the Central Plateau at Bienne (Biel). On the other side, it climbs above the other summits of the folded part of the Jura chain.

Recommended routes

Looking southeast from Villeret in the Vallon de St-Imier, you can already see the Chasseral ridge through the deep-cut gorges of the Combe-Grède. A walk through the valley will bring you to the Combe Grède nature reserve (1). The way through this spectacular cutting in the landscape lies several hundred metres below the level of the Chasseral's northwest flank. This is a Peregrine site and Wallcreepers also live on the rock faces. There are many woodland species too, such as Ring Ouzel or Crossbill.

After a walk of about 3 km through the gorges, you come to a fork. Take the path to the left and it's about 2.5 km from there to the Petit Chasseral (2). The track leads to two houses which lie at the end of a narrow road. Follow the latter as far as the Chasseral (3) or take the poorly marked, more direct route which leads between the two peaks of the Petit Chasseral (1571 m).

The mountain meadows have breeding Woodlark and Skylark, Water Pipit and Wheatear, but you should also see finches such as Citril Finch, Goldfinch and Linnet. Migrating raptors occasionally pass over the summit region and various species stop off here on migration. The latter sometimes include rarities such as Dotterel (end of August to early September), Alpine Accentor and Snow Bunting (chiefly late autumn and spring). On a fine clear day, the magnificent panorama of the Alps is simply breathtaking sight from the Chasseral summit.

Follow the track along the ridge for about 1 km until you get to the Hotel du Chasseral. From there, follow the signposted way to Nods. The trail (*c*.4 km) crosses the wooded southeast flank (4) of the Chasseral. The elusive Hazel Grouse occurs here: listen out for its characteristic high-pitched whistle. Green, Black and Great Spotted Woodpeckers, Ring Ouzel and Nutcracker are easier to find.

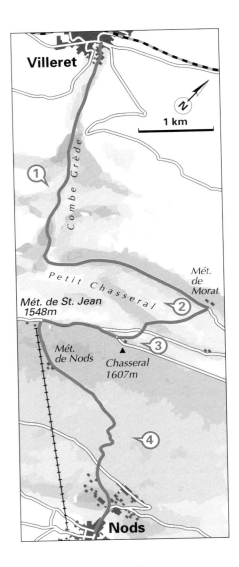

Calendar

Many typical breeding birds of the Jura heights. Conspicuous passerine migration and a few raptors at appropriate times (March–May and August–October). The impression is of slightly more conspicuous migration in autumn than in spring.

Winter: Relatively few species. Peregrine, Goldcrest, tits, Raven, Snow Bunting (occasionally).

Spring and Autumn: Various migrating raptors, Dotterel (rare; end of August to early September), Woodcock, Skylark and Woodlark,

Swallow, Sand, Crag and House Martins, Tree, Meadow and Water Pipits, Yellow Wagtail, Redstart, Whinchat, Wheatear, Ring Ouzel, Redwing and various other thrushes, Brambling, Citril Finch, Goldfinch, Linnet, Crossbill, Snow Bunting (rare).

Breeding season: Black and Red Kites, Goshawk, Sparrowhawk, Kestrel and Peregrine, Hazel Grouse, Woodcock, Stock Dove, Tawny, Long-eared and Tengmalm's Owls, Green, Black and Great Spotted Woodpeckers, Woodlark and Skylark, Crag Martin, Tree, Meadow and Water Pipits, Wheatear, Ring Ouzel, Fieldfare, Song and Mistle Thrushes, Bonelli's and Wood Warblers, Wallcreeper, Raven, Serin, Citril Finch, Goldfinch, Siskin, Linnet, Crossbill.

Useful tips

Slightly away from the itinerary described above (*c.*5 km east of the Chasseral summit) lie Les Prés Vaillons, between the Chasseral and Mont Sujet. There's a chance of hearing Tawny, Long-eared and Tengmalm's Owls here in the evening.

Access

Villeret station is on the Bienne–La Chaux-de-Fonds line (225) on which there is a regular regional train service. From Bienne, you sometimes have to change at Sonceboz. A regular postbus service (210.75) operates between Nods and La Neuveville with connections to Neuchâtel (Neuenburg) and Bienne.

There is also a private toll-road up to the Chasseral.

Accommodation

The Hotel du Chasseral, 2518 Nods, is situated about 1 km southwest of the summit (tel: 032/751 24 51 or 032/751 32 86). For further information, contact the Office régional du Tourisme Chasseral-La Neuveville, rue du Marché 4, 2520 La Neuveville (tel: 032/751 49 49).

Site protection

The dense network of tracks and trails on the Chasseral is the main reason why shy woodland birds such as Hazel Grouse or Woodcock suffer disturbance. Pressure from visitors is considerable at certain weekends. What would be desirable is measures to control visitors and a plan for appropriate careful management of sensitive parts of the forest.

The La Tscharner gorge, a couple of kilometres east of the summit, is threatened by the plan to make a limestone quarry for a cement works.

Disabled access

Access to the summit region for disabled visitors is via the private road. However, the surrounding area is difficult terrain and for the most part unsuitable.

Nearby sites

The region around the Chasseral is impressive with its many sites of outstanding natural beauty. Other places certainly worth a visit in the area include La Combe Biosse (canton of Neuchâtel), the small wetland of Les Pontins (2 km east of Combe Grède) and La Tscharner (at the altitude of La Heutte).

Dotterel (drawing by J. Laesser)

12 CLOS-DU-DOUBS

Canton:	Jura
Grid reference:	570/240
Height a.s.l.:	between 420 and 480 m along the Doubs; slopes up to 1000 m
Start:	St Ursanne rail station
Finish:	Soubey
Itinerary:	St Ursanne station–St Ursanne village–Tariche–Chervillers–Soubey
Duration:	allow 1 day; distance *c.* 16 km
Best time:	spring
Status:	nature reserve
Map:	LdS 1:25,000; sheets 1085 (St Ursanne) and 1105 (Bellelay) or 1:50,000, sheet 222 (Clos-du-Doubs)
Equipment:	walking boots

Over thousands of years, the River Doubs has carved out a deep furrow in the limestone rocks of the Jura. At St Ursanne, the course of the river is diverted abruptly to the west. This great meander almost forms an 'island', the Clos-du-Doubs. This is the only section of the river where both banks lie on Swiss soil.

Hitherto, the region has been spared from over-development for tourism and housing. The unspoilt landscape thus provides the opportunity to discover species typical of the Jura's forests and rivers. The medieval village of St Ursanne is a delightful starting-point for an exploratory tour of this lovely region.

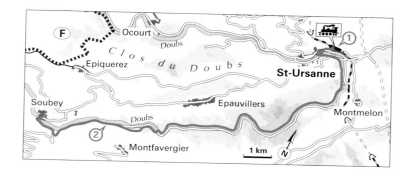

Recommended routes

Start at St Ursanne station (1). Crag Martins and Peregrine breed on the overhanging cliffs and Wallcreepers are seen here in winter. Woods on the south-facing slopes have Bonelli's Warbler and Honey Buzzard and many species of reptiles and orchids are found on the dry slopes. The route leads through the old part of St Ursanne, where a Wallcreeper sometimes winters on the church. Cross the River Doubs and head left towards d'Epauvillers. After 400 m, the road makes a sharp hairpin bend to the right; from here, continue along the footpath which follows the Doubs. The path runs along one or other side of the Doubs as far as Soubey. On the last stage, from Chervillers to Soubey, you can walk only on the left bank (2). The walk of about 15 km passes through one of the scenically most attractive parts of Switzerland. Breeding birds likely to be seen on the way include Grey Heron, Black and Red Kites, Peregrine, Moorhen, Black, Great Spotted, Green and (rarer) Grey-headed Woodpeckers, Grey Wagtail and Dipper.

Calendar

Birds of the river and rocky cliffs in one of the most spectacular and loveliest landscapes in Switzerland.

Winter: Little Grebe, Cormorant, Grey Heron, Mallard and sometimes other dabbling ducks, Pochard and Tufted Duck, Goosander, Moorhen; Dunnock, occasionally Firecrest, Long-tailed Tit, Grey Wagtail; various finches.

Spring: Many birds begin nesting very early. Occasional interesting passage migrants: Cormorant, various dabbling ducks, Pochard and Tufted Duck, Goosander, Osprey, gulls, Whinchat, Grasshopper Warbler, various *Sylvia* and *Phylloscopus* warblers.

Breeding season: Grey Heron, Black and Red Kites, Sparrowhawk, Goshawk, Peregrine, Kingfisher, Great Spotted, Green, Black and Grey-headed Woodpeckers, Crag Martin, Grey Wagtail, Dipper, Bonelli's Warbler, Red-backed Shrike, Raven, etc.

Autumn: Raptors and a few waders (e.g. Common Sandpiper) regularly on passage; usually only resident species present in good numbers.

With its birds and its stunning scenery, an excursion to Clos-du-Doubs is an
unforgettable experience (photo: S. Theytaz)

Access

St Ursanne is on the Porrentruy–Delémont line (240) and is regularly
served by regional and fast trains.

A postbus runs between St Ursanne and Soubey (240.50) and there is
another postbus connection from Soubey to Saignelégier (236.10); several postbuses daily, including Sundays and holidays (check timetables).

Accommodation

The campsite in Tariche (tel: 032/433 46 19) is halfway along the route
described above and is open from 1 March to the end of October.

Various other campsites in the area: e.g. Camping à la ferme (tel:
032/461 31 43) or Moulin-Jeannottat, 2727 Pommerats, Camping rus-
tique 7 km from Soubey (open from 1 April to the end of September;
with adjacent dormitory accommodation (tel: 032/951 13 15)); or the
Moulin du Doubs campsite, 2889 Ocourt, 6 km downstream from St
Ursanne (open from 1 May to the end of September (tel: 032/461 32
98)).

Hotels available: Hotel de Tariche (with dormitory accommodation)
at the same address as the campsite (see above); Hotel du Cerf, 2887
Soubey (tel: 032/955 12 03) and various others in St Ursanne.

Further information from: Jura-Tourisme St Ursanne et Clos-du-
Doubs, rue du Quartier 18, 2882 St Ursanne (tel: 032/461 37 16).

Site protection

The site has managed to retain its wild, unspoilt character.
Nevertheless, the pressure from the large numbers of visitors—bathers,
anglers, canoeists, etc.—clearly has an impact. Visitors are urged not to
pick plants, to keep dogs on the lead and to light fires only at places designated for that purpose.

More and more unused agricultural land is becoming overgrown
with scrub and trees on the edges of the site.

The water level of the artificially-regulated River Doubs can vary
markedly and this has a negative effect on both plants and wildlife in
the river.

Disabled access

The paths and tracks are not really wheelchair-negotiable and visitors
with walking impairments have access to the site at only a few places
such as Soubey or St Ursanne. Tariche can only be reached by private
car.

Nearby sites

The picturesque landscape makes the region, which has a wide network of hiking trails, well worth a visit. Upstream from Soubey, the path
continues as far as Moulin and on to Jeannottat and Goumois. The number of hotels and campsites make it easy to plan your route and arrange
accommodation for each stage. Towards the south, the Neuchâtel
(Mont-Racine chain) and Vaud Jura (Le Suchet and Vallée de Joux)
ranges are worth seeing. Anyone who feels like it can continue the walk
to Saint Jacques de Compostelle. Downstream, there is a path on the far
side of St Ursanne which leads to Ocourt and La Motte (postbus connection with St Ursanne).

South of the Doubs, you can ramble in the Freiberge mountains.

Especially worth mentioning are the Etang de la Gruère with its nature trail and the Cerlatez visitor centre between Saignelégier and Tramelan. The Sommêtres crags near Noirmont are of interest for the autumn raptor migration (also Woodpigeons, etc).

Goosander (drawing by J. Laesser)

13 VINGELZBERG

Canton:	Bern
Grid reference:	583/220
Height a.s.l.:	430–600 m (1000 m)
Start:	Bienne rail station
Finish:	Bienne rail station
Itinerary:	Bienne station–Felseck–Vingelz Wood–Hohflue–Vingelz Wood–pavilion–Felseck–Bienne station
Duration:	allow *c.*2 hours; distance *c.*4–5 km
Best time:	March to June
Status:	the dry slope at Felseck is a nature reserve
Map:	LdS 1:25,000; sheet 1125 (Chasseral)
Equipment:	sturdy footwear

The wooded, south-facing slope of the Vingelzberg drops down gradually over 1000 m to Lake Bienne (German *Bielersee*). The slope is subject to intense solar radiation, both directly and indirectly through reflection from the lake. The wood is of varied composition and contains mainly beech, downy oak, ash and, in places, pine. There is a dense understorey, with many breeding passerines. The magnificent view over Lake Bienne and its environs from the Hohflue and other vantage points cannot fail to impress. At the foot of the slope, the so-called Felseck, there is a flourishing dry, rocky and steppe-like area of mesobromion grassland. Unfortunately, many interesting former breeding birds have disappeared. The site has none the less retained its character and is certainly worth a visit.

Recommended routes

From Bienne (Biel) station, go along the Rue du Débarcadère in the direction of Neuchâtel (Neuenburg). At the car park 400 m after the

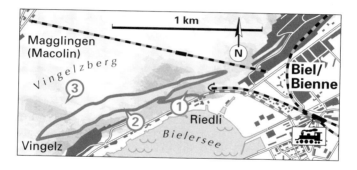

roundabout, go up the wooden stairway which leads across the dry slope of Felseck (1). This nature reserve has sadly lost its main ornithological attractions (Nightjar, Cirl and Rock Buntings). Despite this, the site is an important refuge for many plants, reptiles and insects (e.g. praying mantis) which are adapted to this special hot microclimate.

At the first point where the path divides, branch off right and, shortly afterwards, turn left. Vingelz Wood (2) is rich in birdlife: Black Kite, Tawny Owl, Cuckoo, six species of woodpeckers, Bonelli's Warbler, Golden Oriole.

Bear right at all the following forks and this will bring you to the Hohflue (3). The wood is crisscrossed by countless hiking trails, so it's worth checking the map frequently. There's a marvellous view from the Hohflue of the town, the lake and the western part of the Central Plateau. This vantage point is also a good place for watching migrating and local raptors: Honey Buzzard, Black Kite, Goshawk, Sparrowhawk, Buzzard and Peregrine are all seen regularly.

To continue the circuit, follow the path east for about 1 km. Just before the rack railway, turn right and take the path which leads west past the pavilion. This path will bring you back to the starting point.

Calendar

The varied, south-facing wood has raptors and several other interesting woodland species.

Winter: Sporadic records of interesting species: Raven, occasionally Peregrine.

Spring: Raptors, Raven, Sand and Crag Martins, Swallow and House Martin; certain species such as Tawny Owl or woodpeckers start breeding early (March).

Breeding season: Black Kite, Woodpigeon, Cuckoo, Tawny Owl, Grey-headed, Green, Great Spotted, Middle Spotted and Lesser Spotted Woodpeckers, Garden Warbler and Blackcap, Bonelli's and Wood Warblers, Chiffchaff, Dunnock, Pied Flycatcher, Nuthatch, Golden Oriole.

Autumn: Black Kite, Buzzard, Sparrowhawk, Peregrine, various hirundines, all four *Phylloscopus* species breeding in Switzerland.

Useful tips

As the south-facing slopes warm up rapidly, an early-morning visit is recommended.

The dry mesobromion meadow below the pavilion (Felseck) has long been known to entomologists as a very valuable site. A rare butterfly, the great banded grayling, still occurs along the woodland edge. There are also few sites in Switzerland for the saddle-backed bush-cricket which lives here in the scattered bushes on the meadow.

Access

Bienne is situated at the main traffic intersection of Lausanne/Geneva–Neuchâtel–Olten–Zürich. The site is on the Jura slopes, only about 600 m from Bienne rail station. A regular rack-railway service operates between Bienne and Magglingen (Macolin). The itinerary described above can easily be combined with a journey by rack railway (for the ascent or descent).

Accommodation

The town of Bienne has all kinds of accommodation available. For further information, contact: Tourisme Bienne Seeland, Place de la Gare 12, 2502 Bienne/Biel (tel: 032/322 75 75).

Site protection

As the Vingelzberg is a popular recreation place for people from the surrounding area, there is a lot of pressure from visitors, especially at weekends. The very dense network of footpaths, tracks and trails makes the resulting disturbance even more problematical, since the birds have virtually nowhere to go for peace and quiet. Whatever you do, please keep strictly to the existing paths.

Disabled access

The steep terrain means that you need to be fit and pretty good on your feet. None of the footpaths is suitable for wheelchairs.

Middle Spotted Woodpecker (drawing by J. Laesser)

Nearby sites

The town of Bienne itself can be fairly interesting ornithologically at certain times of the year. In winter, there are often lots of waterbirds in the area between the lakeshore and the mouth of the Schüss: Great Crested Grebe, various diving ducks, Goosander, Common and Yellow-legged Gulls; occasionally rarer species such as Red-necked Grebe or Smew. Swifts and Alpine Swifts, also Jackdaws, nest on buildings in the old town.

14 FANEL AND CHABLAIS DE CUDREFIN

Canton:	Bern, Vaud, Neuchâtel, (Fribourg)
Grid reference:	570/202
Height a.s.l.:	430 m
Start:	La Sauge
Finish:	La Sauge
Itinerary A:	La Sauge–right bank of the Broye–'Gamshoger'–Bernese Tower–Fanelhaus–Witzwil Wood–La Sauge
Itinerary B:	La Sauge–left bank of the Broye–Broye embankment–Chablais (fen)–Chablais Wood–La Sauge
Duration:	allow half a day for each route; route A 4–5 km; route B 5–6 km
Best time:	interesting all year (apart from very cold winters when lagoon and lakeshore freeze over)
Status:	nature reserve, Ramsar site; reserve for waterbirds and migrants of national and international importance; IBA
Map:	LdS 1:25,000; sheet 1165 (Murten)
Equipment:	telescope, wellington boots (in spring)

The Fanel/Chablais de Cudrefin Reserve lies at the northeast end of Lake Neuchâtel (Lac de Neuchâtel, Neuenburgersee), by the mouth of the Broye Canal. The site is situated at the easternmost extremity of the Grande Cariçaie, the largest reedswamp in Switzerland. It extends along the southern shore of Lake Neuchâtel: What makes the site, both within and beyond the limits of the actual reserve, extremely interesting for birds is the variety of attractive habitats: islands with gull and tern colonies, the sandbanks needed by waders, the shallows, the pools, the bordering woodland and the fields of the hinterland.

The fame of the Fanel and the Chablais de Cudrefin speaks for itself. Large numbers of people interested in birds visit it throughout the year. The main attractions in winter are the numerous ducks and geese and in summer the important colonies of gulls and Common Terns. It is even more fascinating and varied in spring and autumn when an extraordinary wealth of migrant birds greatly enriches the site. SVS—BirdLife Switzerland will open a visitor centre at La Sauge in 2000/2001.

Recommended routes

Route A: straight away, at the La Sauge car park, it's worth briefly checking the fields: Curlews, Lapwings, single herons or raptors regularly feed there. Go under the road-bridge which passes over the Broye

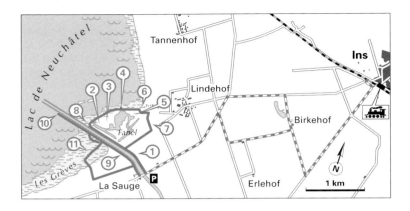

Canal and follow the path along the right bank (1) for about 1.5 km. In the spring and summer, you can hear Cuckoo, Turtle Dove and Nightingale along the way. From the signposted entrance to the reserve onwards, you must keep to the footpaths.

The path leads to the right and there is soon a clear view over a lagoon (2). Smew are regular visitors here in the winter. Look for Night Herons in spring and summer. There is a good chance of seeing beaver at dusk.

The Gamshoger (3) is a small earth mound which you can climb on to and, from it, you get a good view across the reedbed to the lake and the islands. In the reeds: Savi's, Reed and Great Reed Warblers, Bearded and Penduline Tits, Reed Bunting. On the islands: breeding colony with Black-headed and Yellow-legged Gulls, Common Terns and (rarer) Common and Mediterranean Gulls. In winter, Cormorant, Grey Heron, Bean, White-fronted and Greylag Geese, ducks and waders take over the islands. On the lake: grebes, Cormorant, various dabbling and diving ducks. The side of the Gamshoger facing away from the lake is especially interesting when the water level is high: Purple Heron, dabbling ducks and various waders are possibilities. Raptors such as Black Kite, Marsh and Hen Harriers, Buzzard, Merlin (occasional), Hobby and Peregrine hunt here.

Continue towards the Bernese Tower (4). Looking down from the tower, you have a view over the islands, the lagoon with the nesting platforms and the reedbed. There's also the chance of spotting elusive species at the edge of the reeds: Bittern, Little Bittern, Water Rail, Spotted or (rarer) Little Crake. All three marsh terns can sometimes be seen in spring, with Black Tern by far the most numerous.

Go further along the so-called Scherbenweg and you come to a small wood (5) where, among other birds, you may find Lesser Spotted Woodpecker and Long-tailed Tit. When you come out of the wood, climb up onto the old embankment (6) which will take you past the Fanelhaus. On the lake side of the embankment, you overlook the 'Schweinebucht' (Bay of Pigs), a favourite locality for Great Crested Grebes, ducks, Greylag Geese (in winter) and foraging Grey Herons. There is a pond on the other side of the embankment where Teal and Moorhen are regular and Smew sometimes occur in winter. Teal, Garganey, Gadwall and Shoveler feed there in spring. Depending on the water level and the height of the vegetation, a variety of waders can be seen at this pond. From the embankment, you can regularly observe various species of herons: most commonly Grey Heron, but Purple Heron, Great White and Little Egrets are also regular visitors; Squacco Heron and Cattle Egret remain very rare vagrants. At the Fanelhaus, go back down onto the path and take the track that leads off at right angles to the embankment through the spruce wood (7) where there is a Grey Heron colony. Fork right at the junction and this will bring you back to the Broye Canal; turn left and follow the canal path back to the car park at La Sauge.

The Neuchâtel (Neuenburg) Tower (8) is similarly an excellent observation point, affording a marvellous view over the vast reedbed, the islands and the lake. A telescope will even allow you to check the distant sandbanks in Chablais de Cudrefin on the other side of the Broye embankment. However, the tower is only open at irregular times and, in spring, access to it is often blocked by flooding.

Route B: from the jetty at La Sauge, on the left bank of the Broye Canal, follow the path along the canal towards the lake. To the left of the path is Chablais Wood (9). Golden Oriole or Nightingale sing there in the breeding season and frequent calls come from Cuckoo and Lesser Spotted Woodpecker. Goosander and Common Sandpiper can be seen along the canal.

From the embankment (10), the view to the right takes in the Fanel and the islands (see under 3, above). On the left, when the water level is low, you will see the sandbanks as well as the rows of posts poking out of the water. During migration, this area holds many waders: all the *Calidris* and *Tringa* species, Ruff, plovers, Lapwing, Whimbrel and Curlew; occasionally Oystercatcher, Avocet, Black-tailed and Bar-tailed

The Fanel is one of the most important wetlands
in Switzerland (photo: B. Renevey)

Godwits. Turnstones are more likely to be seen among the stones of the jetty. Other species which can be seen on the sandbanks: Little Egret, Shelduck, Gadwall, Teal and Pintail. The posts are used as perches by Cormorant, Grey Heron, various gulls and terns, including mainly Common Tern, but also marsh terns; rarer are Caspian, Sandwich and Little Terns. Great White Egret sometimes at the edge of the reeds. Birds still present at the site in winter include Cormorant, Grey Heron and Great White Egret, various ducks, Curlew, Lapwing, occasionally Dunlin; Black-headed, Common and Yellow-legged Gulls and Water Pipit. Whooper Swans winter, but only irregularly.

The end of the jetty is a good spot from which to scan the water surface for divers and grebes, Eider, Long-tailed Duck, Velvet and Common Scoters. Interesting passage gulls and waders occasionally turn up.

On the return walk, it's worth making a detour through the Chablais Reserve (11). Turn off right at the first fork, as you move from reeds to woodland. Slightly further on, you come to another spot where the path divides. If you take the right-hand fork through the areas where the reeds have been cut, you may see some good birds. Waders gather here when there are floods. A good place for interesting observations at dusk is the small mound, but this lies somewhat hidden among the bushes. Walking on the areas of cut reeds is forbidden. At this time of day, mammals such as foxes, deer and wild pigs are frequently encountered. For the return walk, face away from the lake and turn off first left where the path divides; this will take you to the canal (a few hundred metres) where you turn right for La Sauge.

Calendar

One of the most important and interesting birdwatching sites in Switzerland. In spring (March–May) and autumn (August–October), many migrants stop off here to rest and feed. Many interesting breeding birds in the reeds. Large gull colony on the islands; raft for nesting Common Terns in the lagoon.

Winter: Divers (occasionally), Little, Great Crested and Black-necked Grebes, Bittern, Cormorant, Great White Egret, Whooper Swan, Bean, White-fronted and Greylag Geese, Shelduck, various dabbling ducks, many Red-crested Pochard, Pochard and Tufted Ducks, also Ferruginous Duck and Scaup; Eider, Velvet Scoter and Goldeneye; less commonly Long-tailed Duck and Common Scoter; Red-breasted Merganser and Goosander, Hen Harrier, Goshawk, Sparrowhawk, Merlin, Peregrine, Water Rail, Lapwing, Curlew, sometimes Dunlin; Snipe, Common and Yellow-legged Gulls, Kingfisher, Meadow and Water Pipits, Grey Wagtail, Bearded Tit, Great Grey Shrike, Rook, finches, Reed Bunting.

Spring and Autumn: Little Grebe, Cormorant, Bittern, Little Bittern, Night Heron, Little and Great White Egrets, Grey and Purple Herons; occasionally Squacco Heron and Cattle Egret; White Stork, Shelduck, various dabbling ducks, Red-crested Pochard, Pochard and Tufted Duck, occasionally Ferruginous Duck and Scaup; Eider, Red-breasted Merganser and Goosander, Honey Buzzard (mainly autumn), Black Kite, Marsh and Hen Harriers, Osprey, Hobby and Peregrine, Water Rail, Moorhen, Spotted and Little Crakes, Oystercatcher, Black-winged Stilt,

Avocet, Little Ringed and Ringed, sometimes Kentish, Plovers; Lapwing, occasionally Golden and Grey Plovers; Turnstone, various sandpipers (*Calidris*), Ruff, Whimbrel and Curlew, Black-tailed and (rarer) Bar-tailed Godwits, *Tringa* species, Snipe, Mediterranean, Little, Common, Lesser Black-backed and Yellow-legged Gulls, Common and (rarer) Black, Whiskered and White-winged Black Terns; Turtle Dove, Cuckoo, Kingfisher, occasionally Hoopoe and Wryneck; Swallow, House and Sand Martins, Yellow Wagtail, Nightingale, Bluethroat, Whinchat and Stonechat, Wheatear, Grasshopper and Savi's, Sedge, Reed and Great Reed Warblers, Lesser Whitethroat and Whitethroat, Spotted and Pied Flycatchers, Bearded and Penduline Tits, Red-backed Shrike, Golden Oriole, Rook, various finches, Reed Bunting, Ortolan Bunting (mainly spring).

Breeding season: Little and Great Crested Grebes, Cormorant (summering, not breeding), Little Bittern and Grey Heron, Red-crested Pochard (only a few pairs breed), Eider (a few breeding records since 1994), Red-breasted Merganser (breeding exceptional), Goosander, Black Kite, Marsh Harrier (not breeding), Goshawk, Sparrowhawk, Water Rail and Moorhen, Lapwing, Woodcock; large colony of Black-headed and Yellow-legged Gulls, occasionally Mediterranean and Common Gulls, Common Tern, Turtle Dove, Cuckoo, Kingfisher, Grey-headed and Lesser Spotted Woodpeckers, Nightingale, Savi's, Reed, Great Reed and Willow Warblers, Bearded Tit, Reed Bunting.

Useful tips

The very best place for observations in and around the lagoon is the Bernese Tower. Members of the Bernese Ala and the Ala (Swiss Society for Ornithology and Bird Protection) may collect the keys from the Ins rail station. Only members of Nos Oiseaux are allowed to use the Neuchâtel Tower and visits must be booked in advance. For regular visitors to the Fanel, it is worth becoming a member of one of the societies mentioned above. The SVS—BirdLife Switzerland visitor centre will open in 2000/2001.

Access

Ins, where bicycles can be hired (booking recommended (tel: 032/313 15 29)), is reached via Bern or Neuchâtel (Neuenburg) (220). A bike is the best way of getting around at this site. If you cycle, you can take in a brief visit to the Birkehof Pond (see 'Nearby sites', below) on your way to the main site. From Ins station, follow the rail track for about 500 m in the direction of Neuchâtel, then cross the track at the first level crossing, turn sharp left and and go along a narrow road which bends to the right after about 200 m. Go straight on then for about 2 km and take the sharply-angled right turn at the fourth fork. The Birkehof Pond is on the left-hand side of the road after about 1.5 km and just before this joins the major road.

On the major road, proceed to the next main crossroads, turn left again there and carry on to La Sauge bridge over the Broye Canal. There's a large car park just before the bridge. From this point, you have to walk (no vehicles are allowed in the reserve and that includes bicycles).

The scheduled boat service from Neuchâtel to Murten stops at La Sauge (May to October only; check timetable).

Accommodation

Members of the Bernese Ala (Bernese Society for Ornithology and Bird Protection) can stay at the Fanelhaus. Very basic accommodation is available for a maximum of three people in the Neuchâtel Tower (see 'Useful tips', above). The forthcoming visitor centre at La Sauge will have a few guest rooms. The campsite in Cudrefin, about 2.5 km from La Sauge, is open from 15 March to the end of October (tel: 026/677 32 77).

Site protection

Visitors come to this site in very large numbers on certain weekends. In the Fanel, the pathways are designed to cope with the number of visitors and, at critical spots, bushes have been planted to screen the areas sensitive to disturbance. The latter is a problem mainly in the Chablais de Cudrefin. The sandbanks near the Broye canal embankment are regularly taken over by bathers and, later in the year, by inconsiderate photographers.

Disabled access

This is not a good site for those with walking impairments. The paths are not wheelchair-accessible.

Nearby sites

The Birkehof Pond is worth visiting and is situated by the road connecting Ins and Witzwil. Interesting migrants can be observed there: Wigeon, Gadwall and Teal, Goosander, *Tringa* species, occasionally Black-winged Stilt and other waders; Stonechat, Ortolan and Corn Buntings. The surrounding fields also have great potential for interesting species. Birds you can see feeding there in winter include various geese, Hen Harriers, occasionally Cranes, Curlew and Rooks. During the rest of the year: Black Kite, Peregrine, Lapwing, Curlew, less commonly Golden Plover; Turtle Dove, Stock Dove and Woodpigeon, Skylark and Woodlark, all the pipits, Yellow Wagtail, Wheatear, Rook, finches, Ortolan and Corn Buntings. Inundated fields in the area often attract a range of waders.

To get to the pond from La Sauge, take the road to Neuchâtel as far as the signposted right turn to Ins. After about 1 km (just after the high-tension cables), turn right and you will see the pond on the right-hand side next to the road. There is no entry to the pond itself, but you can get a relatively good view from the road. Species that feed on the fields are not concentrated in any one particular spot. It's worth scanning the farmland with a telescope.

15 AURIED AT KLEINBÖSINGEN

Canton:	Fribourg
Grid reference:	582/193
Height a.s.l.:	490 m
Start:	Bösingen, Laupen or Kleinbösingen
Finish:	ditto
Itinerary:	Laupen–along River Saane–Auried
Duration:	allow 1–3 hours; distance *c.*1.5 km
Best time:	April–June
Status:	nature reserve
Map:	LdS 1:25,000; sheets 1185 (Fribourg) and 1165 (Murten)
Equipment:	telescope

Roughly 2 km downstream from the artificially-dammed Schiffenensee lake lies the nature reserve of Auried. Where the River Saane has eaten away at the subsoil over centuries, seeking to create its own bed, man began to excavate gravel in 1969. Even while gravel extraction was going on, many plants and animals colonized the pit which was steadily increasing in size. The local authority (commune) plan to use the hole as a rubbish dump was thwarted by Pro Natura, particularly Pro Natura Fribourg. In order to preserve the rich species diversity, the two organizations launched an appeal in 1981 and the donations received enabled them to purchase 15 hectares of this site and to declare it a nature reserve with protected status.

The mosaic of pools, ponds, hedgerows and woodland, wet and dry meadows, gravel banks and reedbeds now harbours an astonishing range of species, a total of almost 190 having been recorded to date. Among the breeding birds are rarities such as Little Bittern, Great Reed Warbler, Whitethroat or Penduline Tit and as many as 28 different wader species have stopped off in the Auried on migration.

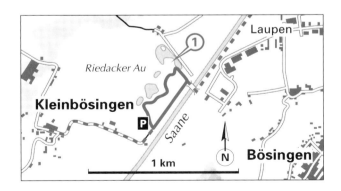

Recommended routes

If you come by public transport, you will still have a short way to walk from Kleinbösingen. After about 700 m, the access road runs parallel to the River Saane right up to the small reserve information centre and the car park on the edge of the site. This is the starting-point for a circular walk through the site of about 1.5 km (see map). Permitted paths are marked. There is a well-developed infrastructure, with several new boardwalks and a nature trail having recently been opened to the public. In the northeastern part of the reserve, an observation mound (1) gives you a good view of what is happening down on the water and next to it. This is the area with the most important and largest ponds and these are the best for waders. In the breeding season, the mound is an ideal place for observing Little Ringed Plovers, Lapwings and Little Grebes, first their courtship displays, later their attempts to rear young. At nightfall on warm evenings from April to June, a loud and impressive chorus of sounds comes from tree frogs, toads and green frogs. At some ponds, you are even allowed to catch small aquatic animals in order to observe them closely, but it goes without saying that they must be released afterwards. Little Bittern and Great Reed Warbler can be found in patches of old reeds in the middle of the reserve while Tufted Duck broods are best looked for in July or August on one of the three large expanses of open water. Migrant and breeding passerines can be seen throughout the reserve.

Calendar

Great importance for rare breeding birds such as Little Bittern, Tufted Duck, Great Reed Warbler, Whitethroat, etc.; important staging site for migrant waders (28 species recorded).

Spring: Several species of heron such as Night and Purple Herons, Little Egret (all rare); Teal and Garganey, Honey Buzzard, Black Kite, Marsh Harrier, Sparrowhawk, Osprey, Hobby and Peregrine, Quail, several rails and crakes, Snipe, Green and Wood Sandpipers, Greenshank and occasionally other waders, Black Tern (rare), Hoopoe, Wryneck, Yellow Wagtail, Bluethroat, Whinchat and Stonechat, Savi's and Sedge Warblers, Icterine Warbler (rare), Lesser Whitethroat, Penduline Tit, Golden Oriole, Ortolan Bunting (irregular).

Breeding season: Little Grebe, Little Bittern (irregular), Tufted Duck, Water Rail and Moorhen, Little Ringed Plover, Lapwing, Cuckoo, Green, Black, Great Spotted and Lesser Spotted Woodpeckers, Skylark, Nightingale, Grasshopper, Marsh and Reed Warblers, Great Reed Warbler (irregular), Whitethroat, Garden and Willow Warblers, Penduline Tit (irregular), Yellowhammer and Reed Bunting.

Autumn: Similar to spring; mainly waders, passerines such as Whinchat, Pied and Spotted Flycatchers.

Access

The easiest way to reach Auried is via Laupen, from where it's just a short walk along the River Saane. To get to Laupen, take the regional train from Bern or the bus from Gümmenen. From Bern, there is also a regional train service to Kerzers (220) or to Düdingen (S1; 290), where you have to change to a bus (290.48). The bus journey from Kerzers to Kleinbösingen takes around 20 minutes, from Düdingen six minutes. If you're coming from Western Switzerland, change at Fribourg to a regional train for Düdingen (S1; 290). From the station, it's only about a minute's walk to the bus-stop where the bus will be waiting for people arriving by train who want to make the connection.

If you're travelling by car, leave the A12 (Bern–Fribourg) at the motorway exit Düdingen. From there, head towards Murten, then take the second right for Kleinbösingen after the dam (Schiffenensee). Continue as far as the River Saane, then northeast towards the reserve information centre.

Accommodation

Hotel possibilities are the Hotel Bären, Bärenplatz 5, 3177 Laupen (tel: 031/747 72 31) or the Hotel des Alpes, Hauptstrasse 29, 3186 Düdingen (tel: 026/493 32 40). All are at least 2 km from the site. Camping: Schiffenen, Düdingen (open 1 April to 31 December (tel: 026/493 19 17)).

Site protection

Dogs must be kept on the lead. There are signs indicating which paths are permitted and which not.

Disabled access

For disabled visitors, the site is very suitable owing to its small size, but it is not wheelchair-accessible because the paths do not have a firm, made-up surface and in places they are rather narrow.

Aerial view of Auried and the River Saane (photo: Yvar Wider)

16 MARAIS DE GRÔNE

Canton:	Valais
Grid reference:	599/121
Height a.s.l.:	500 m
Start:	St-Léonard/Le Pont
Finish:	St-Léonard/Le Pont (or Pramagnon)
Itinerary:	St-Léonard/Le Pont–Rhône embankment–hide–return by same route (or continue via small lake of La Brèche–Pramagnon)
Duration:	allow 1 hr to half a day (for route as far as Pramagnon); distance to hide and back *c*.2 km; to Pramagnon *c*.4–5 km
Best time:	interesting throughout year (except winter when ponds frozen over); spring is most interesting season
Status:	nature reserve
Map:	LdS 1:25,000; sheets 1306 (Sion) and 1286 (St-Léonard)
Equipment:	telescope

In the otherwise cleared and developed landscape of the Rhône valley between Sion and Sierre, a small wetland has managed to survive. The Marais de Grône (also called Poutafontana) is a relict from the time when the previously-meandering Rhône was regulated and it is now a strict nature reserve. Entry into the reserve is not permitted, but you can look into this unique site from a specially-constructed hide. The Marais de Grône is the last fairly large wetland in the former alluvial floodplain of Lower Valais.

Recommended routes

The hide (1) gives you the best views into the site. Any birds present can be watched from here without causing any disturbance. Several different herons, ducks and other waterbirds are likely to be seen. In the bushes along the embankment (2), there are often passerines of various kinds—some local breeders, others stopping off here on migration. Nightingale is one of the breeding birds. To the right of the path lies the nature reserve (no entry). After about 2 km, you come to the small lake of La Brèche (3). This is slightly less interesting than the ponds of the Marais de Grône. All the same, species such as Great Crested Grebe, Cormorant and a variety of ducks do stop off there on migration.

To get to Pramagnon, go round the lake and, on the opposite side, fol-

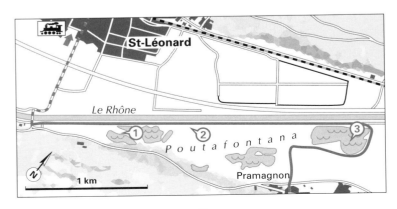

low a canal which runs parallel to the Rhône for about 500 m. Then turn left, cross over the canal and go straight on to reach the village of Pramagnon.

Calendar

An important stopover and breeding site for many wetland species. One of the last wetlands in Lower Valais, attracting many migrant birds; especially interesting in April and May.

Winter: When the ponds are not frozen: Little and Great Crested Grebes, Grey Heron, Teal and Mallard, Water Rail, Moorhen and occasionally Reed Bunting.

Spring: Cormorant, Night Heron, Little Egret and Purple Heron, Gadwall, Teal, Pintail, Garganey, Shoveler and Pochard, Black Kite, Marsh Harrier, Osprey, Little Ringed Plover, Green Sandpiper and occasionally other waders; Sand, Crag and House Martins and Swallow.

Breeding season: Little Grebe, Little Bittern, Mallard, Water Rail, Hoopoe, Wryneck, Green and Lesser Spotted Woodpeckers, Nightingale, Marsh and Reed Warblers, Reed Bunting. Occasional or exceptional breeders in the past include: Teal, Pintail, Garganey and Shoveler, also Penduline Tit.

Autumn: Cormorant, Teal, Pochard and Tufted Duck, Penduline Tit.

Access

From Sion, travel by the postbus service for Siders via St-Léonard–Chalais (100.80). This service runs regularly from Monday to Saturday and less frequently on Sundays. The place to get out is just beyond the village of St-Léonard at the stop St-Léonard/Le Pont. To get to the hide in the Marais de Grône, follow the left (southeastern) Rhône embankment for about 800 m upstream.

From Siders, take the postbus for Sion and alight at the same stop (right after Grône/Pramagnon). There is also a postbus service to Pramagnon.

Another possibility would be to cycle the distance of about 8 km from Sion to the Marais de Grône (bike-hire at Sion rail station). From the station, follow the signposts in the direction of 'Nendaz' as far as the bridge over the Rhône. Then turn off left almost immediately and go along the left bank of the Rhône into the site.

Accommodation

Campsite in Granges/Grône (tel: 079 214 06 55). The nearest youth hostel is in Sion on the rue de l'industrie 2 (tel: 027/323 74 70); there are various hotels in Sion, Siders and the surrounding area.

For further information, contact: Office du tourisme, 3979 Grône-Loye (tel: 027/458 24 67) or Office du tourisme de Sion & environs, place de la Planta, 1950 Sion (tel: 027/322 85 86) or Office du tourisme de Sierre, Salgesch & environs, place de la Gare, CP 404, 3960 Sierre (tel: 027/455 85 35).

Site protection

As there is no entry to the reserve for the general public, its wildlife is protected from disturbance caused by visitors.

However, this wetland is threatened by a continuous process of silting-up and consequent drying-out as well as by eutrophication via a drainage ditch which has been laid to feed into the site.

Disabled access

The official paths in the reserve are wheelchair-accessible and other visitors with walking impairments should have no problems.

Nearby sites

Around 35 km downstream lies the area of cultivated farmland known as El Capio, between Martigny and Fully in the sharp bend of the River Rhône. This is an attractive stopover site for many passage-migrants. In particular, passerines such as Short-toed Lark (rare), several species of pipits and wagtails, Whinchat and Stonechat, Wheatear, Red-backed Shrike, Ortolan Bunting and others can be seen on the fields.

17 LEUK

Canton:	Valais
Grid reference:	615/129
Height a.s.l.:	620 m
Start:	Leuk rail station
Finish:	Route A: Leuk station. Route B: Turtmann station
Route A:	Leuk station–crossing the Rhône–Blagghalde–foot of the Platten Slope–Platten Slope–Hohe Brücke–Brentjong–Leuk station
Route B:	Leuk station–Gampinen–Leukerfeld (arable fields)–ponds–Turtmann station
Duration:	allow half a day for each route, but longer stay recommended; distance c.10 km (A); c.6 km (B)
Best time:	mid-April to June
Status:	no special protection status; IBA
Map:	LdS 1:25,000; sheets 1287 (Sierre) and 1288 (Raron) for Turtmann region
Equipment:	walking boots, telescope

The region around Leuk has been known to experts for some years. It is characterized by a great range of different habitat types. Ponds, cultivated farmland, rocky steppe, hedgerows, meadows, pasture, pinewoods, orchards, vineyards and the Rhône form a relatively small-scale mosaic landscape in which many interesting animals and plants are found. The unique rocky steppe on the southern slopes with its dry, mesobromion grassland rich in plants and insects is reminiscent of the Mediterranean. Apart from the many interesting breeding birds, including several mountain species, the numbers of exciting passage migrants make every excursion here a superb birding experience.

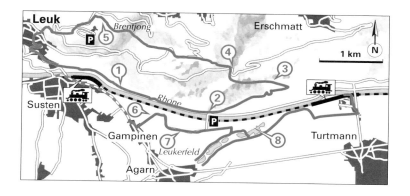

Recommended routes

The two itineraries described above are just two possibilities for excursions. The entire area north of the main road connecting Leuk and Turtmann is ornithologically very interesting.

Route A (slope and Brentjong): Cross the Rhône by the old bridge about 150 m west of Leuk station and then immediately branch off right. The path runs upstream along the foot of the Blagghalde (1). Within the first kilometre, you can hope for Rock Thrush, Bonelli's Warbler and Rock Bunting. After about 2 km, you come to the next bridge (2) which is at the foot of the Feschelbach Gorge. In the small delta of the stream with its trees and shrubs, you will hear the song of Nightingales, Melodious Warblers and various *Phylloscopus* warblers.

Branch off left and, after another good kilometre, you reach the waste-water treatment works at the bottom of the Platten Slope. From there, proceed along the stream for 400 m (path not very obvious) as far as the shed. The route is then across the slope to point '873' and from there to the road. The climb up the Platten Slope (3) (an ascent of 280 m) is the most interesting part of this route. It's worth trying to spend the morning here, in order to see Honey Buzzard, Rock Thrush, Rock Bunting and Ortolan Bunting. There's a chance of Short-toed Eagle or Mediterranean *Sylvia* warblers (e.g. Subalpine Warbler), but these are far rarer and occur only irregularly. This is also the habitat of the Nightjar, which is active only at dusk. The path ends on the link road between Leuk and Erschmatt; turn left there and then carry on to the two parallel bridges over the imposing Feschelbach Gorge (4). The old stone bridge is a good spot for Crag Martins and Wallcreeper and there are sometimes Choughs around the gorge in winter.

On leaving the bridge, follow the signs for about 2.5 km to the Brentjong Plateau (5). Near the satellite ground-station (huge satellite dishes—you can't miss it), you will find a small, traditional farming area with a patchwork of arable fields, meadows and hedges. This has a lot of interesting species in the breeding season: Hoopoe, Wryneck, Woodlark, Lesser Whitethroat, Red-backed Shrike, Cirl Bunting. Orphean Warbler and Barred Warbler are much rarer and these breed only irregularly at the site. From Brentjong, it's not far to Leuk and to the station (follow the signs).

Route B (the plain and ponds): From Leuk station, follow the main road for 1.5 km in the direction of Brig (eastwards), but only as far as Gampinen. Turn left there into a small side-road (6) which is fringed with trees for part of the way. On the stretch up to the stream, you should see the first interesting species such as Hoopoe, Wryneck or Red-footed Falcon (at migration time). Having crossed the stream, continue on the same narrow road to the right and, by the building (200 m further on), to the left. The grassland and arable fields of the Leukerfeld (7) have many fascinating species. Among those regularly recorded are Quail, Yellow Wagtail (of the race *cinereocapilla*), Whinchat and Stonechat, Wheatear and Corn Bunting, with Red-footed Falcon, Short-toed Lark, Tawny and Red-throated Pipits being slightly rarer. Something unexpected can turn up at any time! Good birds can be found not just along the recommended route, but right across the Leukerfeld. Turning off down some of the farm tracks is therefore certainly recommended. To reach the fishponds (8), continue along the same path and when you get to the point where it turns left for the Rhône bridge (2), carry straight on. At the stream, the path bends to the right and after about 150 m, you come to the ponds. The easternmost pond usually has the most interesting birds: Little Grebe, Moorhen, occasionally waders and passerines on passage. All the herons and egrets can be seen here. Little Bittern nests on the island. The other pools are also quite interesting, but they are used by fishermen.

The path running along the south side of the fishponds will take you to Turtmann station. Follow this as far as the railway track and the little river 'Turtmänna' which you then cross on the first bridge (about 300 m before it joins the Rhône). From here, it's straight ahead to the T-junction, then left for 300 m to the station.

Calendar

Many breeding birds, which are now rare or already extinct in the rest of Switzerland, are still regular here. An impressive range of species stop off here on migration.

Winter: Less interesting ornithologically; sometimes Hen Harrier, Rock Partridge, Stonechat, Great Grey Shrike, Chough (Feschelbach Gorge), Hooded Crow, Cirl and Corn Buntings.

Spring: Little Bittern, Night Heron, Little Egret, Purple Heron and (rarer) Squacco Heron, occasionally Short-toed Eagle, Marsh, Hen and Montagu's Harriers, Red-footed Falcon, Short-toed Lark (regular), Tawny Pipit (mainly on passage; rare and irregular breeder), Red-throated Pipit, Yellow Wagtail, Nightingale, Whinchat and Stonechat, Wheatear, Grasshopper Warbler, sporadic and rare records of Mediterranean *Sylvia* warblers; Red-backed Shrike, Hooded Crow (and many Carrion/Hooded Crow hybrids), Ortolan Bunting.

Breeding season: Little Grebe, Little Bittern, Honey Buzzard, Quail, Nightjar, Hoopoe, Wryneck, Lesser Spotted Woodpecker, Woodlark, Crag Martin, Whinchat and Stonechat, Rock Thrush, other (*Turdus*) thrushes, Melodious Warbler, Lesser Whitethroat and Whitethroat, Bonelli's Warbler, Golden Oriole, Red-backed Shrike, Yellowhammer, Cirl, Rock, Reed, Corn and Ortolan Buntings.

Autumn: Lapwing, Yellow Wagtail, Stonechat, Wheatear.

The rocky steppes of Leuk (in the background) and the fishponds in the Leukerfeld are a Mecca for ornithologists (photo: W. Wettstein)

Useful tips

Cockchafers (maybugs) develop in a three-year cycle. In the years when they reach the flying stage, these beetles occur in huge numbers during the months of May and June. This phenomenon is equally fascinating for entomologists and ornithologists alike. For birders, the reason is that a cockchafer year regularly also becomes a Red-footed Falcon year too as these raptors are very partial to cockchafers as prey. Small parties of up to a dozen (sometimes more) falcons can then be seen at the site.

The Ornithologists' Almanack forecasts the next cockchafer years as 2001, 2004...

Access

There is a regular fast train service to Leuk station on the Lausanne to Brig line (100) and it is also served by regional trains on the Sion to Brig line (see timetable). Regional trains operating on the Sion–Brig line stop at Turtmann station every hour. It makes good sense to have a bike in the Leukerfeld, but you can't use it on the slope. Most paths and tracks are negotiable on a bicycle.

Accommodation

Hotels in Susten, Leuk or in the health spa of Leukerbad. Campsites: Camping Gemmi (near Agarn), 3952 Susten (tel: 027/473 11 54). Camping du Monument in the Pfynwald forest (tel: 027/473 18 27).

For further information, contact: Tourist Information Office for Sierre, Salgesch and environs; Place de la Gare (tel: 027/455 85 35).

Site protection

The site is not specially protected. There are a number of threats, above all in the Leukerfeld. A motorway is planned on the left bank of the Rhône. The industrial zones of Gampinen and Turtmann are growing steadily and eating up land. A golf course is also planned. With this lack of legal protection, it is the responsibility of each and every visitor not to damage the vegetation and to have due regard for the needs of wildlife. On the especially sensitive slopes, keep to the existing paths and do not venture into planted fields or uncut meadows.

Disabled access

The Leukerfeld and the fishponds are suitable for wheelchair-users and easily accessible for other visitors with walking impairments. Other wheelchair-friendly places are the satellite station and the road between Leuk and the Hohe Brücke (4).

Nearby sites

The huge Pfynwald forest and the unregulated Rhône between Sierre and Leuk are extremely impressive landscapes, unique in Switzerland. The pinewood is an eldorado for botanists and entomologists. Typical birds likely to be seen include Little Ringed Plover, Common Sandpiper, Woodcock (roding over the clearings at Preisen), Nightjar and Nightingale (common around the campsite). Further east on the Lötschberg South Slope lies Ausserberg. For visitors travelling from Bern, this is a good alternative. Especially recommended is a walk from Ausserberg to St Germann (signposted) or into the dry pinewoods above the village. Buntings, *Phylloscopus* warblers, Hoopoe, Stonechat, also a variety of raptors, can be seen here.

18 ALETSCH

Canton:	Valais
Grid reference:	644/136
Height a.s.l.:	2080 m
Start:	Riederalp (Greicheralp)
Finish:	Riederalp (Greicheralp)
Itinerary:	Riederalp (Greicheralp)–Riederfurka–Hohflüe–Unterweg (Aletsch Forest)–Riederfurka–Riederalp (Greicheralp)
Duration:	allow 1 day (c.8–9 km)
Best time:	breeding season (June–August)
Status:	strict Pro Natura reserve; IBA
Map:	LdS 1:25,000; sheet 1269 (Aletsch Glacier)
Equipment:	walking boots, map 1:25,000,picnic lunch

The Aletsch region lies in the magnificent Alpine landscape of Upper Valais. Pro Natura's aim, in placing the Aletschwald (Aletsch Forest) under protection in 1933, was to preserve a characteristic part of the region.

This is a true larch-Arolla pine forest with an understorey of bilberry and rhododendron. Together with the Great Aletsch Glacier (at 24 km the longest glacier in continental Europe), the Aletsch Forest is certainly the most imposing landscape feature of the site. Not only is it easily accessible and has good tourist facilities, but the many typical Alpine birds means it has much to offer ornithologically.

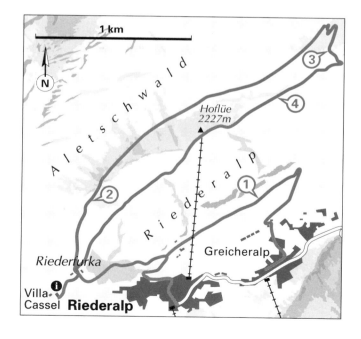

Recommended routes

From the top station of the cable car (gondola) at Greicheralp, first go along the little road to the right, then branch off left after about 250 m onto the hiking trail heading towards the slope (see map). With a bit of luck, Rock Thrush may be found on the scree and rock ledges (1) as you make your way towards the Riederfurka. Wheatear and Black Redstart also occur here.

On the Riederfurka, take the track which leads along the slope (2) parallel to the ridgeway path on the upper edge of Aletsch Forest Although you are only just touching Aletsch Forest on this route, there's nevertheless a fair chance of seeing the typical forest species: wood-peckers, tits, Treecreeper, Nutcracker, Citril Finch and Redpoll, Linnet and Crossbill. You can also get good views of chamois and red deer, the latter drawing attention with their loud roaring or bellowing during the autumn rut.

The characteristic bird along the mountain meadows with scattered trees is the Tree Pipit. At the second fork (15 m before the signpost), turn right and climb up through the dwarf-shrub heath (3) onto the ridge. This is Ptarmigan country. Once on the ridge, you could contin-ue left as far as the Mossfluo (Rock Partridge, Alpine Accentor) or go straight on to the Blausee lake.

For a circular tour, continue along the ridge (4) towards the Riederfurka. On the way, you will pass a number of bog pools which are the haunt of characteristic dragonflies and damsel flies such as com-mon hawker, alpine emerald or white-faced dragonfly. Birds likely to be seen there are Wheatear and Water Pipit.

Anyone with an interest in this site is advised to visit Pro Natura's Aletsch Nature Conservation Visitor Centre ('i') on the Riederfurka. Apart from looking after, managing and watching over the Aletsch Forest, the centre offers a range of attractions and activities from mid-June to mid-October: exhibition, tape-and-slide show, Alpine garden, guided tours, excursions, camps, courses and even an open-air cinema.

For all information, contact Pro Natura Centre Aletsch, 3987 Riederalp (tel: 027/928 62 20).

Calendar

All the typical Alpine bird species are found at the Aletsch site.

Breeding season: Goshawk, Sparrowhawk, Golden Eagle, Kestrel, Ptarmigan, Black Grouse, Rock Partridge, Pygmy and Tengmalm's Owls, Green, Black, Great Spotted and (rare) Three-toed Woodpeckers, Crag Martin, Tree and Water Pipits, Alpine Accentor, Redstart, Whinchat, Wheatear, Rock Thrush, Ring Ouzel, Willow, Crested and Coal Tits, Treecreeper, Nutcracker, Alpine Chough, Chough (rare), Citril Finch, Linnet, Redpoll, Crossbill.

Useful tips

The terrace of the Pro Natura Centre on the Riederfurka is one of the few places where you can watch Blackcocks lekking without disturbing them: this wonderful spectacle takes place in the Alpine garden at dawn. Please do not attempt to get any closer to these birds!

Access

The starting-point is Mörel rail station. This is served by trains of the

Furka–Oberalp–Bahn and connects Brig with Graubünden (the Grisons) (Disentis, via Andermatt) (610). Just opposite Mörel station is the joint valley station of the two cable-car railways, one to the Greicheralp and the other to the Riederalp. The two top stations are situated about 200 m apart. There are also two chair-lifts, to the Hohflüe and to the Mossfluo. Although they operate throughout the year, all the cableways and lifts are shut down for an annual inspection and service. You can only get as far as Mörel by car.

Accommodation

Pro Natura Centre (dormitory and hotel accommodation (tel: 027/928 62 20)), Hotel Riederfurka (dormitory and hotel accommodation (tel: 027/927 21 31)) and various other accommodation possibilities on the Riederalp and the Bettmeralp. For further information, contact: Tourist Office, 3987 Riederalp (tel: 027/927 13 65) or Tourist Office, 3992 Bettmeralp (tel: 027/927 12 91).

Site protection

Although the Aletsch Forest is strictly protected, it is still exposed to many threats even now. The site suffers to some extent from being so popular and the large number of visitors requires that there should be a clear code of conduct for walkers. The most conspicuous damage, and something which is virtually irreparable in this ecosystem, is soil erosion caused by people tramping thoughtlessly along the many unofficial paths and tracks. Walkers must therefore keep strictly to the official hiking trails throughout the site. Browsing by excessive numbers of red deer also has an impact on the vegetation.

Disabled access

The Aletsch site is not suitable for disabled visitors.

Nearby sites

Apart from the itinerary described above, further interesting tours and excursions are possible at this site. For example, a walk (allow a day) to the Massa Gorge (Golden Eagle, Wallcreeper, Crag Martin, Rock Bunting), to the Aletsch Glacier (with a guide!) or along the ridge towards Bettmerhorn (Rock Partridges, Alpine Accentor). The glory of the Aletsch Forest itself can be experienced on several other routes. A short walk up onto the Riederhorn also offers a superb view of the Matterhorn, the Villa Cassel and the entire Aletsch region. A walk round the Riederhorn is also interesting: Black Redstart on scree, Pygmy Owl in the forest, also Crag Martin, Tree Pipit and occasionally Rock Partridge on the west side.

19 HAHNENMOOS PASS

Canton:	Bern
Grid reference:	604/144
Height a.s.l.:	1940 m
Start:	top station Hahnenmoos Pass
Finish:	top station Hahnenmoos Pass
Itinerary:	observations near top station and along ridge; duration depends on what you want to do and the weather (half a day or up to several days possible)
Best time:	mid-September to mid-October
Status:	not a protected site
Map:	LdS 1:25,000; sheet 1267 Gemmi
Equipment:	telescope, something to sit on, picnic lunch

The cable-car journey up to the Hahnenmoos Pass already gives you an opportunity to enjoy the wonderful view on the left—a grandiose mountain panorama, with the peaks of the Ammenterspitz (2681 m), Fitzer (2458 m), Rotstock (2622 m) and the Wildstrubel (3243 m). Wedged between them, the Ammerten Glacier can be made out. As you travel over the mountain meadows and pastures, the wide valley becomes noticeably narrower towards the pass and you will understand how the mountain slopes on either side have a funnelling effect on approaching migrants. Meadows and pastures predominate on the saddle of the relatively wide pass. From here, the view opens out in a southwesterly direction. Standing out against the sky on the horizon are Les Diablerets (3209 m) and the Wildhorn (3251 m). The sparse dwarf-shrub communities and green-alder bushes offer very little cover for birds, which makes the latter much easier to see as they pass through on migration.

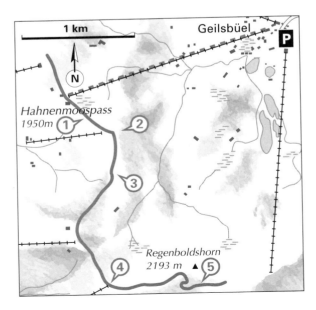

Observation points

As the pass is rather wide, migration may extend, depending on the weather conditions, over a front of up to 2 km: from the Lavey Ridge (2132 m) in the north as far as the Bummere Ridge (2150 m) in the south. The best and most convenient observation point with distant all-round views is probably the hollow 200 m southeast of the mountain hotel (1). To get a good view into the hollow, you need go no further than the forecourt of the cableway top station. Another good place, very popular with model-aircraft enthusiasts, is about another 200 m further southeast, on the top of the small hill (2). There are also other observation points (3, 4, 5).

Calendar

Concentration of migrating birds, especially passerines, because of special topographical features. Similar range of species to that of the watershed at the Gantrisch site (see Site 20).

Breeding season: Kestrel, Black Grouse, Quail, Water Pipit, Garden Warbler, Alpine Chough, Citril Finch and Redpoll.

Autumn migration: Large numbers of hirundines (mainly Swallows and House Martins; a few Sand Martins), also Cormorant, Grey Heron, Woodpigeon, Woodlark, etc. Raptors such as Red Kite, Marsh, Hen and Montagu's Harriers, Sparrowhawk, Osprey, Hobby and Peregrine are regular.

Useful tips

If you want to do a long migration watch without getting tired, we recommend bringing a folding chair or something else to sit on. A telescope is useful for keeping raptors in view for a longer period as they can be picked up early and all observers present can focus in on them.

The Hahnenmoos Pass is equally popular with both model-aircraft enthusiasts and ornithologists. A little tolerance is called for, especially in fine weather at weekends. Neither group really spoils the enjoyment of the other.

Access

By train from Bern to Frutigen (300) and from there by postbus to Adelboden (300.20). Change there to a bus (operates only up to mid-October) or walk to Geils via Gilbach (2 hrs). From Geils (1707 m) on foot (40 min) or by cable car up to the Hahnenmoos Pass (1956 m). If you travel to Geilsbüel via Adelboden and Gilbach by private car, you will need to get a travel permit to continue beyond Gilbach (these cost Sfr8 and are available from a ticket machine by the Gilbach restaurant). No private vehicles are allowed up to the Hahnenmoos Pass! Parking possible in Adelboden, Gilbach and Geilsbüel.

Mountain-bikes can be hired at the top station Hahnenmoos Pass, but they need to be booked in advance (tel: 033/673 12 57); after riding down, you can hand in your bike at the post-office in Adelboden or at any rail station.

Accommodation

Berghotel Hahnenmoospass, The Spori Family, 3715 Adelboden (tel: 033/673 21 41) (hotel rooms and dormitory accommodation, including with self-catering facilities). For information on other overnight accommodation possibilities, contact the Tourist Centre in Adelboden (tel: 033/673 80 80) or the Tourist Information Office in Lenk (tel: 033/733 31 31).

Site protection
No special protection status.

Disabled access
The Hahnenmoos Pass is very suitable for visitors with walking impairments. The best observation point is the forecourt right by the top station of the cableway, next to the hotel (Berghotel Hahnenmoospass). Disabled visitors can buy a special permit (costs Sfr10) at the Gilbach restaurant which allows them to drive their own vehicle up to the top station. Wheelchair-users can travel by cable car only if their wheelchair is collapsible. Accommodation is available for wheelchair-users and others at the Hahnenmoos Pass hotel; phone to make a reservation.

Nearby sites
The small Lenkerseeli lies near Lenk in the Simmental valley, on the far (southwest) side of the Hahnenmoos Pass. This is an artificial lake built around 1913 and situated about 1 km southwest of the centre of the village at a height of 1068 m above sea level. As suitable sites for waterbirds are rare in the Alps, the small lake (2.3 ha) has developed into an interesting passage and staging site for such species. Particular weather conditions can cause hold-ups for migrating birds and it is then that exciting species are often found. In addition, the Lenkerseeli has in recent years become one of the most important breeding localities for Tufted Duck in Switzerland.

Swallows on migration (drawing by J. Laesser)

20 GURNIGEL-WASSERSCHEIDE

Canton:	Bern
Grid reference:	600/176
Height a.s.l.:	1590 (1200–2175) m
Start:	Wasserscheide between Selibüel and Gantrisch
Itinerary:	no special route; observations at a few particular points. For mountain birds, circular walk round Gantrisch possible
Duration:	allow 1–3 days
Best time:	autumn (end of August to beginning of November), May–July for mountain birds
Status:	no special legal protection status; IBA
Map:	LdS 1:25,000; sheet 1206 (Guggisberg)
Equipment:	telescope, folding chair

The Gurnigel is situated on the northern edge of the impressive Stockhorn chain in the Gantrisch region southwest of Thun. The Wasserscheide (watershed) at just 1600 m is wedged between the Selibüel (1750 m) and the Gantrisch summit (2175). All around the top of the pass, the landscape is one dominated by alpine pastures and subalpine spruce forests.

Its special position on the northern edge of the Alps means that masses of small birds and a wide range of raptor species cross the watershed on their flight to the wintering grounds. Ornithologists thus have unique

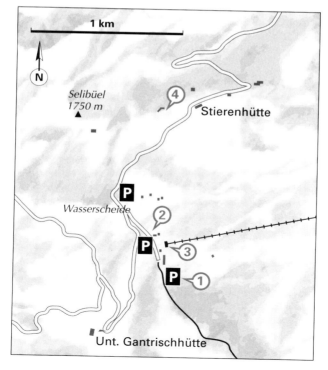

possibilities for observing the autumn migration in action, and to see a Black Stork migrating through against the backdrop of the Alps is surely a marvellous experience in itself. The mass migration of commoner species is also most impressive. Anyone wanting to watch mountain birds will find good hunting grounds in the woods, pastures and among the rocks around the Gurnigel.

Observation points

The best watchpoint is the uppermost army shooting platform (1). If you get there early in the morning, you should see small birds passing through in large numbers. Then, as soon as the sun warms the mountain slopes, the raptor migration begins, these birds using the lift of thermals to soar and gain height. They often cross the Wasserscheide along the slope, which is orientated southeast, between the Zigerhubel and the Selibüel. September sees the greatest variety of species, while large numbers of the commoner ones (Buzzard, Sparrowhawk) pass through in October. The lowest point in the watershed (2), where the paths cross in the direction of the ski-lift, is best for watching passerine migration in the early morning. Wagtails, pipits, thrushes and finches pass through in large numbers and are most easily identified by their flight-calls. Finches such as Siskin and Citril Finch are fond of resting in the spruce trees of the surrounding area, while wagtails and pipits use the nearby meadows to recover from the stresses of migration. There is a noticeable decline in the strength of the migration towards midday, but it sometimes picks up again as evening approaches.

On workdays in the autumn, the military often carries out tank shooting practice from the upper shooting platform (1). It is then, of course, strictly forbidden to enter the danger zones and to go to Point (1) and you should make sure you obey the prohibition without fail if you value life and limb. The alternative observation points on such occasions are the wooden platform by the top station of the ski-lift (3) and another shooting platform near the Stierenhütte (4).

For a change, you could take a walk through the sprucewoods which lie below the Gurnigel towards Thun. Apart from the commoner species of mountain forests—tits, Citril Finch, Ring Ouzel or Nutcracker—such a walk may, with a slice of luck, also produce the more elusive birds of this habitat such as Hazel Grouse, Three-toed and Black Woodpeckers, Tengmalm's and Pygmy Owls or Woodcock. In the Gantrisch area, just below and just above the tree-line, live typical Alpine species such as Golden Eagle (also to be seen from the other migration watchpoints mentioned), Black Grouse (autumn lekking display can be heard from Point (1) and can be seen regularly in the little wood above the Wasserscheide), Alpine Accentor as well as, on south-facing slopes, Rock Partridge and Rock Thrush. A little patience may be rewarded with views of Wallcreeper on vertical rock faces of the Gantrisch.

Calendar

In the autumn, an intersection for streams of birds migrating along the Alps, with a wide range of raptors and mass gatherings of small birds. Watching active diurnal migration. Mountain birds in the surrounding Gantrisch area.

Breeding season: Golden Eagle, Hazel Grouse, Ptarmigan, Black Grouse and Rock Partridge, Woodcock, Pygmy and Tengmalm's Owls, Black

Gazing east full of expectation from the Gurnigel: this is the direction from which the migrants come (photo: H. Schmid)

and Three-toed Woodpeckers, Water Pipit, Alpine Accentor, Wheatear, Rock Thrush, Ring Ouzel, Lesser Whitethroat, Willow and Crested Tits, Wallcreeper, Nutcracker, Citril Finch, Crossbill.

Autumn: Cormorant, Black Stork, 14 raptor species, including Honey Buzzard, Black and Red Kites, all three harrier species, Goshawk, Sparrowhawk, Buzzard, Osprey, Kestrel and Hobby, Merlin, Peregrine; Stock Dove and Woodpigeon, swifts, Woodlark, several species of pipits and wagtails (e.g. Tawny Pipit), hirundines, Ring Ouzel, Song Thrush, Redwing and Mistle Thrush. Coal Tit (masses in invasion years), Brambling, Citril Finch, Siskin and Redpoll, Linnet, Crossbill, Bullfinch, Reed Bunting.

Useful tips

For those who also want to see some mountain birds, a walk round the Gantrisch or over towards the Stockhorn is to be recommended. From the Wasserscheide via the Lower and Upper Gantrisch Huts–Chummli Hut–the pass at Schibenspitz (2020 m)–Leiteren (the pass between Gantrisch and Nünenenflue)–Obernünenen–Wasserscheide. Both Wallcreeper and Rock Partridges are found on the Nünenenflue. This is a fairly tough walk for which sturdy footwear and the recommended LdS map are required!

Access

By public transport: a few postbuses (290.40) run up to the Gurnigel Wasserscheide daily from Bern (bus-stop right by the main rail station). Reservation obligatory (tel: 031/386 65 65). Journey time is about 75 minutes.

By private car, travel via Bern–Belp–Riggisberg or Fribourg-Plaffeien-Riggisberg. You can park on the Wasserscheide.

Accommodation

Nauturfreundehaus Selibüel, 3099 Rüti bei Riggisberg (tel: 031/809 08 72), Berghaus Gurnigel (tel: 031/809 04 30). Hotel Schwefelbergbad (1380 m a.s.l.), c.3 km away (tel: 026/419 33 66).

Disabled access

The Gurnigel is both wheelchair-accessible and also ideal for other visitors with walking impairments. There are no problems in using a wheelchair on the upper platform. The Gwatt reserve and long walk in the mountains are not really accessible to disabled visitors.

Nearby sites

If the weather is bad, leave the top of the pass and travel into the Thun region. The nature reserve 'Gwattlischenmoos' (Gwatt, for short) south of Thun is usually quite interesting. However, for the observation tower in the reserve you do need a key, but this can be obtained on request at Gwatt rail station (tel: 033/336 11 57). There are also good observation points outside the reserve: the Bonstettenpark and the Seeallmend afford good views out over the lake and the reedbed. Passage waders regularly stop off to rest on the gravel island in front of the Gwatt campsite. In the autumn, apart from some waterbirds, there's a chance of finding migrant passerines in the reeds. Other regular species to watch out for include Black-necked Grebe, Red-crested Pochard, Hobby, Black Tern and Little Gull.

21 WAUWILERMOOS

Canton:	Lucerne
Grid reference:	644/225
Height a.s.l.:	500 m
Start:	Wauwil rail station or Kottwil
Finish:	ditto
Itinerary:	various routes possible at the site
Duration:	6–7 km; allow 3–4 hrs
Best time:	spring and autumn
Status:	in part, nature reserve
Map:	LdS 1:25,000; sheet 1149 (Wolhausen)
Equipment:	telescope, boots (in spring), bicycle, something to sit on

The Wauwilermoos is an extensive plain of around 16 km² in the Lucerne (Luzern) part of the Central Plateau. It lies in the Kottwil-Wauwil-Schötz triangle west of the Sempachersee (Lake Sempach). A prominent range of hills, of which the highest point is the Santenberg at 677 m, forms the northern limit of the site. Lying in the heart of the Central Plateau of Switzerland, the Wauwilermoos is important above all for the large number of passage migrants it attracts. Around 240 species have been recorded there so far. In the autumn especially, the raptor migration can be impressive. The habitat type covering the largest area is intensively-farmed meadows and arable land and, in

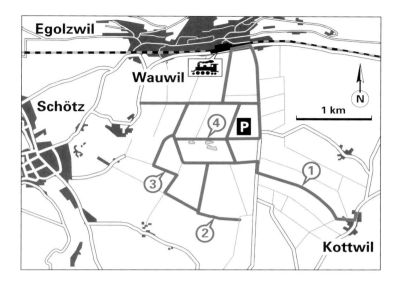

order to enhance the ecological value of the site, strips of fallow land have been set aside since 1995, these providing food and cover for both breeding birds and migrants. In the middle of the plain lies the nature reserve, which comprises marshy areas and the encircling belt of reeds. Other elements of the landscape are the tall mature hedges of varying composition that divide up the agricultural fields.

Recommended routes

The many farm tracks are good places to watch birds and also provide a whole range of possibilities for walks into the Wauwilermoos. The best place to start is Kottwil. Head west and, on the edge of the village, bear right to follow a farm track straight across the fields (1) until you reach the Wauwil–Ettiswil link road. At migration time, there will be various small birds flitting about in the fields and meadows on both sides of the track; Lapwings too, in the breeding season. Red-footed Falcons can occasionally be seen perched on overhead cables in the spring. A further important part of the plain is the Ettiswiler Moos (2), which is one of the best places for watching the autumn migration of birds of prey. To get to the best spot, follow the shelter-belts for about 600 m from the main road, then turn off left and, after a further 700 m, left again. If you turn left, this will bring you to the Schötzermoos (3). The fields are usually flooded in the spring and consequently attract large numbers of waders, including chiefly *Tringa* species, Black-tailed Godwit, Ruff and Lapwings. Various larks and harriers can often be seen as well.

The centrally-placed nature reserve in the plain (4) is, unfortunately, not very good for watching birds as you can't really see into it from the various tracks and paths. Entry into the reserve is not allowed from March onwards. Since 1993, Highland cattle from Scotland have been introduced to graze the reserve and to keep the vegetation down. Nevertheless, there are well-built paths all round the reserve. Wauwil is easy to find. Either follow the main road (not very attractive, but the quickest way), or take one of the farm tracks that run parallel to the road.

Calendar

Conspicuous raptor migration in the autumn, with up to 13 species. Mass migration of small birds such as finches and larks, which sometimes gather in thousands on harvested fields. Important breeding site for Lapwing (1996: c.15 pairs).

Winter: Ducks of various kinds, Hen Harrier, Goshawk, Sparrowhawk, Merlin, Peregrine, Jack Snipe, Snipe (in the reserve if ponds not frozen).

Spring: Garganey, Honey Buzzard (up to 100 per day from mid-May), Marsh, Hen and Montagu's Harriers, Osprey, Red-footed Falcon, Quail, Golden Plover (March), Ruff, Black-tailed Godwit, Whimbrel, *Tringa* species, Short-toed Lark (annual since 1987), Yellow Wagtail, Bluethroat (on the edge of the reserve), Whinchat and Stonechat, Wheatear, Penduline Tit, Golden Oriole, Red-backed Shrike, Ortolan Bunting.

Breeding season: Little Bittern (irregular), Water Rail and Moorhen, Lapwing, Savi's Warbler, *Acrocephalus* warblers, Reed Bunting. Since 1995, a small rookery (1–4 pairs).

Autumn: Black and White Storks, Honey Buzzard (up to 480 birds per day), Black and Red Kites, Marsh Harrier, Sparrowhawk, Buzzard, Osprey, Hobby, Merlin, Crane (rare), waders (if fields flooded), various larks, Whinchat and Bluethroat, *Phylloscopus* warblers and finches.

Useful tips

The autumn raptor migration follows a line from northeast to southwest Most birds of prey which overfly the Wauwilermoos pass through north of Wauwil, across the middle of the plain or southwest of Kottiswil. From the observation point in the Ettiswiler Moos, most of the birds seen will be those taking the direct route over the fields.

Access

There is an hourly regional train service on the Olten–Lucerne line (510) and all trains stop in Wauwil (1.3 km from the site). Olten and Lucerne give you guaranteed connections to Zürich, Basel and Bern. Kottwil, on the eastern edge of the plain, is reached by bus (510.78) from Sursee rail station, which lies on the same stretch of line as Wauwil. Sursee is served by fast trains from Lucerne and Basel.

To get to Wauwilermoos by car, use the A2 Olten–Lucerne and leave the motorway at the Sursee exit. From there, continue to Kottwil–Ettiswil. A link road runs from Ettiswil (turn off right before the village) to Wauwil; after about 2.5 km, turn left onto a farm track and park after about 400 m.

Accommodation

In the vicinity: Hotel Pinte, Schmiedegasse 13, 6247 Schötz (tel: 041/980 13 33); a further possibility in Sursee. The nearest campsite is situated to the east of the idyllic Mauensee lake (Camping 'Waldheim' (tel: 041/921 11 61)), but it is open only from 1 April to 30 September.

Site protection
Only the small reserve in the middle is designated as a protected area and there is strictly no entry to the reserve in the period from the end of February to 1 November. Dogs must be kept on the lead only in the area round the reserve itself. Although the agricultural crops are not specially protected, you should not go into such fields.

Disabled access
As the paths are wet and muddy in places, it can be rather difficult to negotiate the Wauwilermoos in a wheelchair, and for those who have difficulty in walking, it is not very suitable either.

Nearby sites
The Hagimoos, c.1 km northeast of Kottwil on the main road to Mauensee, is a good place for staging Bluethroat and passage waders in spring. It is also known as a paradise for dragonflies and damsel flies. Further east still lies the Mauensee lake with its wintering Smew, several different dabbling ducks and Bitterns (regular since 1994).

22 REUSS DELTA

Canton:	Uri
Grid reference:	689/194
Height a.s.l.:	436 m
Start:	Flüelen rail station
Finish:	Seedorf
Itinerary:	Flüelen station–sports ground–'Weg der Schweiz' path–Seedorf (walk from there or take the postbus back to Flüelen)
Duration:	allow 2 hrs to half a day
Best time:	spring (mid-March to May)
Status:	cantonal nature reserve no-hunting area
Map:	LdS 1:25,000; sheet 1171 (Beckenried). There are several information boards at the site with good, easy-to-use maps
Equipment:	possibly a telescope, wellington boots (only if water level exceptionally high), bicycle not necessary (cycling *is* permitted)

Since the end of the last ice age, the Reuss has deposited an extensive alluvial plain at the southern end of the Urnersee, the southern tip of Lake Lucerne (Lac des Quatre Cantons, Vierwaldstättersee). As recently as the beginning of this century, the Reuss floodplain was characterized by large tracts of fen and marshland, but a major highway now cuts across it and there have been large-scale drainage and land-improvement schemes. At the mouth of the river, an important fen-mire has survived as the last remnant of this rich habitat. In this varied natural and cultivated landscape, we find a mosaic comprising remnants of riverine forest, fen-meadows and both mesobromion grassland (on nutrient-poor soils) and improved grassland of low plant diversity on nutrient-rich soils, reedbeds, gravel- and mudbanks, as well as old river arms and ox-bow lakes, streams, pools, canals and the lake. A large popula-

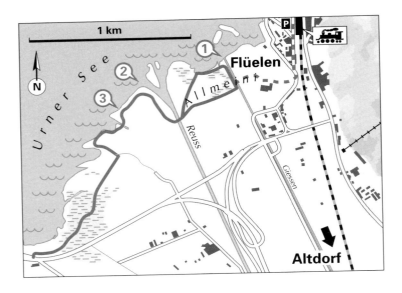

tion of the Siberian iris, many species of orchids and sedge as well as rare aquatic plants in the various ditches and pools help to explain why this site has such enormous appeal for botanists.

Recommended routes

From Flüelen station, follow the national footpath marked 'Weg der Schweiz' past the sports ground to the stream. Having crossed the latter, continue to where it flows into the lake, at which point you will find an observation platform (1). This gives a good view over the offshore islands. At migration time especially, it's worth checking these for waders. From this point, the network of tracks and trails offers you various possibilities for exploring the area on both sides of the Reuss (see map). Further good birding spots are marked on the map (2, 3). You should, at any rate, check the meadows, hedges and the riverine woodland for migrant passerines. When you reach Seedorf, take the postbus back to Flüelen or return on foot by a different route.

Calendar

An attractive site for passage, staging and breeding birds, especially interesting during the migration period. The new gravel islands provide an ideal stopover site for passage waders. If there are late snowfalls in the spring, several species of mountain birds are driven down and seek refuge at the site.

Winter: Relatively few winter visitors (site is shaded and cold): grebes, Bittern, certain ducks, Red-breasted Merganser, various gulls, Kingfisher, Great Grey Shrike.

Spring and Autumn: Night Heron, Little Egret and Purple Heron, Osprey, Marsh and Hen Harriers, 19 species of waders, gulls and terns, Turtle Dove, Hoopoe, Wryneck, Woodlark, Tawny and Red-throated Pipits,

Bluethroat, Whinchat and Stonechat, Grasshopper, Sedge (occasionally), Icterine and Willow Warblers, Pied Flycatcher, Ortolan and Corn Buntings.

Breeding season: Little Grebe (2–3 pairs), Tufted Duck, Eider (irregular breeder), Goosander (1–5 pairs), Peregrine (regularly overflies the site), Water Rail (irregular; bred 1993), Moorhen (1–2 pairs), Little Ringed Plover (breeding attempts since 1990), Yellow-legged Gull, Dipper, Marsh and Reed Warblers, Great Reed Warbler (occasionally), Garden Warbler, Spotted Flycatcher, Red-backed Shrike, Scarlet Rosefinch (irregular breeding bird; e.g. 3–4 territories in 1994), Reed Bunting.

Useful tips
The most interesting sightings are often recorded during hold-ups caused by the weather conditions, when many migrating birds are forced to come down at the site for a stopover of varying length.

Access
The Reuss Delta is easy to reach by public transport. Flüelen rail station (600, 601) makes a good starting-point and it's only a few minutes' walk from there into the delta. Car drivers are advised to park at the station or at the sports ground. At weekends, when the weather is fine, lots of visitors come to the area and parking can become a problem.

Accommodation
Flüelen has quite a large selection of hotels. Private homes offering bed & breakfast and dormitory-style accommodation are also available. Information can be obtained from the Flüelen Tourist Office, Kirchstrasse 88, 6454 Flüelen (tel: 041/870 42 23). There are campsites in Flüelen (Surfcenter-Camping (tel: 041/870 92 22)) and Altdorf (Remo-Camp (tel: 041/870 85 41)).

The Reuss Delta is an important stopover for migrant birds before or after crossing the Alps (photo: M. Sacchi)

Site protection

A large part of the Reuss Delta is designated as a cantonal nature reserve. Apart from the instruction not to stray from the official marked paths and to keep dogs on the lead, visitors are especially reminded that bathing is prohibited in the reserve zones (but there *are* areas where swimming is explicitly allowed). Certain zones at the site are excluded as strict nature reserves with no entry under any circumstances.

Disabled access

With its flat terrain and the relatively short distances to be covered, the site is well suited to visitors with walking impairments. The signs to indicate wheelchair-friendly paths are an exemplary feature.

Nearby sites

Eiders can almost always be found somewhere on the Urnersee and there are often Peregrines, Crag Martins and Bonelli's Warblers on the surrounding slopes.

23 NUOLENER RIED

Canton:	Schwyz
Grid reference:	708/229
Height a.s.l.:	407 m
Start:	Lachen
Finish:	Nuolen (or return to Lachen)
Itinerary:	Lachen rail station–Wangen airfield–via farm track to Nuolen–along the bay to the lake–return to Nuolen–Lachen
Duration:	walking from Wangen airfield c.3 hrs; total distance c.4 km (including return)
Best time:	April/May and September–November
Status:	nature reserve
Map:	LdS 1:25,000; sheets 1132 (Einsiedeln) and 1133 (Linthebene)
Equipment:	telescope, possibly bicycle

The Nuolener Ried lies on the southern shore of the Obersee—the upper or eastern part of Lake Zürich (Lac de Zurich, Zürichsee)—between the Buechberg and Lachen by the mouth of the Wägitaler Aa river. With an area of 40 ha, it is one of the last extensive open fen-mires in Switzerland. As with many other such fens in the country, this is more of a cultivated than a natural unspoilt landscape. Over the centuries, the local farmers have worked the land and created a relatively small, but diverse patchwork of sheep pastures, fen-meadows, and both unimproved mesobromion and improved (fertilized) grassland. Separating the fen from the lake is a narrow belt of *Phragmites* reeds. The different types of meadows also provide habitat for fox, brown hare and stoat and are, in addition, very interesting botanically (many orchids, irises).

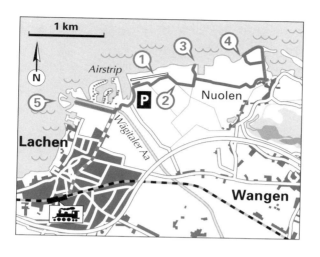

Recommended routes

A good starting point for a tour is Lachen rail station. Walk from there or cycle through Lachen and over the Wägitaler Aa river in the direction of Lake Zürich to Wangen airfield (1). There's a chance of hearing the characteristic call of the Quail here in May. These shy meadowland birds have been regularly recorded in the meadows and mesobromion grassland near the airstrip in recent years.

Along the farm track (2), which has an asphalt surface on some stretches, there are lots of possibilities for watching birds in the meadows (e.g. Corn Bunting) and on the adjoining cultivated farmland. It's worth checking this nationally-important wader staging site very carefully. In the breeding season, 2–3 male Great Reed Warblers are regularly present and loudly advertise their territories in the narrow belt of *Phragmites*. The best place to watch these birds is halfway between the airfield and Nuolen. Turn left at the fork and take the time to walk the short distance (*c.*200 m) down to the lake (3). On calm days, the Great Reed Warblers often sing from the very top of the reed stems where they can be easily observed. Watch out for Bitterns in the winter. When you get to Nuolen, follow the little road leading along the left-hand side of the bay to the lake. The nesting platform for Common Terns (4) has been regularly used by 1–3 pairs for several years now. These elegant and graceful birds are easy to watch from the lakeshore as they perform their spectacular flying and diving manoeuvres.

Calendar

Passage migrants resting and feeding in the open fen landscape and on the adjoining farmland, often easy to observe. Wader stopover site of national importance with up to 200 Curlews.

Winter: Bittern, occasionally Whooper Swans and geese, many diving ducks, Hen Harrier, Curlew, Kingfisher.

Spring: Red-throated Diver, Purple Heron, Marsh Harrier, several wader species, Yellow Wagtail, Tawny and Red-throated Pipits, Bluethroat,

Wheatear, Penduline Tit, Ortolan Bunting. Rare species turning up unexpectedly are not that infrequent.

Breeding season: Great Crested and Little Grebes, Water Rail, Lapwing, Quail (regularly heard calling near the airstrip), Common Tern, Great Reed Warbler, Corn Bunting (up to five singing males).

Autumn: Various waterbirds, waders on adjoining improved grassland (Curlew, Ruff, Lapwing, Snipe and, in November, often Golden Plover), pipits, Yellow Wagtail, Whinchat, Woodlark, Great Grey Shrike. Occasionally raptors such as Peregrine, Merlin and Osprey.

Useful tips

At weekends in fine weather, the airfield is at its busiest and walkers, dog owners, anglers and bathers take over the nature reserve during the day. The best time for birdwatching is therefore early morning or in the week.

Access

The Nuolener Ried is easily accessible by public transport. Lachen station is served by regional and occasional fast trains from Pfäffikon (SZ) and Ziegelbrücke (720). A bus service also operates between Pfäffikon and Lachen (720.92). You can park at Wangen airfield. It's easy to explore the site on foot or by bike.

Accommodation

In Lachen: Hotel Bahnhof, Bahnhofplatz 2 (tel: 055/442 13 27) or Hotel al Porto, Hafenstrasse 4 (tel: 055/451 73 73).

Site protection

The nature reserve is very open and, because of the lack of cover, the birds generally do not allow a close approach. For that reason, visitors should stick to the marked paths and trails throughout the site. The path along the lakeshore, used mainly by anglers and bathers, is illegal and should be strictly avoided. On the lakeside, only authorized persons are permitted to drive in the lake-protection zone which is about 150 m wide.

Disabled access

This a flat area and well suited to visitors with walking impairments. The path across the meadows is wheelchair-accessible and has an asphalt surface for part of its length. Access to the reedbed (3) and to the lake is likely to be difficult because the path is narrow and uneven.

Nearby sites

West of the Nuolener Ried, a walk of only 15 minutes along the left bank of the Wägitaler Aa will bring you to the river delta (5). Icterine Warblers occasionally breed in the delta area, in habitat similar to riverine woodland. Interesting migrants are sometimes seen. Meadows, gravel islets, riverine wood and reedbeds (with Great Reed Warbler) form a diverse habitat.

The Kaltbrunner Riet (see Siter 30) is a bike ride of about 40 minutes from the Nuolener Ried.

24 ULMETHÖCHI

Canton:	Baselland
Grid reference:	616/247
Height a.s.l.:	973 m
Start:	Lauwil
Finish:	Lauwil
Itinerary:	stationary observations at the top of the pass, approach from Reigoldswil via Lauwil or Bretzwil
Duration:	allow at least 1 day
Best time:	September/October
Status:	no special protection status; IBA
Map:	LdS 1:25,000; sheet 1087 (Passwang)
Equipment:	telescope, windproof and warm clothing (icy wind sometimes in October)

The site is on the northern edge of the Chain Jura in a cleft formed by the eastern and northernmost hills in this range. Adjoining the area in the northeast is the Tabular Jura with plateaux and not very deep valleys. Southwest of Lauwil, the Ängiberg and the Aletenchopf form the sides of a funnel-shaped opening which merges with the narrow valley of the Ulmet. In the south, the Passwang rises to 1204 m. The typical vegetation is composed of mixed woods of silver fir and beech and grassland—from the mesobromion type to improved, nutrient-rich meadows.

The special attraction of the Ulmethöchi is the active diurnal migration, mainly of finches, tits (in invasion years), Woodpigeons and birds of prey. Every autumn, thousands of raptors are counted as they pass through on the way to their wintering grounds. The total of 17 raptor

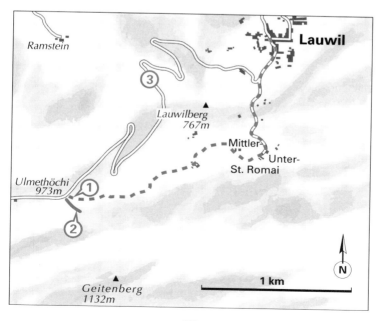

species recorded to date, including such rarities as Booted or Spotted Eagles, is evidence for the great potential of Ulmethöchi as an important migration watchpoint. To study the bird migration, annual ringing programmes carried out by the Basellandschaftlicher Natur- und Vogelschutzverband BNV (the SVS cantonal society for Baselland) have been in operation since 1962.

Observation points

The observation points are restricted to the top of the pass, the Ulmethöchi (1). If visibility is limited because the light is against you, another possibility is to position yourself c.150 m further south on the opposite slope (2). Both watchpoints allow a clear view east-northeast and west-southwest, which is the main flight direction taken by migrating birds (compare map). Another migration watchpoint is at map reference 617100/248600 (3) halfway up between Lauwil and Ulmethöchi.

Calendar

A locally important leading line for bird migration with sometimes mass movements of small birds and raptors. To date, 17 species of birds of prey recorded. Spectacular migration of Woodpigeons.

Breeding season: Local breeders include Peregrine, Black Woodpecker and Nutcracker.

Autumn (in brackets, the average counts for the last six years): The total number of birds ringed in the years 1962–1996 stands at 56,000 of 91 different species, including Merlin, Quail, Snipe, Woodcock, Tengmalm's Owl, Dipper, Penduline Tit and Rock Bunting. Among the passage migrants are Black Stork (19 birds), Honey Buzzard (589), Black Kite (116), Red Kite (874), all three harriers, Buzzard (4,302), Osprey (19), various falcons, Woodpigeon (53,000), wagtails, pipits, thrushes, finches. In invasion years, tits and Jay.

Useful tips

Hirundines and pigeons fly high, especially in fine weather, and hardly use the Ulmet valley as a leading line. Raptors behave similarly, though smaller species such as Kestrel and Sparrowhawk often fly low, following the edge of the Aletenchopf Wood. However, wagtails, pipits, tits, finches and thrushes do fly along Ulmethöchi, using it locally as a leading line, and these passerines make up the bulk of the passage migrants.

Access

Travel by public transport via Liestal. There is an hourly fast train service to the station from Olten, Zürich or Basel and from Liestal an AAGL bus No.70 to Reigoldswil (500.10). The rest of the journey has to be on foot via Lauwil (c.1 hr). As an alternative, take the train from Liestal to Waldenburg (502), where the Lauwil–Bretzwil bus (502.20) waits for the connection. If you're travelling by car, the best route is Liestal–Bubendorf–Reigoldswil–Lauwil. Cars have to be left in Lauwil as no vehicles are allowed on the narrow little road up to Ulmethöchi!

Accommodation

There is no special accommodation available in the area around Ulmethöchi. Camping is not permitted.

Anyone wishing to spend a week as a voluntary assistant at Ulmethöchi should apply to the BNV, c/o Werner Schaffner, Rössligasse 43, 4467 Rothenfluh (tel: 061/991 02 90).

Site protection

The Ulmethöchi has no special legal protection status. As the site is 'only' a point where large numbers of migrants pass through, negative human influences have very little impact.

Disabled access

Because of the long walk and 300-m altitude difference that have to be tackled from Lauwil, the Ulmethöchi is not really suitable for wheelchair-users or for others with walking impairments.

Nearby sites

Chamois can be seen in the surrounding area, occasionally also asp vipers.

Hawfinches (drawing by J. Laesser)

25 KLINGNAUER STAUSEE (KLINGNAU RESERVOIR)

Canton:	Aargau
Grid reference:	660/270
Height a.s.l.:	350 m
Start:	Koblenz rail station
Finish:	Klingnau-Döttingen rail station
Itinerary:	Koblenz station–Giriz riverine wood–Aare upstream over dam and along lakeshore path to Klingnau road bridge–Klingnau-Döttingen station
Duration:	allow at least half to 1 day. Distance *c*.5 km
Best time:	all year
Map:	LdS 1:25,000; sheet 1050 (Zurzach)
Status:	nature reserve, reserve for waterbirds and migrants of national and international importance; Ramsar site; IBA
Equipment:	telescope, picnic lunch

The Klingnau Reservoir lies north of the Baden–Brugg–Wettingen conurbation at a point just before the confluence of the Aare and the Rhine. Following its construction with the damming of the Aare in 1935, this artificial lake has developed into an internationally-important site for waterbirds and ranks as one of the most interesting sites in Switzerland. The number of species recorded there stands at 270. Extensive shallows, mudflats, reedbeds and remnant riverine forest together create within a small area a mosaic of habitats which provide feeding grounds and nest-sites for a rich variety of birds. It is worth visiting the reservoir at any time of the year and you can be sure of seeing something interesting.

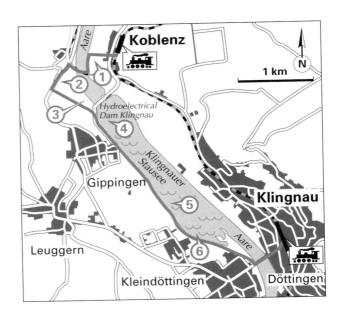

Recommended routes

As the relict of a once very dynamic river system, the riverine wood of Giriz (1) near Koblenz offers a good chance of seeing Lesser Spotted and Grey-headed Woodpeckers, Nightingale, Golden Oriole and other woodland species in the breeding season between the end of March and July. There have also been irregular sightings of Middle Spotted Woodpecker. A similar habitat, the Gippinger Grien (2), is situated on the other side of the Aare and can be reached by crossing the rail bridge. Afterwards, follow the Gippingen road for a short distance. From the edge of the road, you have the best views over the open ox-bow lakes along the Aare, before you take a gravel path to the left and go back into the closed riverine wood. Female Gadwall and Tufted Ducks with their broods are a regular sight in August The favourite spot for Kingfisher and Green Sandpiper is directly below the waste-water treatment works (3). After about 800 m, you leave the wood and climb up onto the left bank above the power station. Common Terns and Black-headed Gulls rear their young on artificial platforms in the lower part of the lake (4), while Reed Warblers and Reed Buntings nest in the dense reeds. A highlight in winter is the regular occurrence together of Whooper and Bewick's Swans, as well as a range of ducks, all of which feed by upending close to the bank. We recommend keeping an eye on the canal which runs parallel to the path along the lake, as Common Sandpiper, Kingfisher, Grey Wagtail and Dipper are regular there and tend to reveal their presence by their characteristic calls. West of the canal, there are orchards and open fields and species typical of cultivated land such as hirundines, Black Redstart and Redstart, Serin and Tree Sparrow can be seen there. Check the winter flocks of small birds for Redwings, Bramblings and Water Pipits. Grey-headed Woodpeckers occasionally come to the orchards to feed.

The shallow-water zone (5), which begins about 1.5 km up the lake, is usually the most interesting, as it tends to have the greatest variety and number of birds and associated activity. In spring and autumn especially, this part of the reservoir is the haunt of many different kinds of ducks and a range of wader species. The latter are particularly numerous when the water level is low. Waders regularly observed include Lapwing, Curlew, Ruff, *Tringa* and *Calidris* species. Hundreds of Cormorants rest on the electricity pylons in the middle of the lake. In the river channel towards the opposite bank, Goldeneye, or the rarer Scaup or Long-tailed Duck, dive for food in winter. This is also the best place to see the raptors which fly along the Acheberg heights or cross the lake (usually very high up) in the autumn. Further up the lake (6), the bankside vegetation becomes ever denser. Oaks, poplars and thick scrub block your view out onto the water and the areas of mud. The upper part of the lake, which is characterized by its extensive reedbeds, can therefore be viewed from only a few points. One good watchpoint is a concrete slab jutting out into the water near the old observation tower. It's worthwhile scanning along the edge of the reeds from there, Spotted Crakes and Snipe being easy to see, especially on August evenings. Lots of herons, dabbling ducks and waders are found in the bays between the patches of reeds and Night Herons occasionally roost during the day in the massive white willows which tower up out of the reeds. Between this point and the Klingnau-Döttingen link road, there are only a few places from which to take a last look at the reeds, mud and open water. Closer to the Aare bridge a white-willow wood

The Klingnau Reservoir is an interesting site throughout the year
(photo: Schweizer Vogelschutz SVS, Zürich)

replaces the reeds and this has a number of woodland birds such as Nuthatch, Short-toed Treecreeper or Chiffchaff.

Calendar

A waterbird site of international importance with many different species and large numbers of birds. Especially important as a staging site for waders, a good migration watchpoint for raptors.

Winter: Black-necked Grebe, Cormorant, Bewick's and Whooper Swans, Shelduck, Wigeon, Gadwall, Shoveler, Pintail, Red-crested Pochard, Scaup, Velvet Scoter (irregular) and Goldeneye, Goosander; Hen Harrier, Sparrowhawk, Lapwing, Snipe, Curlew, Kingfisher, Grey-headed Woodpecker (in the poplars or orchards), Water Pipit, Grey and White Wagtails, Dipper, tits and finches.

Spring: Night Heron, Little Egret, Shelduck, various dabbling ducks such as Wigeon, Pintail, Garganey and Shoveler, Red-crested Pochard, Black and Red Kites, Osprey, Spotted Crake, Little Crake (irregular), waders: *Calidris* species, plovers, Ruff, Snipe, Curlew, *Tringa* species; Mediterranean and Little Gulls, terns, Stock Dove and Woodpigeon,

Alpine Swift, Kingfisher, hirundines, Tawny, Tree and Meadow Pipits, Yellow Wagtail, Whinchat and Bluethroat, Redwing, Sedge Warbler, Lesser Whitethroat, Bearded Tit, Penduline Tit, Jackdaw, Rook, finches.

Breeding season: Little and Great Crested Grebes, Gadwall, Pochard and Tufted Duck, Red Kite, Water Rail and Moorhen, Lapwing, Black-headed Gull, Common Tern, Cuckoo, Kingfisher, Grey-headed, Green and Lesser Spotted Woodpeckers, Nightingale (irregular), Marsh, Reed, Garden and Willow Warblers, Long-tailed Tit, Short-toed Treecreeper, Golden Oriole, Reed Bunting.

Autumn: Similar range of species to spring, some more numerous: Great White Egret, Wigeon, Black and White Storks, conspicuous raptor migration with Honey Buzzard, all three harrier species, Goshawk, Sparrowhawk, Merlin, Hobby and Peregrine; rails and crakes, *Tringa* and *Calidris* species.

Useful tips

In autumn, from mid-August onwards, it's worthwhile paying special attention to the migration of birds of prey over the foothills of the high Jura. Spectacular mass migration of raptors can occasionally be witnessed in favourable weather conditions. At the end of August and in early September, large numbers of Honey Buzzards pass through and then, in October, their place is taken by Buzzards. In between, you may have have scarcer migrants such as Black Stork, Osprey, Peregrine or Goshawk.

Access

The site is easy to reach by regional train service from Baden or Wettingen (701). Get out at Koblenz or Klingnau-Döttingen. Restricted parking is available by the rail stations and the Gippingen bridge (see map).

Accommodation

There is rather little accommodation in the surrounding area. Hotel accommodation is available in Koblenz (for example: Hotel Blume, Landstrasse 2, 5322 Koblenz (tel: 056/246 17 80)) and Döttingen (Hotel Bahnhof, Hauptstrasse 13, 5312 Döttingen (tel: 056/245 10 50)). The thermal spa of Zurzach has a bigger supply of beds available. It's only if you want to be at the site very early in the morning that you need to stay overnight.

Site protection

The Klingnau Reservoir is well enough protected, but there are more and more leisure activities taking place all around the lake especially at weekends, and infringements of various rules are the order of the day (e.g. failure to keep dogs on the lead). It is therefore all the more important for ornithologists to set a good example and to obey the law. Please leave room for other people to enjoy themselves and don't block the path with telescope tripods.

Disabled access

The path along the Klingnau Reservoir embankment is very much to be recommended for wheelchair-users and other disabled visitors. The areas of riverine woodland are less suitable as the paths do not have a firm surface.

26 FLACHSEE UNTERLUNKHOFEN

Canton:	Aargau
Height a.s.l.:	380 m
Grid reference:	670/241
Start:	Rottenschwil Bridge
Finish:	Rottenschwil Bridge
Itinerary:	depending on where the sun is: in the morning, anti-clockwise, in the afternoon, clockwise round the lake
Duration:	allow about 3 hrs (c.6 km); longer variant about 5 hrs (c.10 km)
Best time:	spring (breeding birds, migrants); winter (winter visitors)
Status:	cantonal nature reserve, site for waterbirds and alluvial habitat of national importance, BLN
Map:	LdS 1:25,000; sheets 1110 (Hitzkirch) and 1090 (Wohlen)
Equipment:	telescope

The Reuss plain in the canton of Aargau is rich in near-natural land-scapes. This comes about because the site, which has been given its characteristic stamp by the meandering Reuss river, is situated away from the great communication routes and has never been opened up and developed to the same extent as much of the rest of the Central Plateau. In the middle of this varied landscape lies the Flachsee lake, which was created as recently as 1975 when the Reuss was artificially dammed. The aim was to establish a waterbird reserve containing as many typical fluvial habitats as possible. The aim has been achieved: we now find here a mixture of flowing and standing water with shallow-water zones, both fen-meadows and unimproved mesobromion grass-land, reedbeds, riverine woodland, islands of bare gravel and others with plant cover, sand- and mudflats—a site of rich diversity supporting correspondingly varied birdlife.

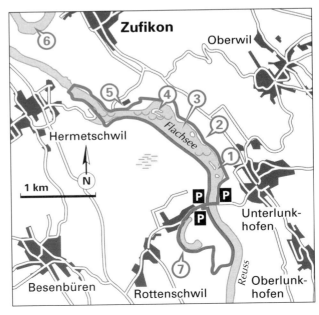

Recommended routes

The starting point for a circular walk is the car park by the bridge in Rottenschwil. Choose your route depending on the position of the sun (morning anti-clockwise; afternoon clockwise). Because it's quite a narrow lake, the Flachsee offers the chance to get outstanding views of various waterbirds. From the bench in the meadow, you can easily look across to the mudbanks (1), which vary in size, of course, depending on the water level. At migration time especially, various species of waders can be seen there. The best view of the small Grey Heron colony (2) is from several metres north of the green gate where a stream flows into the lake from the side.

The dead oaks in the middle of the lake (3) are taken over by Cormorants as roosting trees each year from late summer up until the spring and this has become a characteristic Flachsee scene. Little Ringed Plovers tend to be on the gravel islands (4) during the breeding season. A little further on, it's worth stopping at the Geisshofweiher pond (5), where there's a remnant of riverine woodland. Test your knowledge of bird sounds from the path there (40 breeding species, e.g. Lesser Spotted Woodpecker). The return walk is via the other side of the lake. If you feel like it, continue your walk to Bremgarten.

An especially good stretch of the Reuss (6) for waterbirds lies between Zopfhau and the dam.

Calendar

Important site for breeding birds with 58 species. Many migrants, especially waders and occasional rarities. Observers prepared to work long and hard for their birds have found many exciting species, from Marsh Sandpiper to Thrush Nightingale.

Winter: Cormorant (roosting in trees), Greylag and (rarely) Bean Geese (check surrounding fields!), Wigeon, Gadwall, Teal, Pintail, Shoveler, Pochard, Tufted Duck and Goldeneye, Goosander, Hen Harrier (occasionally), Goshawk, Sparrowhawk, Kingfisher, Water Pipit, Grey Wagtail.

Spring: Black-necked Grebe. Almost all the waders on the Swiss list have also been recorded at the Flachsee in recent years (but only in small numbers). Osprey, Marsh Harrier and many passerines pass through regularly on migration; occasionally Red-footed Falcons by the Stille Reuss.

Breeding season: Little and Great Crested Grebes, Grey Heron (small colony near Rottenschwil Bridge), Greylag Goose (established 1981, up to 40 birds present throughout the year; regular breeder), Mallard, Pochard and Tufted Duck, Black and Red Kites, Water Rail, Little Ringed Plover (2–4 pairs on the four gravel islands), Lapwing, Kingfisher, Lesser Spotted Woodpecker, Marsh and Reed Warblers, Golden Oriole, Reed Bunting.

Autumn: Various ducks and waders (mainly Lapwing, Snipe).

The Flachsee in the Reuss valley is essentially man-made (photo: B. Schelbert)

Access
The easiest way to get there is to take the direct postbus service from Zürich's Wiedikon rail station (tram No. 9 or 14, or fast train S8 for the station) to the bridge at Rottenschwil (720.15). An alternative route would be to take the train to Bremgarten (654) and to start your circuit of the lake from the other side (see map). If you're travelling by car, the recommended route is from Zürich to Rottenschwil via Birmensdorf–Aesch–Oberlunkhofen. There are public car parks on both sides of the bridge.

Accommodation
Bremgarten has a range of hotels. Campsite by the bridge at Ottenbach (*c.*5 km); information at the Reussbrücke restaurant in Ottenbach (tel: 01/761 20 22).

Site protection
The wildlife and landscape of this reserve enjoy protection through a variety of different regulations and arrangements. Visitors should use only the designated paths in all nature reserves on the Reuss plain. In addition, they are requested to keep dogs on the lead and to light fires only where this is expressly permitted. Bathing and water sports are prohibited.

Disabled access
This is a level site with wide, well-maintained paths and as such is suitable for disabled visitors. The wheelchair-friendly asphalt path on the northeastern shore of the Flachsee is especially recommended.

Nearby sites

For visitors wanting to learn more about the site, there is an exhibition on its ecology in the 'Zieglerhaus' Nature Conservation Centre at Rottenschwil. There are also regular guided walks starting from the centre (for more information, telephone 056/634 21 41).

Directly in front of the Zieglerhaus lies the Stille Reuss (7), an ox-bow lake with a large reedbed and fen-meadows as well as all all stages of silting-up and successive invasion by vegetation (fen succession). The rare Little Bittern breeds here sporadically. With a total of 42 mostly rare and endangered species, the Stille Reuss is one of the richest wetlands for dragonflies and damsel flies in Switzerland, and Hobbies hunting these insects in the breeding season here often provide a marvellous wildlife spectacle. Other creatures found at the site are tree frog, natterjack toad, grass snake, viviparous lizard and several fascinating kinds of grasshoppers and crickets (13 species, including the rare marsh-cricket). Access to the Stille Reuss is easy: there is a gravel path allowing you to complete a circular walk of about 1.5 km.

The Siebeneichen ('Seven Oaks') nature reserve in Merenschwand (near the Ottenbach campsite, c. 6 km south of the Flachsee) is another interesting wetland with a valley bog of national importance. This is a good site in particular for various species of waterbirds.

27 PFÄFFIKERSEE AND ROBENHUSERRIET

Canton:	Zürich
Grid reference:	701/245
Height a.s.l.:	540 m
Start:	several, depending on access route (e.g. Aathal)
Finish:	as above
Itinerary:	several on made-up paths through the fen
Duration:	distance from 3 km; allow half a day
Best time:	April/May and September
Status:	nature reserve, fen-mire (bog) of national importance
Map:	LdS: 1:25,000; sheet 1092 (Uster)
Equipment:	telescope, wellington boots (in spring, when paths under water)

Lake Pfäffikon (Pfäffikersee) lies, embedded between ranges of low hills, in the Zürich Oberland (Zürcher Oberland). The Robenhuserriet fen covers an area of around 330 ha, extending across the southern end of the lake from Seegräben to Auslikon, and is one of the richest of Swiss wetlands. The uniquely wide expanse of different vegetation types—they range from belts of floating plants through luxuriant reedswamp up to areas of raised bog—is, of course, the main factor determining the site's bird fauna. Typical birds of *Phragmites* reedbeds and other fenland vegetation occur here in good numbers and are usually easy to find. Nevertheless, some species have declined markedly owing to disturbance from various noisy and obtrusive human leisure

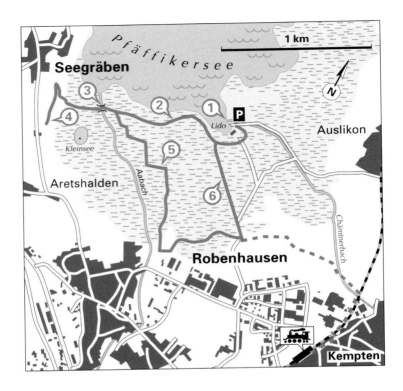

activities and because of encroachment by scrub onto their favoured habitats. The Snipe was pronounced extinct at the site, but returned in 1994. Let's hope that this characteristic species will now become permanently established in the Robenhuserriet.

Recommended routes

The most interesting places are the southern end of the lake, the area around the Auslikon lido (bathing beach), the Kleinsee and the central part of the Robenhuserriet. A circular walk right round the lake may also spring a few ornithological surprises.

The Auslikon lido (1) offers a good view over large sections of the lake as well as the adjoining reedbeds where Bitterns are regularly found in the winter. During the autumn migration period, Black Terns and Little Gulls and also waders can be seen from the same point. From the lido, the path leads towards Seegräben, all the time keeping fairly close to a belt of reeds (2). The rare Little Bittern can be heard there in the breeding season and both Great Reed and Savi's Warblers are among the breeding birds easy to locate by their songs. After around one kilometre, turn right after the small bridge across the creek (Aabach) onto a small jetty (3). The low mound (4) near Seegräben overlooks the Kleinsee, a small reed-filled pool of standing water on the western edge of the fen. A nesting raft, specially made and put in place for Common Terns, is currently used by Black-headed Gulls.

The Robenhuserriet at the southern end of the Pfäffikersee is one of
the biggest and most important fen-mires in Switzerland
(photo: Schweizer Vogelschutz SVS, Zürich)

Two trails (5 and 6) lead through the central part of the
Robenhuserriet. These are especially interesting in the breeding season
as typical species of this fenland habitat such as Reed Bunting, Willow
Warbler, Tree Pipit and Snipe have their territories there. Marsh
Warblers are present at high densities and, in recent years, even singing
Scarlet Rosefinches have been noted. Lesser Spotted and Grey-headed
Woodpeckers breed in the areas with more trees.

Calendar

Extensive mire with a number of typical features such as valley, transitional and raised bogs. A wide spectrum of bog- and fenland species in the
breeding season. Autumn and spring migration periods also interesting.

Winter: Bittern (especially on passage in November), Bean Goose (rare
on fields at the northern end of the lake), Shoveler, Smew, Hen Harrier,
Snipe, Long-eared Owl, Meadow and Water Pipits, Great Grey Shrike,
Bearded Tit.

Breeding season: Little and Great Crested Grebes, Little Bittern, Pochard
and Tufted Duck, Pheasant, Water Rail and Moorhen, Lapwing, Snipe
(up to 1991, displaying again from 1994), Black-headed Gull (5–30
pairs), Long-eared Owl, Cuckoo, Grey-headed and Lesser Spotted
Woodpeckers, Tree Pipit, Grasshopper, Savi's, Marsh, Reed, Great Reed
and Willow Warblers, Scarlet Rosefinch (irregular), Reed Bunting.

Spring and Autumn: Herons, various ducks, Marsh Harrier, rails and crakes, waders (on mown meadows in spring, Auslikon lido in autumn), Little Gull, Common and Black Terns, passerines such as pipits, wagtails, Whinchat, Redstart, thrushes (autumn), Pied Flycatcher, various finches.

Access

The nearest rail stations are Aathal (fast train S14 from Zürich every half hour) (740), Kempten or Pfäffikon (S3 from Zürich via Effretikon, daily every half hour) (753). From Winterthur with the S7 or S8 to Effretikon (750), change there to the S3 for Pfäffikon or Kempten.

Accommodation

There's no need to stay overnight as a day trip is normally enough. Campsite Pfäffikersee, 8331 Auslikon (tel: 01/950 13 29). Hotel Bahnhof, Bahnhofstrasse 18, 8330 Pfäffikon (tel: 01/950 14 42).

Site protection

In order to protect the mire, certain paths are closed during the breeding season. On no account stray from the officially designated pathways: the vegetation is extremely sensitive to crushing from human feet. Dogs must be kept on the lead. Please obey the rules and set a good example for other visitors. The point is that up to 10,000 people seeking recreation come flooding into the area on weekends with fine weather and there is then virtually no one else to set an example apart from you!

A nature trail was deliberately placed on the edge of the site, in an area less sensitive to disturbance.

Disabled access

The track along the edge of the lake is suitable for wheelchair-users and other visitors with walking impairments. However, most of the other tracks are often swampy and not suitable for wheelchairs. The only difficulties arise from the relatively long access routes.

Nearby sites

The neighbouring Greifensee, especially the upper end of the lake between Riedikon and the lido at Egg, is interesting at migration time and in winter and has a similar range of species to the Pfäffikersee. It has had an observation platform since the summer of 1997. The lower end of the lake near Schwerzenbach has various *Acrocephalus* warblers, Little Bittern and Common Tern, but also Nightingale, which does not breed at the Pfäffikersee. It's difficult to get good views into this site, at least in places.

28 NEERACHER RIED

Canton:	Zürich
Grid reference:	678/261
Height a.s.l.:	410 m
Start:	Riedt near Neerach
Finish:	Riedt near Neerach
Itinerary:	several possible routes for doing a circuit of the site
Duration:	allow 3 hrs to half a day; 3.5–4.5 km
Best time:	spring (April–June) or autumn (August–October)
Status:	nature reserve, valley bog of national importance; IBA
Map:	LdS: 1:25,000; sheet 1071 (Bülach)
Equipment:	telescope, bicycle (for trips into the surrounding area)

The Neeracher Ried lies in the Höri-Neerach-Niederglatt triangle and, with a surface area of over one square kilometre, is one of the largest valley bogs in the country. Unfortunately, this 'child of the Ice Age' is bisected by two busy cantonal highways. Despite this, the sedge-beds (Macro *Carex* fen) are, for Swiss conditions, unique and provide rare fenland birds, including all the European rail and crake species, with superb nesting habitat. The water level is artificially regulated over a weir and can therefore be adapted to the needs of the birds. It is lowered in the autumn and the exposed mudflats are used for feeding and resting by waders. Despite the considerable efforts of conservationists, Snipe, Lapwing, Whitethroat and Tree Pipit have sadly become extinct as breeding birds in recent years.

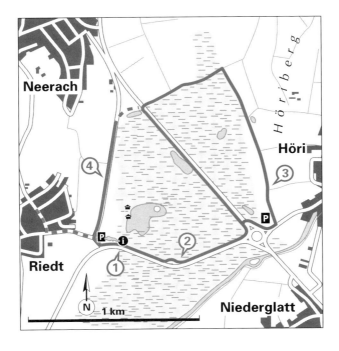

Recommended routes

A tour of the reserve usually begins at the observation tower (1) next to the SVS—BirdLife visitor centre. The tower affords superb views over the extensive marshy meadows and *Phragmites* reedbeds, stands of alder and the shallow lagoon. This is also the access point to the hides that are situated directly by the lagoon. The hides provide an opportunity to watch birds on the mudflats and in the reeds without disturbing them. Reed Buntings and Savi's Warblers flit about in the reeds and, at the lagoon, 1–3 pairs of Great Reed Warblers find conditions to their liking. At dusk, on spring nights between May and June, there's a good chance of hearing the whiplash call of the Spotted Crake. Up to 200 pairs of Black-headed Gulls nest on the sedge tussocks. In autumn, you can also get good views of waders on the mudflats from the tower: regular visitors include various *Tringa* species and plovers, also Snipe. The high-pitched calls of Penduline Tits can be heard in the reeds and a typical sight, in August especially, is Hobbies hunting dragonflies over the fen-mire. Among the centre's many attractions, the visitor can choose from an exhibition, a nature laboratory and a multi-media show. The centre also offers access to the hides and regular guided tours (for all information, SVS Nature Information Centre, 8173 Neerach, telephone 01/858 13 00).

There are a number of different ways for doing a circular tour of this site. However, they do involve mostly walking along roads and the noise of the traffic can be considerable. It is therefore best to visit the site early in the morning. If you first head east towards Höri (2), you will regularly hear the songs of Savi's and Grasshopper Warblers. After around 900 m, you come to the big roundabout; continue along the Höri road, then turn left after about 50 m onto a farm track (3). This track is higher than the mire, so that there are good views over the extensive wet meadows. In the winter, you might spot a Great Grey Shrike from this track as it watches for prey atop a bush or tree. Between the fen-mire and the gravel path lies a wide buffer-zone which is farmed only extensively and which is designed to protect the mire against the incursion of harmful substances from agriculture. Turn left again after about 800 m and follow the northern edge of the protected area. As soon as you reach the road again, you have a choice: you can either continue along the road which cuts acros the mire (in the direction of the roundabout), or you follow the Neerach–Riedt link road which runs along the western limit of the site (4). The range of species likely to be encountered is similar to that on the rest of the route. There are often Penduline Tits in the bushes and trees, a species which has attempted to breed in the Neeracher Ried. From here, it's about one kilometre to the car park next to the visitor centre.

Calendar

Stopover site of national importance for waders, which are numerous, especially in autumn. Important valley bog with rare rails and other bog and fenland species.

Winter: Only few species: Cormorant, Wigeon and Teal, Sparrowhawk, Red Kite (roost of up to 200 birds in the nearby woods in winter), Hen Harrier, Snipe, Water Pipit, Great Grey Shrike (irregular).

Spring: Purple Heron, White Stork, Gadwall and Shoveler, Marsh

The lagoon in the Neeracher Ried is a good place for passage waders
(photo: Schweizer Vogelschutz SVS, Zürich)

Harrier, Honey Buzzard, Hobby, various waders, Kingfisher, Sand Martin, Tree and Meadow Pipits, Yellow Wagtail, Bluethroat, Whinchat, Sedge Warbler, Lesser Whitethroat, Penduline Tit, Linnet.

Breeding season: Little Grebe, Little Bittern, Garganey, Teal, Water Rail, Spotted, Little and Baillon's Crakes (the last two species irregular), Black-headed Gull, Yellow Wagtail, Nightingale, Savi's, Grasshopper, Marsh, Reed and Willow Warblers, Penduline Tit (irregular), Golden Oriole, Yellowhammer and Reed Bunting.

Autumn: Similar to spring, but usually more interesting for waders as the water level in the lagoon is lowered: Little Ringed and Ringed Plovers, Lapwing, various *Calidris* and *Tringa* species (especially in August), Ruff, Snipe, Black-tailed Godwit (25 wader species recorded to date); Little Gull, Black Tern, pipits and wagtails, Redwing, Rook, Siskin and other finch species.

Useful tips

In the winter, from 100 to 200 Red Kites gather at a feeding and roosting site on the Heitlig above Neerach. The kites can be seen very well as they circle close to the observer. Several dozen soaring Red Kites are a magnificent spectacle.

Access

The fast S-Bahn rail service (S5) will get you quickly from Zürich to Oberglatt from where a postbus (ZVV-line 510) operates to Riedt or (760.10) to Neerach.

Trains and buses run hourly. It's only a few minutes' walk to the observation tower and the visitor centre from the village of Riedt. For those travelling by car, the recommended route is Zürich–Regensdorf–Dielsdorf–Neerach.

Accommodation

There are no hotels or campsites close to the reserve. The nearest possibilities are Dielsdorf, Bülach or Steinmaur. As only short walks are possible at the site, there's normally no need to spend the night locally.

Site protection

The observation tower, the hides, paths and tracks and roadsides offer excellent views into the reserve; please keep strictly to the paths—leaving them is prohibited. Since June 1997, an experiment has been running with Highland cattle from Scotland. These animals can subsist on very little and it is hoped they will open up the vegetation and thus create favourable conditions for plants and animals needing more light.

Disabled access

The exhibition in the SVS visitor centre and the hides are easily accessible to wheelchair-users; the observation tower, unfortunately, is not. Only the fairly long distances to be covered within the reserve could potentially cause a problem. The tracks northeast of the roundabout are not suitable for wheelchairs.

Nearby sites

Roughly 2 km north of the Neeracher Ried lies the Strassberg and Middle Spotted Woodpecker breeds in the woods there. Listen for the hooting of Long-eared Owl in the Oberholz near Neerach on clear, still nights in the late winter or early spring. However, the male owl's display-calls barely carry more than 50 m. North of Neerach lies the Rhine power station of Eglisau and this has an Alpine Swift colony in the summer. Wallcreeper is occasionally seen there in hard winters.

29 NIDERHOLZ

Canton:	Zürich
Grid reference:	688/273
Height a.s.l.:	360–440 m
Start:	Marthalen rail station
Finish:	Marthalen
Itinerary:	Marthalen–Nider Marthalen–Buechberg–Hörnlispitz Ellikerholz–Chachberg–Watt–Radholz–Wattbüel–Marthalen
Duration:	allow half a day to one day; distance around 13 km
Status:	no special protection status; IBA; BLN
Best time:	March–May
Map:	LdS: 1:25,000; sheets 1051 (Eglisau) and 1052 (Andelfingen)
Equipment:	binoculars, picnic lunch, tick repellent!

The Niderholz lies in the northern part of the canton of Zürich, in the triangle Marthalen, Rheinau and Flaach. It is bounded in the north and west by the Rhine, in the south by the Thur. The climate of this region, which is also known as the 'Wine Country', is drier and warmer than in other parts of the canton.

This is one of the most valuable oak-hornbeam forests in Switzerland. Extensive tracts of continuous woodland, with oak predominating, are well preserved over wide areas. In places, there is typical coppice-with-standards: scattered trees (oaks) allowed to grow to their full height and

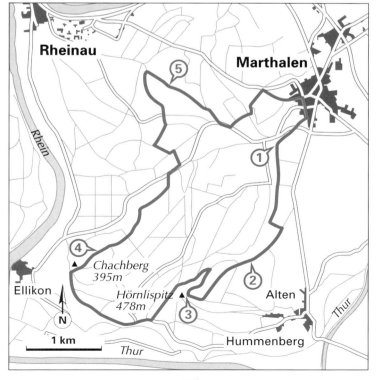

a coppice layer formerly used for fuel. These woods support an especially wide range of bird species and provide ideal habitat conditions for six species of woodpeckers, including Middle Spotted, as well as other rare woodland birds.

Recommended routes

Begin your walk in the centre of Marthalen (c.1 km from the station), then follow the yellow markers through the village to its southern edge and turn right. From that point, it is simply a question of following the trail with the yellow rhomb-shaped markers. The path goes along the side of a rise from which there's a good view over large parts of the Niderholz (1). After a few metres, the first block of woodland extends away on your right. On the left, agricultural desert—monocultures. Look up for soaring Red Kite, Kestrel and Buzzard. After about an hour's walk across the more or less open fields, you come to the start of the continuous forest (2). Hawfinches are easily picked up by their calls. Tits, *Sylvia* warblers, Spotted and Pied Flycatchers sing almost without pause, especially in early May. After a walk of about 800 m through a first splendid piece of oak woodland, you reach quite a large area of young growth. Leave the official hiking trail by turning right onto the gravel path before the hiking trail then continues on a narrower path. The hill called 'Hörnlispitz' (3) which follows is probably one of the best places in the Niderholz to find Middle Spotted Woodpeckers. Stock Doves and Jackdaws also occur there and both Black and Grey-headed Woodpeckers are easily identified on fine days in March thanks to their far-carrying calls. Next comes a long bend to the right and, after about 300 m, the road through the forest branches off sharply to the left. Continue straight on for about 1 km until you reach a well-built forest track which you then follow for about another 1.2 km. After that, another road through the forest branches off right and, 400 m further on, a road leads up to the right and onto the Chachberg plateau (4). The forest road goes straight ahead through in places good Middle Spotted Woodpecker habitat and, after 1.6 km, you are back to the official hiking trail heading in the direction of Rheinau-Dachsen. A piece of coppice-with-standards 'straight out of the textbook' is followed by a short stretch on the link road between Marthalen and Ellikon am Rhein. The wood which then comes into view on the other side of the road is the complete opposite: stands of alien tree species are no longer suitable habitat for the highly specialized Middle Spotted Woodpecker. In marked contrast, the parts of the forest called 'Watt' and the Radholz (5), which lie alongside the hiking trail, are a real delight for ornithologists. Gnarled old oaks, hornbeams and beeches form a picture-book coppice-with-standards woodland where to see Middle Spotted and other woodpeckers is not just a matter of luck. Other species present include Pied Flycatcher, Wood Warbler and Stock Dove. Don't become so engrossed in your birdwatching that you miss the great dividing of the ways, with one fork going to Rheinau-Dachsen and the other (right-hand) fork to Marthalen. For a distance of about one kilometre, the forest is extremely interesting, but then a quite large open plain brings the fairy-tale woodland scene to an abrupt end. Continue along the hiking trail to return to the starting point at Marthalen.

Ancient, gnarled oaks are the characteristic feature of the Niderholz Forest near Marthalen (Zürich) (photo: P. Rüegg)

Calendar

One of the most extensive and unbroken tracts of mixed oak-hornbeam forest in Switzerland. Wide range of woodland birds with important population of Middle Spotted Woodpeckers.

Breeding season (March–June): Honey Buzzard, Black and Red Kites, Goshawk, Sparrowhawk, Hobby and Kestrel, Woodcock, Stock Dove, Woodpigeon and Turtle Dove, Cuckoo, Tawny Owl, Alpine Swift (visits the site, breeds on Eglisau power station), Grey-headed, Green, Black, Great Spotted, Middle Spotted and Lesser Spotted Woodpeckers, Skylark (on fields all round the Niderholz), Song and Mistle Thrushes, Garden Warbler (young plantations), Wood Warbler, Firecrest, Pied

Flycatcher, Long-tailed Tit, various other tits, Short-toed Treecreeper and Treecreeper, Golden Oriole, Serin (in the villages), Hawfinch, Yellowhammer (open areas, young growth).

Access
By Swiss Federal Railways (SBB) via Zürich–Winterthur or Schaffhausen to Marthalen (hourly service from Winterthur; 762). Postbus service from there to Marthalen Dorf and to Rheinau (762.20).

Accommodation
There are single hotels in each of Flaach (Hotel Engel, Wesenplatz 6 (tel: 052/318 13 03)), Marthalen (Restaurant Rössli, Oberdorf 54 (tel: 052/319 13 37)) and in Ellikon (Restaurant Schiff (tel: 052/319 34 34)) and these are the only possibilities for overnight accommodation close to the Niderholz Forest Otherwise, you'll have to look for somewhere in Schaffhausen, Andelfingen or even in Winterthur.

Campsites: Rassenwies, Kleinandelfingen (open from 30 March to 29 September (tel: 052/317 24 08)) and Steubisallmend in Flaach (open from 3 April to 29 September (tel: 052/318 14 13)).

For information, contact the Wyland Tourist Information Office, Thurtalstrasse 4, 8450 Andelfingen (tel: 052/317 13 40).

Site protection
The Niderholz Forest is a BLN site (BLN: Federal inventory of landscapes and natural monuments of national importance), but still does not enjoy any special protection. There are campaigns to protect and foster the oak and to ensure the proper coppice-with-standards woodland management. Anyone who believes they have to chase after the Middle Spotted Woodpecker with a tape-recorder has no right to be in this forest. Tape-lures seriously upset this species and can lead to reduced breeding success.

Disabled access
The site is not wheelchair-accessible and the distances are too great for other visitors with walking impairments.

Nearby sites
On the western edge of the Niderholz Forest lies Ellikon am Rhein. Mixed flocks of Swifts and Alpine Swifts can often be seen over the little village and Hobbies nesting in the forest use the more open areas for hunting.

The Oerlinger Ried (fen), lying east of the Niderholz, is not very big, but has proved to be a good site for unusual species. Breeding birds there include Water Rail, Lapwing, Yellow Wagtail, Reed and Marsh Warblers, Red-backed Shrike (sporadic) and Reed Bunting. The total number of species recorded stands at 150. The site is situated to the east of Oerlingen (on the far side of the Schaffhausen–Winterthur motorway), which is only a few kilometres from Marthalen. Northeast of there are the Husemer lakes, glacial relicts with an interesting flora and fauna. Despite the rumpus associated with the numbers of people swimming there in the summer months, the original character of the lakes has survived largely intact.

Beavers live in the remnants of old river channels and ox-bow lakes north of Rüdlingen. On request, a ferry will take passengers from Ellikon am Rhein to the opposite bank and the beaver site lies downstream from there.

Canton:	St Gallen
Grid reference:	717/230
Height a.s.l.:	410 m
Start:	Uznach rail station
Finish:	ditto
Itinerary:	from Uznach along road–after 1 km, turn right, observation tower–Entenseeli–pumping station–across arable land–cross over railway and back to Uznach along the Bösch canal
Duration:	distance *c.*5 km; allow half a day to whole day
Best time:	spring (mid-March to end of May) and late summer (mid-August to mid-September)
Map:	LdS 1:25,000; sheet 1113 (Ricken)
Status:	nature reserve, Ramsar site
Equipment:	telescope, picnic lunch (nowhere to buy food on the way)

As the last remnant of a once extensive area of fen and marsh, the Kaltbrunner Riet now ranks as one of the most important wetlands for rare animals and plants in eastern Switzerland. Its location in the middle of the intensively-cultivated Linth plain gives this nature reserve of some 45 ha the character of an oasis. The diversity of the birdlife at the site means that the Kaltbrunner Riet has now become a popular destination for ornithologists from all over the east of the country. Few other sites have such good facilities as the Kaltbrunner Riet. An observation tower at the edge of the lagoon, several observation platforms and a Pro Natura visitor centre ('i') are open and available for the benefit and enjoyment of visitors.

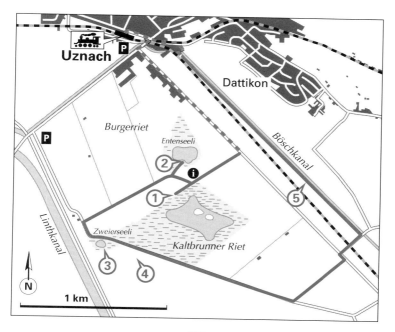

Recommended routes

The best way of getting to know where the many different birds are and of observing them is do a walk all round the Kaltbrunner Riet reserve. To get to the site, cross over the rail tracks after Uznach station, follow the Grinau road for just 50 m and then turn left onto the road to Benken. After one kilometre, a gravel path branches off right and leads along a shelter-belt directly into the fen. Some 500 m further on, you reach the observation tower (1) and the temptation is to stay there for a prolonged watch. From the top platform, there is the spectacle in the breeding season of the Black-headed Gull colony and always the chance of something new: herons, ducks, waders, *Acrocephalus* warblers or Bluethroat, which is easy to see especially in the spring.

The birds are usually more difficult to see from the raised observation platform at the Entenseeli lake (2) because of the tall vegetation. Reed and Great Reed Warblers sing in the reeds in the breeding season. In the spring, Water Rails and Spotted Crakes are regularly to be seen at close quarters on wet patches by the foot of the platform. From the Entenseeli lake, follow the small canal south as far as the pumping station where the path leads off left to the Zweierseeli lake (3). This observation point gives you another chance to watch typical birds of the reeds such as Water Rail, Reed Warbler and Reed Bunting. Birds of open country prefer the adjoining meadows and pastureland (4): Quail, Stonechat, Grasshopper Warbler, Red-backed Shrike and Corn Bunting (rare) are (relatively) easy to find there. About one kilometre further on, a gravel road branches off to the left from this track and this takes you through intensively-used meadows back to the Uznach–Kaltbrunn road. From there, either take the direct way to Uznach or end the day by making a slight detour along the Bösch canal (a canalized stream). Approaching on the farm track across the fields, cross over the road and follow the yellow hiking-trail markers to reach the top of the Bösch canal embankment (5). It's worth going for this alternative route as several rare plants of semi-dry mesobromion grassland grow on the canal embankments. These sunlit banks also suit the Stonechat. In the afternoon, the sun's rays strike the banks strongly from the side so that it's advisable to follow the left bank of the canal.

Calendar

Site of international importance for breeding birds and as a stopover for migrants, with a wide range of species. Attracts waders, especially in the spring and late summer when the water level is lowered. In the autumn, interesting for only a brief period (mid-August to mid-September).

Winter: The site has rather few birds in this season: Long-eared Owl (often in the shelter-belts), Water Pipit, Great Grey Shrike (irregular).

Spring: Various herons and dabbling ducks, Marsh and Montagu's Harriers, Goshawk, Sparrowhawk, Red-footed Falcon, Hobby and Peregrine, Water Rail, Spotted Crake, Little Crake (irregular), Crane, Little Ringed Plover, Lapwing, Ruff, Snipe, Curlew, *Tringa* species, Whiskered Tern, Black Tern (irregular), Turtle Dove, Kingfisher, pipits and wagtails, Crag Martin (if there are cold snaps in the mountains), Bluethroat, Ring Ouzel (comment as for Crag Martin), Sedge Warbler, Aquatic Warbler (very rare), Penduline Tit.

The Kaltbrunner Riet is just a remnant of the once extensive fen- and marshlands of the Linth plain (photo: M.Sacchi)

Breeding season: Little Grebe, Black-necked Grebe (irregular), Little Bittern (irregular), White Stork (breeds in Uznach), Teal, Garganey and Pochard, Hobby, Water Rail and Spotted Crake, Lapwing (outside reserve), Black-headed Gull (50–100 pairs), Cuckoo, Barn Owl (in the general area), Long-eared Owl (in the shelter-belts), Whinchat and Stonechat, Grasshopper, Savi's, Marsh, Reed, Great Reed, Garden and Willow Warblers, Reed Bunting, Corn Bunting (rare and irregular).

Autumn: Similar range of species to that in spring, but passage lighter. More waders as water level is lowered in August: Ruff, Snipe, Curlew, *Tringa* species, less commonly plovers and *Calidris* species, occasionally rails and crakes (at the edge of the reeds).

Access
The nearest rail station is Uznach (distance *c.*1.5 km) to which SOB (Südostbahn) and SBB trains run half-hourly from Rapperswil and hourly from St Gallen (870). You can also get to the fen from Ziegelbrücke (735) with connections from there to Zürich and Chur.

Useful tips
The fascinating valley-bog vegetation with yellow flag-iris and cowbane, a highly poisonous plant of the family Umbelliferae, certainly also deserves attention. Stoats are a common sight. Special rarities are the two blue butterflies, the alcon blue and the scarce large blue, which still

survive in the Kaltbrunner Riet, but are in the category 'critically endangered' in Switzerland as a whole.

Accommodation

Overnight accommodation is not normally needed as the site can be covered in a day, but if you want to make a very early start, try the Hotel Ochsen, Zürcherstrasse 1 (tel: 055/280 40 70) or the Linthof, Bahnhofstrasse 2 (tel: 055/290 16 26) in Uznach. Other accommodation is available in Kaltbrunn, Schmerikon and Rapperswil (with youth hostel (tel: 055/210 99 27)).

Site protection

In order to make the protection as effective as possible, the usual rules for nature reserves apply thoughout the site and visitors must keep to the official paths and tracks all year round. Certain paths are closed to visitors during the breeding season.

Some tall poplars have been felled in places with the aim of providing suitable conditions for birds favouring more open habitats. The stumps of these trees are still visible at the southern end of the protected areas. Lapwings and other meadowland nesters have benefited from this measure, as they have regained the clear all-round view which is so crucially important to them when breeding.

Disabled access

The Kaltbrunner Riet is a good site for disabled visitors to explore, but it is not very wheelchair-friendly, certain paths (between the Entensee lake and the pumping station) being rather narrow. Almost all the farm tracks across the fields lack a firm, made-up surface.

Nearby sites

Many northern waterbirds, including Eider or Red-breasted Merganser, are regular at Rapperswil in winter. Terns and gulls occcasionally turn up on passage. The bay and the Allmend of Schmerikon with their wetland areas are situated near the point where the Linth flows into the Obersee (part of Lake Zürich) and can produce the odd unusual sighting.

31 STEIN AM RHEIN

Canton:	Schaffhausen/Thurgau
Grid reference:	706/279
Height a.s.l.:	390 m
Start:	Stein am Rhein rail station
Finish:	Eschenz rail station
Itinerary:	Stein am Rhein station–over bridge–through 'old town' to harbour–return, turn left shortly after bridge–along riverbank to Werd Island, from there, official hiking trail to Eschenz lido–Eschenz rail station
Duration:	allow 3–4 hrs; 4–5 km
Best time:	winter (December–February)
Status:	reserve for waterbirds and migrants of national and international importance'; IBA
Map:	LdS 1:25,000; sheets 1032 (Diessenhofen) and 1033 (Steckborn)
Equipment:	telescope, warm clothing

The historic little town of Stein am Rhein lies at the point where the Rhine flows out of the Untersee (part of Lake Constance/the Bodensee). The Schienerberg mountain, its highest point crowned by Schloss Hohenklingen, extends along the right bank of the river. Both banks have been heavily built-up and very much altered in places and this somewhat mars the idyllic picture created by the large rafts of ducks. All the same, some parts of the left bank have remained virtually unspoilt and there are reedbeds, scrub and the remnants of other alluvial flood-plain habitats. Beyond this, in the hinterland, lie intensively-farmed fields and meadows as well as some villages and housing estates. The gully of the river widens at the Eschenz lido (bathing beach) and parts of the Untersee come into view.

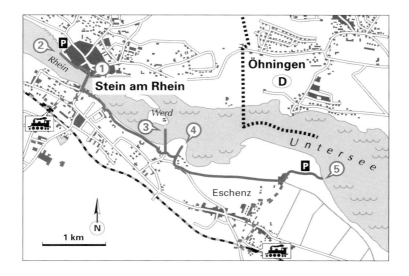

Recommended routes

The first place to check what waterbirds are present is from the great bridge over the Rhine (1) between the new and the historic old heart of the town. This is where you often find the largest concentrations of Little Grebes. Further downstream, large rafts of ducks can be picked out, but you will need to view them from the boat harbour (2) to identify the species with certainty. Goldeneye are especially numerous and, though much rarer, Ferruginous Ducks can sometimes be found among the Tufted Ducks and Pochard. From this point, you have to retrace your steps. To get to Werd Island, turn left shortly after crossing the road bridge and follow the path along the bank upstream to the narrow wooden bridge which leads across to the island (3). On the way to the island, there are frequent opportunities to scan through the rafts of ducks. Flocks of diving ducks resting on the water regularly have scarcer species like Scaup or Ferruginous Ducks hidden among them. Now and again, a Kingfisher will flash past low over the water. Goshawk and Sparrowhawk hunt small birds in the house gardens and among the rows of trees along the bank. Please be especially quiet and considerate here so that the sleeping ducks are not disturbed unnecessarily. Water Rails can often be watched at very close quarters in the belt of reeds by the island. The wooden bridge connecting Werd Island to the bank overlooks the upper river channel and a small bay near Lower Eschenz (Untereschenz). There are further opportunities for watching birds from the tip of the small, reed-covered headland (4) which marks the limit of the bay just mentioned, but under no circumstances venture out onto the open shore as this will flush all the ducks. Responsible and caring observers should go no further than the small bench on the bank. Don't hurry or make a noise! There are usually a couple of dabbling ducks among the diving ducks asleep on the water. Quite large flocks of gulls and Cormorants will be on the gravel islands, while Water Pipits move along the water's edge in search of food and in the alders and poplars that fringe the stream, you'll often find feeding Siskins, Short-toed Treecreepers or woodpeckers.

Having rejoined the tarmac road, go left and then straight on through open grassland. Turn left at the next farms and, barely 100 m further on, right again to the Eschenz lido (5). If you stand by the jetty, you can make out large flocks of ducks on the water at the lower end of the Untersee, even with the naked eye. Red-crested Pochard and Black-necked Grebes are occasionally present and there are usually Reed Buntings in the reeds.

From the lido, take the same way back for a short stretch, then turn left and head for the centre of Eschenz village, where it's just 15 minutes' walk to the station.

Calendar

Internationally-important waterbird reserve with large numbers of ducks. One of the most important wintering sites for Goldeneye in Central Europe. Numerous diving ducks, including rare species such as Ferruginous Duck, Scaup and Smew.

Winter: Little and Black-necked Grebes, Cormorant, Gadwall, Teal and Pintail, diving ducks including Red-crested Pochard, Ferruginous Duck, Scaup, Long-tailed Duck, Smew and Goosander, Goshawk, Sparrowhawk, Peregrine, Water Rail, Snipe, Common and Yellow-legged Gulls, Herring Gull (rare), Kingfisher, Green Woodpecker, Water Pipit, Grey and White Wagtails, Dunnock, Fieldfare, Long-tailed Tit, Short-toed Treecreeper, Brambling, Siskin, Yellowhammer and Reed Bunting.

Access
Regular connections from Schaffhausen and Kreuzlingen (820). From Zürich, travel via Schaffhausen or Winterthur (821).

It takes only half an hour from Eschenz or Stein am Rhein to Ermatingen (see Site 32, Ermatinger Becken), so that you can easily combine visits to both sites in a day.

Accommodation
Stein am Rhein has a few hotels, also a youth hostel at Hemishoferstrasse 87 (tel: 052/741 12 55).

Site protection
The internationally-important waterbird site around the lower end of the Untersee suffers from ongoing disturbance caused by anglers, divers and some other recreational activities. Birdwatchers can, of course, cause disturbance if they venture out onto the gravelbanks and flush the huge flocks of birds and they are therefore urged to make a special effort to behave in an exemplary manner at all times.

Disabled access
The site is wheelchair-accessible and suitable for other visitors with walking impairments.

Nearby sites
The Hemishofen/Bibermühle area, several kilometres further down the Rhine, is known as a site for watching migrating raptors and as a stopover for migrant passerines in the autumn. Honey Buzzards soar overhead, Yellow Wagtails, Tree Pipits and finches refuel in the fields before continuing their journey. Moos near Radolfzell on the German side is not far from Stein am Rhein. From the harbour jetty in Moos, you have a good view of the lake and the adjoining shore around the mouth of the Radolfzeller Aach. There are more dabbling ducks here in winter than at Stein am Rhein. The Aachried (fen) offers favourable conditions for wintering geese, Hen Harrier and Great Grey Shrike. From the end of February, the first passerine migrants—Skylark, wagtails, pipits and thrushes—pass through.

32 ERMATINGER BECKEN (ERMATINGEN BASIN)

Canton:	Thurgau
Grid reference:	724/281
Height a.s.l.:	395 m
Start:	Ermatingen rail station
Finish:	Tägerwilen rail station SBB
Itinerary:	Ermatingen station–Ermatingen harbour–along rail track to Triboltingen lido–Gottlieben–Tägerwilen station (SBB)
Duration:	allow 2–3 hrs; distance 4–5 km
Best time:	winter (November–February), May (Wollmatinger Ried)
Status:	reserve for waterbirds and migrants of national and international importance; some restrictions on hunting; IBA
Map:	LdS 1:25,000; sheets 1033 (Steckborn) and 1034 (Kreuzlingen)
Equipment:	telescope, warm clothing; passport/ID card for trips to Wollmatinger Ried (Germany)

The Ermatingen Basin straddles the border in the upper part of the Untersee (part of Lake Constance/the Bodensee) between the Swiss villages of Gottlieben and Ermatingen and between Konstanz (Constance) and Reichenau island on the German side. The site is characterized by extensive shallow-water zones, mudbanks and reedbeds. Because of its large numbers and great diversity of waterbirds, the Ermatingen Basin has been designated as a wetland of international importance. The Wollmatinger Ried on the German shore of the lake is

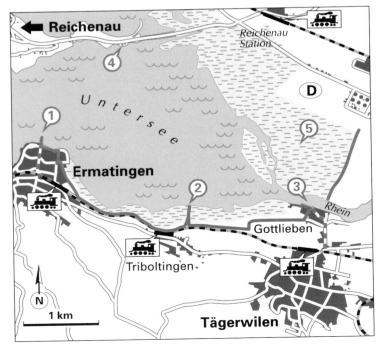

the biggest and most important valley bog in in the Lake Constance region and a trip there can be easily combined with a visit to Ermatingen. An impressive total of 270 bird species have been record- ed in the Wollmatinger Ried.

Recommended routes

For a start, it's worth taking a look from the harbour jetty in Ermatingen (1). The Untersee lake is deeper at this point, so that diving ducks such as Long-tailed Duck or Red-breasted Merganser also occur. In the dis- tance, you can see the poplar-fringed causeway called 'Schopflen' link- ing the mainland with Reichenau island. Loud and far-carrying bugling calls betray the presence of Whooper Swans.

After a walk of around 2.5 km along the railway in the direction of Gottlieben, turn left at a bunker complex which is surrounded by spruce trees, when you are level with Triboltingen, and a further 300 m will bring you to the lido (2). You must be particularly careful here, as you approach the lakeshore. Many species are shy and will flee in panic if you try to move closer too hastily. If there are birds very close to the shore, any thoughtful and considerate observer should resist the temp- tation to go up onto the jetty. Many different species of ducks, mainly dabbling ducks, Red-breasted Merganser or Black-necked Grebe are found close to the Swiss shore of the lake. Whooper and Bewick's Swans are, unfortunately, often some distance away and you will need a powerful telescope to tell them apart with certainty. There will be many Lapwings and Curlews on the mud or in shallow water. Various small birds haunt the reedbeds in winter: apart from 'true' tits, Bearded Tits may also be seen flitting and climbing about the reed stems. The dense stands of reeds provide optimal nesting conditions for *Acrocephalus* warblers and Little Bittern in the summer.

The next good observation point, in Gottlieben (3), is reached by walking across intensively-cultivated fields and along the Gottlieber Riet (fen). From the jetty used by the 'Krüger' shipping company, you have a view over the Rhine as it flows through the lake. The gully of the river is quite narrow at this point and you are likely to see similar species to those at Triboltingen, though the distance is much less. With luck, you can pick up Bearded Tits at the edge of the reeds on the German side. Hunting Hen Harriers or Peregrines occasionally overfly land on the Swiss side and Kingfishers are regular winter visitors.

The Reichenau causeway 'Schopflen' (4) is often a better place for viewing birds in the Ermatingen Basin (shorter distances), but can only be reached via Konstanz.

A site that deserves special mention at this point is the **Wollmatinger Ried** (fen) (5), which has rather extensive reedbeds and other fenland vegetation. The nature reserve stretches from the edge of the town of Konstanz as far as Hegne and includes not only parts of the Ermatingen Basin, but also the Hegnebucht (Hegne Bay). In order to improve habi- tat conditions for breeding ducks, a network of ponds and canals was dug in 1976. Following this, many species of ducks began to breed that are rare in Central Europe, such as the Shoveler for example. In addi- tion, the reedbeds hold breeding Bearded Tits, Great Reed Warblers or Little Bittern. In the high summer, thousands of ducks use areas close to the lakeshore as a moulting site and, when the water level is low, many waders rest and feed on the exposed mud. The Wollmatinger Ried also has something to offer those with an interest in botany. The real treasures of this site include the endemic Lake Constance forget-me-not, which thrives as small blue cushions only in the so-called 'Schnegglisand'. The Siberian iris in full bloom around mid-May or at the end of the month is also a truly lovely sight, a feast for the eye.

This is a strictly protected site and the only entry for the general public is with a guided tour. Information on this can be obtained from the Wollmatinger Ried Nature Conservation Centre (visitor centre) at Kindlebildstrasse 87, D-88097 Reichenau (tel: 0049 7531/788 70). Only a few routes are possible if you want to go it alone and do your own thing. One recommended route, which represents a good alternative to a tour of the fen in winter, leads along the reserve boundary from the Konstanz waste-water treatment works to the Rhine flowing through the lake.

Calendar

Important wintering site for Whooper Swans, dabbling and diving ducks; wintering waders. In the Wollmatinger Ried, rare breeding birds such as Little Bittern, ducks, *Acrocephalus* warblers, Bearded Tit, etc.

Winter: Little, Red-necked and Black-necked Grebes, Cormorant, Bewick's and Whooper Swans, Shelduck, dabbling and diving ducks, Red-breasted Merganser, Hen Harrier, Goshawk, Sparrowhawk, Merlin, Peregrine, Lapwing, Dunlin, Curlew, Yellow-legged and Herring Gulls, Kingfisher, Water Pipit, Grey and White Wagtails, Chiffchaff (sometimes wintering in reedbeds), Bearded Tit, Great Grey Shrike, Rook, Reed Bunting.

Spring and Autumn: Few observers present on the Swiss side during the migration periods. Species that can also be seen in the Wollmatinger Ried: Night Heron, Little Egret, Purple Heron; various ducks: e.g. Garganey, Pintail, Red-crested Pochard; harriers, Osprey, *Calidris* species, plovers and other waders (total 43 species!), terns, a variety of small birds such as pipits, wagtails, Bluethroat, Whinchat, thrushes, Lesser Whitethroat, Pied Flycatcher, Penduline Tit, finches.

Breeding season: Black-necked Grebe*, Little Bittern* (1–2 pairs), Grey Heron, Gadwall*, Garganey*, Shoveler*, Red-crested Pochard, Pochard* and Tufted Duck*, Black Kite, Marsh Harrier*, Water Rail, Lapwing*, Snipe*, Cuckoo, Lesser Spotted Woodpecker, Nightingale, Grasshopper Warbler*, Savi's, Icterine, Marsh and Reed Warblers, Great Reed Warbler*, Willow Warbler, Bearded Tit, Golden Oriole, Reed Bunting.
(* = Wollmatinger Ried only.)

Access

There is an hourly train service to Ermatingen, Triboltingen and Tägerwilen from Schaffhausen via Stein am Rhein and Steckborn or from Kreuzlingen (821). Mittelthurgau Rail runs regular trains between Tägerwilen and Weinfelden (830), from where there are good connections to Zürich. However, the station is well outside the town, so bear in mind that it's quite a long walk to get there.

The 'Seehase' train is a half-hourly service linking Kreuzlingen and Radolfzell (Germany) and this stops at the stations Konstanz, Wollmatingen and Reichenau, from where it's not a very long walk to the Wollmatinger Ried.

Accommodation

Accommodation is available in Ermatingen (a few hotels) and Tägerwilen (only one hotel (tel: 071/669 31 31)).

There's a bigger range of places to stay in Kreuzlingen, including a youth hostel—Promenadenstrasse 7 (tel: 071/688 26 63). Another alternative, for trips in the spring and autumn: the Fischerhaus campsite, 8280 Kreuzlingen (tel: 071/688 49 03; open from the beginning of April to the end of October).

Further information from the Tourist Office in Kreuzlingen (tel: 071/672 38 40).

Site protection

The Ermatingen Basin is of great ornithological importance. However, various interest groups are undermining the efforts of conservationists to bring about better protection for this internationally-important staging and wintering site. Unpleasant encounters with anglers and hunters are not completely out of the question during a visit to the site. The advice is to stay calm and to set the best possible example so that those who are against bird conservation cannot profit from mistakes made by bird-lovers.

Disabled access

The Ermatingen Basin is suitable for visitors with mobility problems as it is possible to park at most of the observation points. However, the paths are not made-up and thus lack a firm surface. The Wollmatinger Ried is not wheelchair-accessible.

Nearby sites

The so-called Konstanzer Trichter (a reference to the funnel-shaped western end of Lake Constance where the Rhine flows through a narrow gap into the Untersee) is another site of international importance for waterbirds, covering the very bottom end of the Obersee lake between Kreuzlingen and Konstanz. This site tends to hold mainly Tufted Ducks and Pochard. Other species that occur rarely are Scaup and Red-crested Pochard as well as a few Black-necked Grebes.

33 ROMANSHORN–KREUZLINGEN

Canton:	Thurgau
Grid reference:	746/270 (Romanshorn)
Height a.s.l.:	400 m
Start:	Romanshorn rail station
Finish:	various possibilities, for example Güttingen rail station
Itinerary:	on foot: Romanshorn harbour–then by regional train to Uttwil, lakeshore path to Kesswil–Güttingen (4.5 km)
Duration:	allow at least 3 hrs (Uttwil–Güttingen), possibly half a day up to a whole day for longer distances
Best time:	November–April
Status:	no special protection status; site of national importance for waterbirds
Map:	LdS 1:50,000; sheet 217 (Arbon)
Equipment:	telescope, bicycle, warm clothing

Among ornithologists, this section of Lake Constance (Lac de Constance, Bodensee) is known as 'the diver stretch'; it extends along the southwest shore of the Obersee from Romanshorn to Kreuzlingen. Although there has been a marked decline in the numbers of wintering Black-throated Divers since the 1970s, the site is still a cast-iron certainty for observing these magnificent waterbirds. The main area of interest is therefore the lake itself, also the adjoining shore. The hinterland, in contrast, has little to offer the birdwatcher: immediately behind the pebble beach are rather exclusive houses, chalets, rather sterile gardens and intensive agricultural land. In some places, the lakeshore way is lined with old avenue trees which have an almost magical attraction for small birds. In clear weather, views from here really bring home to you the huge size of Lake Constance or the 'Swabian Sea' as it is also known.

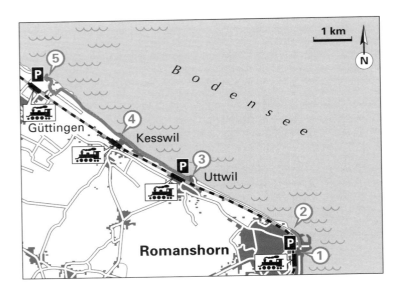

Recommended routes

It's worth stopping briefly to see what's about as soon as you get into the harbour of Romanshorn (opposite the rail station) (1). Black-necked Grebes and various diving ducks are frequently seen feeding in the harbour basin. Before the harbour mouth, towards the small lighthouse that stands offshore, you will occasionally find Velvet Scoters and Long-tailed Ducks. The lido at Romanshorn (2) will give you your first good view of the northwest part of the lake. It's best not to walk, but to take the train on the stretch from Romanshorn to Uttwil, as the best observation points are the harbour installations, moles and jetties at Uttwil (3), Kesswil (4) and Güttingen (5). These points offer in each case good and far-reaching views in all directions and, if the water is calm, then the Black-throated Divers can be spotted at a great distance. Between the points mentioned, there are many other opportunities to scan the water surface for divers, grebes and diving ducks, including sea-ducks. Teal, Gadwall and, less commonly, also Wigeon, are to be found in the shallow water close to the shore. Common Sandpipers and Dunlin over-winter irregularly on the pebbled areas, while even in the depths of winter, Grey and White Wagtails as well as Water Pipits are a regular sight in the washed-up debris along the water's edge. There are lots of buoys and these are favourite perches for gulls; the latter should be checked carefully as rarer species such as Herring or Lesser Black-backed are regularly present among the Yellow-legged Gulls. Kingfishers also winter in the harbours at Kesswil and Güttingen. Anyone who is cycling will have no difficulty in going on to Münsterlingen, but most of the water-birds are found between Uttwil and Güttingen. If you want to get to Kreuzlingen, where there are often dabbling ducks in the harbour area,

Connoisseurs know the section of the lake between Romanshorn and Güttingen as 'the diver stretch'. Black-throated Diver is the most regular wintering species
(photo: P.Rüegg)

on a short winter's day, you'll need to pedal hard and not stop too often to watch birds! The other point to note is that the cycle path does not always run along the lakeside.

Calendar

Most important wintering site for Black-throated Diver in Switzerland. In the winter of 1994–95, all four European diver species were present at the same time. Apart from that, a good place for sea-ducks and fresh-water diving ducks, grebes and large gulls.

Winter: Red-throated and Black-throated Divers, Great Northern Diver (irregular), Red-necked, Slavonian and Black-necked Grebes, Bean Goose, Shelduck (irregular), Wigeon, Gadwall, Teal and Red-crested Pochard, other diving ducks and sea-ducks such as Scaup, Eider, Common and Velvet Scoters, Red-breasted Merganser and Goosander, Dunlin, Common Sandpiper, Common, Yellow-legged and Herring Gulls, less commonly Lesser Black-backed Gull; Kingfisher, Green Woodpecker, Water Pipit, Grey and White Wagtails, Chiffchaff, Firecrest (some wintering), various tits, Siskin, Crossbill, Hawfinch, Reed Bunting.

Useful tips

The best conditions for good birding are a Föhn-type weather situation when the visibility is clear and the water smooth and calm. In strong winds (Bise, Föhn gale) and on dull, gloomy days with high fog (thick, uniform layer or sheet cloud), the birds are simply harder to find and to identify.

Access

Trains run hourly to Romanshorn from Zürich (with connections to Olten–Bienne/Biel and Bern) (840) and from St Gallen with the Bodensee–Toggenburg rail service (870). Along the lake between Romanshorn and Kreuzlingen-Schaffhausen (820), there is a train in both directions every half hour. If you prefer to spend only half a day on this stretch of the lake, you can combine this with a trip to Ermatingen or Stein am Rhein (see Sites 31 and 32).

Accommodation

In Romanshorn: various hotels and a youth hostel at Gottfried-Keller-Strasse 6 (tel: 071/463 17 17). In Uttwil: Bad-Hotel Uttwil (tel: 071/463 17 03).

Disabled access

The site is very suitable for disabled visitors, including wheelchair-users.

Nearby sites

Another site recommended as being worth a visit is the Luxburger Bucht (= Egnacher Bucht or bay) southeast of Romanshorn, where Whooper Swans and Curlew winter. A walk of only about 10 minutes will take you there from Egnach station (regional train service Romanshorn–Rorschach, 820). The Steinacher Bucht (bay) at Arbon is also of interest: in the autumn, when the level of the lake falls, this is a stopover site of national importance for passage waders.

34 RHINE VALLEY IN ST GALLEN

Canton:	St Gallen
Grid reference:	760/247
Height a.s.l.:	420 m
Start:	Altstätten rail station
Finish:	Altstätten rail station
Itinerary	from Altstätten (SBB) by bike, following the red-marked cycle path to Montlingen. On narrow country road to limit of Bannriet–turn right at the 'Dreier' crossroads –Hilpert (hide); possibly continue to Ruggeller Riet or turn back
Duration:	allow 1 day
Best time:	spring/autumn
Status:	part is nature reserve of Swiss Foundation for Bird Reserves (SSVG) and the society 'Pro Riet Rheintal'
Map:	LdS 1:50,000; special combined sheet 5014 (St Gallen–Appenzell)
Equipment:	bicycle (can be hired from Appenzell-Gais Rail; Swiss Federal Rail SBB does not do bike-hire!), telescope

The Rhine Valley in St Gallen is a wide plain, cut through by the river and extending from St Margrethen to Buchs. Quite high mountains rise up on either side. The Rhine forms the border with Austria in the north and Liechtenstein in the south. The widest section of this intensively-used valley floor lies in the Altstätten–Oberriet area. Scattered among meadowland, arable and pasture, there is a network of hedgerows mainly of trees, patches of fen and valley bog, as well as ponds laid down in the years 1995–96 as part of a nature-conservation programme. The slopes between Altstätten and Widnau, which face east and south-east, are covered in places with old orchards and vineyards. An inside tip for ornithologists: many migrants use the Rhine Valley as a leading line and it's certainly possible to discover some unusual species there.

Recommended routes

To reach the Bannriet, first cross the rail track after Altstätten station (in the direction of Oberriet) and immediately afterwards a small stream, then turn right onto the red-marked cycle-path heading for Montlingen–Oberriet. At the next crossroads, take the middle road which leads to Montlingen (follow the red markers for cyclists). After a further 200 m, you cross the Rietbach stream and, about 1 km from where you turned off, you come to the edge of the Bannriet (1). From the main road, you have a good general view over the site and will be able to observe most of the species found there without difficulty. One conspicuous feature in the fen is the stacks of peat. Despite the massive habitat changes wreaked by this peat-digging activity, an astonishing variety of breeding birds have managed to survive here: White Stork, Quail, Stonechat, Grasshopper, Reed and Marsh Warblers, Corn and Reed Buntings. Icterine Warbler and Golden Oriole sing in the patches of scrub and woodland, as do passage Redstart, Whitethroat or Willow Warbler. The edge of the peat-cuttings has been colonized in places by low hedges and both Stonechat and Red-backed Shrike nest in those. The flooded peat-cuttings develop reedbeds with time and are then a favourite habitat for *Acrocephalus* warblers and rails. Partly screened by a small birchwood, the peat-processing plant called the 'Schollenmühle' (2) is situated on the right-hand side. This is where you can get the best views into the western parts of the Bannriet which are

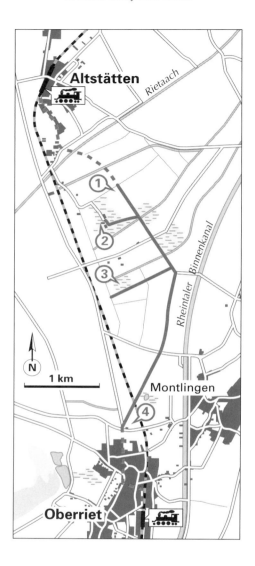

not visible from the road. A pair of White Storks has recently started to breed again on the roof of the processing shed.

If you continue along the main route, you will see the area called 'Spitzmäder' (3) some distance from the road on the right-hand side and about 200 m from the southern limit of the Bannriet. The birdlife there is not so rich as that in the Bannriet, but Stonechat, Red-backed Shrike and Grasshopper Warbler do occur and Bluethroats occasionally stop off there in spring. At the present time, these areas are being improved ecologically and linked to other wetland sites. Such measures also benefit the tree frog of which there are still quite large populations in the Rhine Valley.

In order to get to the nature reserve 'Hilpert' (4) between Montlingen and Oberriet, follow the same road as before, but turn right at the next T-junction. Having crossed the rail track, you will see the former brick-pit with its dense reedbed on the left-hand side. Patches of open water catch the light amongst the reeds. From the hide, you can watch Great Reed Warblers, rails and crakes, Little Grebe and other reedbed birds without disturbing them. Hundreds of Starlings roost in the reeds in the autumn.

Calendar

A rich breeding bird fauna, with White Stork, Quail, Lapwing, Stonechat, Red-backed Shrike and Corn Bunting; great potential for passage-migrants: raptors, waders and passerines.

Spring: Grey Heron, Honey Buzzard, Black Kite, Marsh Harrier, Sparrowhawk, Hobby, Quail, Snipe, Greenshank, Green and Wood Sandpipers, Stock Dove and Turtle Dove, Hoopoe, hirundines, Tawny, Meadow and Water Pipits, Yellow Wagtail, Nightingale, Bluethroat, Redstart, Whinchat, Wheatear, various thrushes, Icterine Warbler, Whitethroat, Wood and Willow Warblers, Pied Flycatcher, Ortolan Bunting.

Breeding season: Little Grebe, Grey Heron (comes to feed), White Stork, Buzzard, Kestrel, Quail, Water Rail and Moorhen, Lapwing, Cuckoo, Stonechat, Grasshopper, Marsh, Reed and Great Reed Warblers, tits, Golden Oriole, Red-backed Shrike, Serin, Corn Bunting, Yellowhammer and Reed Bunting.

Autumn: Similar species to those in spring; migration less conspicuous.

Access

To Altstätten by the fast train from St Gallen–Chur or regional train (hourly service) from St Gallen with connection to the Zürich–Winterthur Intercity (880). Unfortunately, in place of trains, only buses (880.1) run between Oberriet and Altstätten and these do not carry bicycles. If you are cycling, you'll have to ride back to Altstätten. Bikes can be hired from Appenzell Railways, but they have to be booked in Appenzell (tel: 071/787 14 44; book at least two days in advance for bikes to be sent to Altstätten).

Accommodation

You will have no difficulty in finding suitable accommodation in the historic little town of Altstätten. The Sonnensee campsite in the neighbouring town of Kriessern is open from the beginning of April to the end of September (tel: 071/755 12 24).

Site protection

The Rhine Valley in St Gallen is the object of intensive conservation efforts, especially in and around the Bannriet. Some farmers are rather touchy about birdwatchers. All visitors are therefore requested not to enter meadows or planted crops under any circumstances and strictly to obey the rules drawn up to protect the site. The workers at the peat-processing plant ('Schollenmühle') should also be treated with courtesy and respect, as the new protection law means that they have lost their livelihood and have certainly drawn the short straw compared with nature conservation.

Disabled access

The Bannriet is wheelchair-accessible and very suitable for other visitors with walking impairments.

Nearby sites

The vineyards and orchards c. 1 km southwest of Altstätten station (SBB) in the direction of Hinterforst–Eichberg are worth a visit. Wryneck, Lesser Spotted Woodpecker, Red-backed Shrike and Cirl Bunting are all regular breeding birds. In addition, there have been frequent records of unexpected migrants: Nightingale, Bonelli's Warbler or even a Subalpine Warbler discovered here in 1996 give an idea of what might turn up.

Jackdaws nest on the Blattenberg ruin outside Oberriet and the comings and goings of these garrulous birds can be observed from the road to Meiningen (Austria).

Fit and energetic ornithologists could try a day trip from Altstätten to the **Ruggeller Riet** which lies in Liechtenstein. This site still supports a remarkable diversity of birds. Apart from good populations of Whinchats, Grasshopper Warblers, Corn Buntings and other fenland birds, Corncrake is a regular breeder, although its numbers have shown a marked decline. The flora is also extremely valuable. Extensive marshy meadows with an abundance of Siberian iris are a splendid sight. To get there, cross the Sennwald–Ruggell bridge over the Rhine. Branch left c. 200 m after the bridge. About another 500 m further on, turn left onto a well-built farm road and follow this to the end (about 1200 m). From there, you can do a circuit of about 3 km. Please keep strictly to the marked paths (some paths are not open during the breeding season). The well-known **Vorarlberger Rheindelta** is situated in Austria and extends between the mouth of the new and the old course of the Rhine. Among the most important habitats here are extensive reedbeds and other fenland vegetation, mudflats and riverine woodland. The birdlife is extremely rich and varied: it is possible to see over 100 species here in a single day in early May. The Rhine delta is particularly well known for the many waders that occur there and really rare species turn up with surprising frequency. The delta is an absolute must for all keen birders! Access is via St Margrethen or Rheineck to Fussach. Then follow the Rhine embankment right to the end into the delta with its alluvial sand islands. Other places worth a visit are the Fussacher Bucht (bay) and the Rohrspitz as well as the marshy meadows of the Höchster Ried, which can be reached via Fussach and Höchst, respectively.

35 OBERTOGGENBURG

Canton:	St Gallen
Coordinates:	730/220
Height a.s.l.:	980–2200 m
Start:	Starkenbach (Selun), Alt St Johann (Alp Selamatt) or Wildhaus (Gamser Rugg)
Finish:	as above
Itinerary:	various routes possible on marked hiking trails, e.g. Starkenbach–Selunerwald–Alp Vorder Selun–Selun summit (2289 m) and return, with possibility of walks to Iltios (mountain railway) and the Alp Selamatt. Route round the Gamser Rugg through alpine terrain
Duration:	allow 1–2 days
Best time	April–July
Status:	part is protected landscape of outstanding natural beauty; IBA
Map:	LdS 1:25,000; sheets 1134 (Walensee) and 1135 (Buchs)
Equipment:	mountain boots, picnic lunch

The Obertoggenburg extends from Starkenbach as far as Wildhaus in a west-east direction. The massive and jagged Churfirsten peaks tower some 2200 m into the sky. If you approach the area from the north, the extended, partly-wooded ridges of these spectacular mountains are easy to see. There are precipitous cliffs, plunging down for several hundred metres to the Walensee. With around 100 species of breeding birds, this is one of the richest mountain regions in the north of Switzerland. The range of different forest-types and the way forest is closely interwoven in a patchwork pattern with open pasture and grassland as well as rocky terrain explains the great diversity of birds found there. With a good measure of luck and patience, visitors can even see the more elusive species such as Three-toed Woodpecker or grouse.

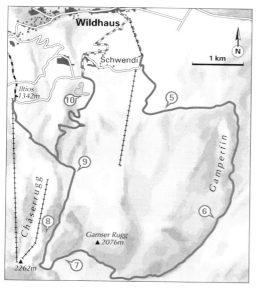
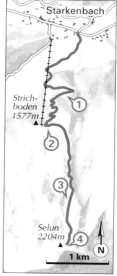

Recommended routes

One itinerary begins at the postbus-stop 'Drei Eidgenossen' in Starkenbach, from where you follow the yellow hiking-trail markers in the direction of Vorderselun–Selun. Having crossed the last pastures, you'll soon find yourself ascending a steep slope in the Selunerwald (Selun Forest) (1). As you climb up the slope, you'll witness the impressive change from montane broadleaved woods with beech and maple to subalpine coniferous forest. Tits, Treecreeper and finches (Crossbill, Siskin) are especially conspicuous and other species such as Black or Great Spotted Woodpeckers and Nutcracker are also regularly encountered. On the Alp Vorder Selun (2), you leave behind the closed forest and will immediately catch sight of Selun summit. The open stands of spruce all round the top station for the goods lift which comes up from Starkenbach are the ideal habitat for Citril Finch. From Alp Vorder Selun, bear slightly left and, after around 300 m, turn off again onto the right-hand path. On a sparsely-wooded mountain ridge, you'll find yourself going uphill again. The higher you get, the smaller and the more stunted the last spruces become. Black Grouse lek in this transitional zone in the spring. Finally, at about 1800 m altitude, you reach the alpine-meadow zone on the treeless, north-facing Selun ridge (3). This is the realm of Water Pipit and you'll also see the odd Linnet and Wheatear. Golden Eagles are regularly observed and you may be lucky enough to find some Ptarmigan. The summit region at 2200 m (4) has only a very small range of species. Alpine Accentor, Snow Finch, Alpine Chough and the rare Wallcreeper on the steep rock faces of the summit are your reward for the effort. Unfortunately, you have no choice but to return by the same route. Anyone who feels strong enough can continue the walk from Alp Vorder Selun via Breitenalp to the top station of the Alp Selamatt chair-lift where Citril Finches are easy to find in the breeding season. The Selamatt is also a good starting point for walks to the other Churfirsten summits.

Another possibility is to start your walk in Wildhaus or Lisighaus from where a chair-lift goes up to Oberdorf. The boggy hollow called 'Älpli' (5) with its open stands of trees lying east of there is a good place for owls (plan your walk for dusk) and for Three-toed Woodpecker. The track leads along the southern edge of the small bog in the direction of the Voralpsee (lake). By way of the Ölberg and the Gamperfin, you come to a fascinating landscape of forest and bog (6). The spruce forests north and east of the Gamser Rugg are important refuges for rare mountain birds and among the rare but regular inhabitants, apart from Three-toed Woodpecker, are Pygmy and Tengmalm's Owls, which also occur in the Rosswald forest south of Wildhaus. The best way to locate the shy Hazel Grouse is by its high-pitched, thin whistling courtship-display call (song). If you are still not satisfied by the time you reach the Voralpsee, you could do a full circuit of the Gamser Rugg. From the Voralp, the track first leads across alpine meadows up into the Obersäss (1800 m). By way of karst-type terrain, you come to the saddle, where the way points ahead across the Schlachtböden (7). Ptarmigan, Alpine Accentors, Snow Finches and the engagingly comical Alpine Choughs are all commonly seen in this area. From here, you can either climb up onto the Chäserrugg or follow the right-hand track to the Plisenalp and in the direction of Hinterrisi along the eastern flank of the Chäserrugg (8). It may be worth searching the rock face on the left as this is a Wallcreeper site, and chamois are often seen on the rock ledges there too. Other typical birds of the Alps may be seen feeding at the edge of the rocks and cliffs: Ring Ouzels, Water Pipits and Wheatears. When you reach Alp Hinterrisi (9), we recommend that you look for Redpolls and Citril Finches as well as other small birds. You can then head off left to the Iltios summit station and travel by funicular from there to Unterwasser. The steep descent to the right through the Seichbergwald (forest) to the Schwendiseen (lakes) (10) might just be worth the effort. In the breeding season, Whinchats and Tree Pipits will be in song all round the lakes.

Calendar
Species-rich mountain bird fauna with raptors, grouse, owls, wood-peckers and a range of small birds. Quite strong movements of birds at the Selamatt Alp in the autumn.

Breeding season: Honey Buzzard (rare), Goshawk, Sparrowhawk, Golden Eagle, Kestrel; Hazel Grouse, Ptarmigan, Black Grouse and Capercaillie, Woodcock, Cuckoo, Pygmy, Tawny, Long-eared and Tengmalm's Owls, Green, Black and Three-toed Woodpeckers, Tree and Water Pipits, Grey Wagtail, Dipper (along the Thur river), Alpine Accentor, Whinchat, Wheatear, various thrushes, Lesser Whitethroat and Garden Warbler, Wallcreeper, Crested and Willow Tits, Linnet, Citril Finch, Siskin and Redpoll, Crossbill, Scarlet Rosefinch (by the Thur).

Autumn: Fairly well-marked migration at this season on the Alp Selamatt: Honey Buzzard, Hen Harrier, passerines such as pipits, thrush-es, finches, especially Citril Finch and Siskin, Linnet, Redpoll, Crossbill.

Useful tips
A trip to the Toggenburg in April is very worthwhile, because it's simpler then to find grouse, Three-toed Woodpecker or the various owls. Later in the year, they are much more retiring and they no longer call. Clear, cold nights are the ideal conditions for hearing Tengmalm's Owls. There is still snow lying higher up at this time of the year, so the area is easily accessible only with snowshoes. However, beware of avalanches!

Access
The simplest way is to take the Intercity service from Zürich to Wil via Winterthur (750, 850). Change at Wil and take the regional train serving Wattwil and Neu St Johann/Nesslau (853). There is also a regular ser-vice to Wattwil from Rapperswil and St Gallen (970), change at Wattwil for Neu St Johann. From Neu St Johann by postbus to Starkenbach, Alt St Johann or Wildhaus (853.70). If you are travelling from the Rhine Valley, take a Swiss Federal Railways (SBB) train to Buchs, then con-tinue by the Neu St Johann postbus service. Chair-lift Alt St Johann to Alp Selamatt (operates daily from 08.00 hrs, beginning of June to begin-ning of November), chair-lift Wildhaus to Oberdorf (beginning of July to mid-October, from 08.30 hrs), funicular railway Unterwasser-Iltios (end of June to beginning of November, from 08.00 hrs).

Accommodation
As a tourist region, the Obertoggenburg is well provided with various kinds of accommodation—hotels, guesthouses, etc. Mountain inns on

the Selamatt (tel: 071/999 13 30) and Voralp (tel: 081/771 38 48) would make an ideal base for short and longer excursions in the Churfirsten area. Tourist Info, Hauptstrasse, 9658 Wildhaus (tel: 071/999 27 27). Toggenburg also has several campsites (Starkenbach, Alt St Johann, Unterwasser, Wildhaus) and a youth hostel at Befang, Wildhaus (tel: 071/999 12 70).

Site protection
On the Alp Selun, conservation efforts are being made by the SSVG (Swiss Foundation for Bird Reserves of SVS—BirdLife Switzerland). Many woods and forests are game preserves where walking off the official paths is forbidden.

Disabled access
This site is not suitable for wheelchair-users or other visitors with walking impairments.

Nearby sites
On the Walensee side of the Churfirsten mountains lies Walenstadt. There are some vineyards on the slopes along the road to Walenstadtberg and these have breeding Cirl Bunting and Red-backed Shrike. Bonelli's Warblers can be heard in the woods above Walenstadtberg. You can climb up into the Churfirsten mountains from this side as well.

If you are interested in insects, there's a real gem to be found on the Chäserrugg and the Gamser Rugg: these mountain tops are namely the only sites for the endemic Swiss gold grasshopper discovered as recently as 1989—it occurs nowhere else.

36 FLIMS

Canton:	Graubünden (the Grisons)
Grid reference:	739/193
Height a.s.l.:	1300–2690 m
Start:	Flims Mountain Railways (Route A); Falera (Route B)
Finish:	Flims Mountain Railways (Route A); Falera (Route B)
Itinerary:	*Route A:* Flims–by Mountain Railways up to Fil da Cassons–follow ridge east for 800 m–and back. Descent to middle station possible on foot.
	Route B: walk through mountain forest from Falera–Ladir–Ruschein
Duration:	allow 1–2 days; *c.*7 km (Route B)
Best time:	May–June and end of August/beginning of September
Status:	no special protection status
Map:	LdS 1:25,000; sheet 1194 (Flims)
Equipment:	mountain boots, warm clothing (for Cassonsgrat)

The striking and distinctive 'Flimserstein' towers up from the magnificent mountain landscape above Flims like some gigantic and crudely-fashioned sculpture. The rounded, windswept top of the Flimserstein—the Cassonsgrat—is more reminiscent of a Scandinavian tundra landscape than of the Swiss Alps: stone- and rock-strewn alpine meadows with short grass, willows (*Salix* sp.) growing underground and other plants that brave the harsh climate are the characteristic features. One species that feels at home in this barren wilderness is the Dotterel. Its preferred habitat for stopovers on migration to the wintering grounds is similar to that of the Scandinavian fjell where it breeds. However, the area around Flims has more to offer the ornithologist than just this one species. Others seen regularly in the alpine zone there include Ptarmigan, Golden Eagle, Alpine Accentor and Snow Finch. The near-natural spruce forests lower down have Hazel Grouse, various owls, Three-toed Woodpecker and an abundance of small birds.

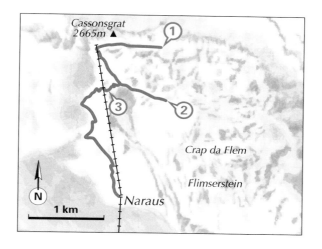

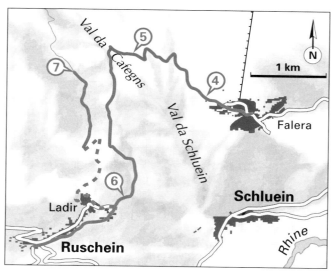

Recommended routes

Dotterel are likely to be found only within a brief time-span from late August to mid-September (20.8.–10.9.). The prerequisite for their presence is that there should be no snow lying on the summit. A cable car will take you directly up on to the Cassonsgrat summit. From the top station, follow the hiking trail to the right, in an easterly direction. After *c.*800 m, the mountain top widens out and there is a small, sparsely-vegetated plateau resembling a mini-tundra (1). A few Dotterel stop off there each year and they can usually be seen from the path, but at the weekend, when there are lots of walkers about, the birds are often slightly warier and it takes quite a long time to find them. Apart from the Dotterel, other birds of the high tops are the main attraction. Snow Finch, Alpine Accentor, Alpine Chough and Wheatear are all regular there and easy to find, whereas you need a bit more patience and luck for the well-camouflaged Ptarmigan and Golden Eagle. Then there is a narrow footpath which leads downhill from the top station to the Alp Naraus station and this will give you a further opportunity to observe Alpine birds. On the saddle about 600 m below the top station, the path divides. One route leads left across the Plaun Sura (2) where Ptarmigan are regularly seen, and don't forget to admire the lovely Alpine flowers, one of the most striking being the Alpine aster. The other path descends steeply in zigzags towards the valley below and, for the first 100 m, runs past high rocky crags (3). With a little luck, you can find a Wallcreeper somewhere on the rock face. After about 20 minutes' walk, you come to an Alpine hut and here the path is lost in the vegetation.

To continue downhill, you have to go straight across mountain pastures, but take care where it's wet underfoot! The last bit before Naraus station is once again a normal footpath. The last cable-car journey downhill at 17.00 hrs will bring you back to Flims.

Near Flims lies Falera and from there you can do a worthwhile ramble through subalpine spruce forest to Ruschein. At the start of the walk (coming from Falera), parts of the large skiing area with the lift installations (4) are visible above the village, but these are shut down in the summer. Whinchats breed in the meadows, the males frequently singing on the gables of the cowsheds. Even Red-backed Shrikes are still found this high up. After about a kilometre, the path bends to the right into the heavily-wooded Val da Cafegns (5) and runs on steadily into the valley carved out by a mountain stream. Very early in the morning, you might be fortunate enough to see a Hazel Grouse here. The male's high-pitched whistling is heard during courtship in March and April and again in September. On the valley floor, cross over the stream and follow the forest road again towards the mouth of the valley in the direction of Ladir. There is an alternating pattern of forest and pastureland and a frequently-heard sound is the harsh screeching caw of the Nutcracker.

The last section is beneath the 'Bual' (6), a striking rocky elevation near Ladir and a regular site for Bonelli's Warbler. In the semi-open landscape below the path, you will see various tits, Yellowhammer or Garden Warbler. There's even a chance of more unusual species during the migration period in May. Take the tarmac road downhill to Ruschein. The woods above Ladir, especially the unbroken stands of spruce on the eastern slope of the Muota (7), are excellent habitat for elusive birds of mountain forests such as Goshawk, Hazel Grouse, Three-toed Woodpecker, Tengmalm's or Pygmy Owl. Evening or early morning in April or early in May is the best time to listen for these species.

Calendar

Rich variety of Alpine and mountain-forest birds around Flims, species characteristic of riverine habitats and passage-migrants near Ilanz. Over 100 breeding bird species in the area. Traditional stopover site for Dotterel on the Cassonsgrat.

Spring: Honey Buzzard, harriers, Quail, Hoopoe, Wryneck, hirundines, Redstart, Whinchat, *Acrocephalus* and *Phylloscopus* warblers, Icterine Warbler, Pied Flycatcher, finches.

Breeding season: Goshawk, Sparrowhawk, Golden Eagle, Kestrel, Hazel Grouse, Ptarmigan and Black Grouse, Cuckoo, Pygmy Owl, Tengmalm's Owl (rare and elusive), Alpine Swift, Green, Black and Three-toed Woodpeckers, Skylark, Crag Martin, Tree and Water Pipits, Grey Wagtail, Dipper, Alpine Accentor, Redstart, Whinchat, Wheatear, Ring Ouzel, Lesser Whitethroat, Bonelli's Warbler, Long-tailed Tit, Willow and Crested Tits, Wallcreeper, Red-backed Shrike, Nutcracker, Alpine Chough, Raven, Snow Finch (only in unwooded areas above 2000 m), Citril Finch, Redpoll, Siskin.

Autumn: Dotterel (a few each year on Cassonsgrat).

Useful tips

If you are keen to observe owls, the best thing to do is to visit one of the places described at dusk. Your best chance of hearing one or even several species is from February into April.

Access

There is a postbus service to Flims from Chur (900.75) where good direct connections are guaranteed to Zürich and Basel (900) and St Gallen (880). A cableway runs from the postbus-stop 'Flims Bergbahnen' via Foppa and Alp Naraus up onto the Cassonsgrat (only from the beginning of July to mid-October and only in good weather). Ascent from 09.00 hrs, last descent 16.45 hrs. A postbus service operates to Falera (920.30) and Ilanz can be reached by trains of the Rhätische Bahn from Chur (920). There are regular postbuses from there to Ruschein and Ladir (920.25) and one from Flims to Ilanz (920.30).

Accommodation

As popular winter-sports resorts, Flims, Laax and Falera have lots of accommodation available. For information, contact Flims Tourismus, 7018 Flims-Waldhaus (tel: 081/920 92 00) or Falera Tourismus (tel: 081/921 30 30).

The Prau La Selva campsite, Flims-Waldhaus (tel: 081/911 15 75 or 081/920 91 91) is open all year.

Site protection

Most areas are not protected. Visitors should stick to the specified footpaths and trails, especially on the Cassonsgrat. And don't attempt to take photographs. There are already enough good photographs of Dotterel to fill whole archives.

Disabled access

The site is not suitable for wheelchairs but, because of the short distances involved, the Cassonsgrat is accessible to other visitors with walking impairments.

Nearby sites

Ornithologists will find other interesting places in the area around Flims. Not far away lies Ilanz on the Vorderrhein (one of the two sources of the Rhine, the other being the Hinterrhein) where fieldwork for the new Swiss breeding bird atlas produced an impressive 107 species of breeding birds in one 10-km square. In the breeding season, it's especially worth visiting floodplain habitats along the Rhine valley and the fields between Schluein and Sagogn. Gravel islands on this natural, unaltered section of the river have breeding Common Sandpipers and Little Ringed Plovers. Quail can be heard in the fields and meadows and you can count on seeing a variety of migrants. On the right bank of the Rhine, between Ilanz and Castrisch, there are several fairly small ponds. Reedbeds and riverine forest alternate with the land used for agriculture in a close-knit patchwork pattern. Apart from waterbirds such as Moorhen and Coot, which are rather rare in this region, Lesser Spotted Woodpecker can be found in the strips of woodland.

37 VALS

Canton:	Graubünden (the Grisons)
Grid reference:	733/163
Height a.s.l.:	1240–3120 m
Start:	Vals Platz
Finish:	Vals Platz or Berghaus Zervreila
Itinerary:	various routes possible in the region
Duration:	allow at least 1–2 days
Best time:	mid-May to mid-July
Status:	no special protection status
Map:	LdS 1:25,000; sheet 1234 (Vals)
Equipment:	mountain boots, telescope, picnic lunch

The Valsertal valley, carved out by the Vals Rhine, extends from Ilanz to far beyond the dammed Zervreilasee lake. Varied habitats in a small area with great altitudinal differences, from the valley floor at 1200 m right up to the highest summits at over 3000 m, support a rich fauna and flora. Farmland of meadows and pastures predominates down in the valley, while subalpine spruce forest covers the slopes. Above the treeline, a barren high-mountain region stretches away with scree and alpine pastures. In order to get to know the somewhat harsh beauty of the mountain landscape and the typical birds of the Valsertal, you should allow at least two days.

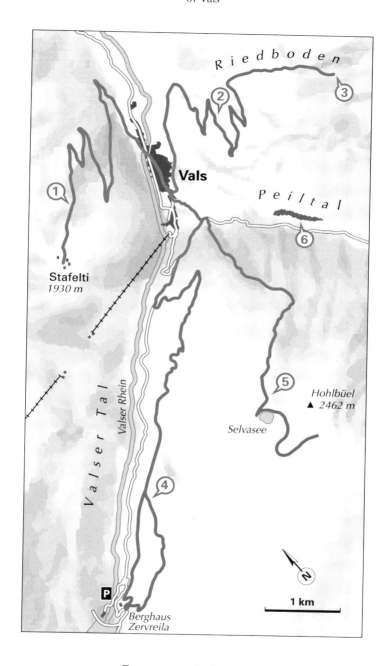

Recommended routes

One interesting walk is from the centre of the village of Vals on a well-built track, which also takes vehicles, as far as the Leisalp. After about an hour's walk, you come to the last left-hand bend in this road from where it's quite a long stretch heading up the valley to the 'Maiensäss' (mountain pasture above the tree-line with one or more huts) of Stafelti (1). The slopes on this part of the walk are strewn with rocks and boulders: this is Rock Partridge habitat and these birds can be easily watched with a telescope from the track. In the breeding season, they give their characteristic display-calls and are often seen standing for quite a long time on a rock ledge. Further attractions of the southern slopes are Peregrine, Rock Thrush and Black Grouse. If you climb higher up, you can see Alpine Accentor.

There's a good chance of finding Pygmy Owl in the woods on the northwest slopes above the village (2). In spring especially, its calls are likely to attract your attention around dawn and at dusk. This hiking trail, which winds uphill in zigzags, leads to the Riedboden (3), where you should look for Wallcreeper on the rock faces.

A walk taking several hours from the Zervreilasee over the 'Kippe' and though the Valéer Wald (wood) to Vals (4) would also provide further worthwhile opportunities for birdwatching. Lesser Whitethroat, Citril Finch or Nutcracker are to be seen straight away, close to the Berghaus Zervreila, where the postbus-stop is situated.

The official hiking trail begins at the end of the car park behind the Berghaus. Apart from tits and finches, Tengmalm's and Pygmy Owls, Black and Three-toed Woodpeckers as well as Hazel Grouse can be observed as you walk through the spruce forest, but you'll need a lot of patience and a certain amount of luck to see these rare species. There's a Golden Eagle's nest in this area and the birds are often seen approaching after only a short time. As an alternative to this route, which is entirely within forest, you could climb up from the Berghaus towards the Alp 'Gross Guraletsch'. At the fork after about 400 m, follow the track which leads straight on and parallel to the slope. There's a rise of a further 40 m over the next kilometre, then the path drops down again as you approach the wood. At 'Calvari', you get back onto the route described above and in the open, partially rocky landscape, you'll find Water Pipit, Black Redstart or Wheatear as a supplement to the forest birds.

Only really fit and energetic ornithologists are recommended to try the route from Vals to the scree slopes above the Selvasee (5). To reach this small lake by walking through the Valéer Wood via the Heinisch Stafel, you face a climb of 1000 m! As a reward for the effort, you should see Rock Partridge, Black Grouse, Ptarmigan, Alpine Accentor, Snow Finch, Ring Ouzel and the mountain hare. The alpine species in particular tend to be found on the scree above and west of the lake. Don't risk climbing up away from the path unless you are very sure-footed.

Calendar

Rich and diverse breeding bird fauna with many rare species characteristic of mountain forest and the high tops.

Breeding season: Goshawk (breeding probable), Sparrowhawk, Golden Eagle (2 pairs in the area), Kestrel and Peregrine, Hazel Grouse, Ptarmigan, Black Grouse and Rock Partridge, Cuckoo, Pygmy, Long-eared and Tengmalm's Owls, Black and Three-toed Woodpeckers, Skylark (often above the tree-line), Crag Martin, Tree and Water Pipits, Grey Wagtail, Dipper, Dunnock and Alpine Accentor, Whinchat, Wheatear, Rock Thrush, Ring Ouzel, Song and Mistle Thrushes, Lesser Whitethroat, Bonelli's Warbler (above the thermal baths), Red-backed

Shrike, Nutcracker, Alpine Chough, Raven, various tits, Wallcreeper, Treecreeper, Snow Finch, Citril Finch, Siskin, Linnet, Redpoll, Crossbill.

Autumn: Light passage: Goshawk, Sparrowhawk, Buzzard, Peregrine, roving Lammergeier (very rare); small birds such as hirundines and pipits.

Access
Hourly train service with the Rhätische Bahn (RhB) from Chur to Ilanz (920), from there by postbus to Vals Platz (920.45). By car via Chur to Ilanz on the cantonal road via Flims or through the Rhine Gorge from Versam. The official postbus service runs as far as the Zervreilasee (Berghaus Zervreila stop), but only in the summer (beginning of July to mid-October). In addition, there's a privately-run shuttle-bus service to the Zervreilasee from Vals post-office (for information, telephone 081/935 11 66).

Accommodation
Vals is well provided with accommodation of various kinds. In the summer season, from July, it's possible to stay overnight in the Berghaus Zervreila. Information from Kur- und Verkehrsverein [Spa and Tourist Information Office] Vals, Poststrasse, 7132 Vals (tel: 081/920 70 70).

Useful tips
Apart from birds, it's relatively easy to see also mountain (Alpine) hares and chamois at the site and there is a rich Alpine flora which is certainly worthy of attention. Wallcreeper can be found in the quarry at the upper end of the village outside the breeding season.

Site protection
The Valsertal has no special legal protection status. Nevertheless, in order to avoid disturbing the sensitive birdlife (especially grouse), you should keep to the footpaths when you are out walking. A telescope is recommended. Better to observe a Rock Partridge at your leisure through a telescope which you have laboriously lugged up the mountain than to have nothing but the brief rear view of a flushed bird somewhere off the beaten track.

Disabled access
The site is unsuitable for all people with mobility problems.

Nearby sites
The nearby Peiltal is also very interesting and definitely worth a visit. The cliff northeast of the road (6) is a good place where Rock Thrush and Wallcreeper are regularly encountered. Another good site for the stunning Wallcreeper is a further kilometre up the road near Balmentachli.

38 SCHANFIGG

Canton:	Graubünden (the Grisons)
Grid reference:	76/18 and 77/18
Height a.s.l.:	600–2700 m
Start:	Langwies
Finish:	Arosa
Itinerary:	Langwies–Medergen–Tschuggen–Grüenseeli–Iselwald–Arosa (can be combined with trips up into the high mountains or to various lakes)
Duration:	allow 1–2 days; c.14 km
Best time:	mid-May to June (depending on snowline); September to mid-October
Status:	part of the site is a specially-protected area for plants
Map:	LdS: 1:25,000; sheet 1196 (Arosa)
Equipment:	mountain boots, picnic lunch

The Schanfigg is a side-valley of the Chur Rhine valley and extends some 30 km from Chur to Arosa, a well-known winter-sports resort. A great diversity of habitats are found together within a small area in this valley—from montane meadowland and pasture to barren high-mountain terrain. The forests, mostly typical subalpine spruce woods, are in some cases very close to a natural state. On both sides of the valley, mountain peaks rise up to more than 2500 m above sea level. The mountain birdlife—the real attraction of the site—is correspondingly rich and varied. Almost 100 species were proved to breed in the whole valley in the period from 1993 to 1996. Most species, such as Golden Eagle, Alpine Accentor, tits or finches, are easy to observe, but you will need a fair amount of luck if you're hoping to see the rare and elusive inhabitants of the mountain forests like the owls or grouse. Because of its proximity to Arosa, the Schanfigg has a well-developed transport network and can be warmly recommended as a place to visit.

Recommended routes

The best and most convenient route, from which a good proportion of the mountain birds can be seen, begins in Langwies at the Rhätische Bahn (RhB) station and ends in Arosa. Even in Langwies itself, it's worth looking up: a few Crag Martins, which breed irregularly on the nearby railway viaduct, may be hawking insects over the village. First follow the Arosa road for a short distance and then, after a sharp right-hand bend, turn off left onto the hiking trail towards Medergen and Mederger Alp. The trail leads steadily uphill and there are several places where it takes you through subalpine spruce forest (1). Here, Black and Three-toed Woodpeckers also occur, alongside various tits and finches. If you are very lucky, you may encounter grouse. At an altitude of around 1900 m, you reach the tree-line (2), which is the preferred habitat of Black Grouse, Ring Ouzels, Nutcrackers and Citril Finches. From the Mederger Alp (1986 m), the route is via Tschuggen (2041 m) (3), where you'll find Black Grouse, Lesser Whitethroat and Bonelli's Warbler, and via Tieja again through forest to the Grüenseeli lakes. From the Tiejer Alp, it's possible to climb higher up and to observe Ptarmigan, Snow Finch, Alpine Accentor and Alpine Chough on the Schwifurgga (4) at 2519 m.

Before you reach the Grüenseeli lakes, you will twice come to places where the track divides (the first of these is in a clearing) and at each you should bear left and continue up the slope. The track runs past two

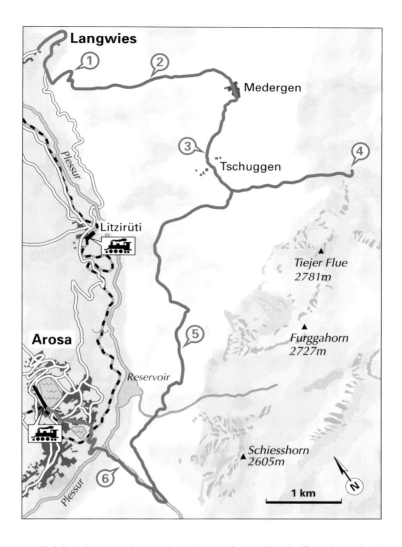

small lakes into an interesting piece of woodland (5), where both Pygmy and Tengmalm's Owls and the Three-toed Woodpecker have been recorded. There is then a fairly steep descent down to Isel, an alluvial floodplain. During migration, a detour to the right to the reservoir (1606 m) may be rewarding. When the water level is low, waders such as Snipe, Ruff, Green and Common Sandpipers occur there. From Isel, continue to the left and follow the Welschtobelbach upstream. The stream can be crossed a good 900 m further on. If you have plenty of time, continue your walk along the stream to the Altein Waterfalls. There, on the sheer rock faces by the falls, a little luck and patience may produce one of the most colourful of mountain birds, the Wallcreeper. Continuing along the same path without this detour, you come through the so-called 'backwood' (6) on the slope facing northeast. In the

Langwies is the starting point for an interesting ornithological tour in the mountains around the Schanfigg (photo: W. Wettstein)

spring up to early May and in the autumn, Hazel Grouse may reveal its presence by calling. After having covered by now around a dozen kilometres through forest and shortly before you cross the Plessur river, you come once again to a well-built access road. From the bridge, Dipper can be seen by the riverbank. Follow the road uphill and this will take you to Arosa. Passing the smaller Untersee lake on your left, you come to the rail station near the Obersee lake which you can't miss.

Calendar
First and foremost, typical birds of the mountains: tits, finches, woodpeckers, also some rarer, more elusive inhabitants of mountain woods. Total of 97 breeding species. Occasionally, waders on passage.

Spring: Little Grebe, Grey Heron, Teal, Honey Buzzard, Marsh Harrier, Sparrowhawk, occasionally passage waders at the lakes; Hoopoe, Willow Warbler, Pied Flycatcher.

Breeding season: Honey Buzzard, Goshawk, Sparrowhawk, Golden Eagle, Kestrel, Hobby and Peregrine, Hazel Grouse, Ptarmigan, Black Grouse and Capercaillie, Rock Partridge, Long-eared, Pygmy and Tengmalm's Owls, Green, Black, Lesser Spotted and Three-toed Woodpeckers, Tree and Water Pipits, Grey Wagtail, Dipper, Dunnock and Alpine Accentor, Redstart, Whinchat, Wheatear, Rock Thrush, various *Turdus* thrushes (for example, Ring Ouzel), Lesser Whitethroat, Bonelli's Warbler, Willow and Crested Tits, Wallcreeper, Treecreeper, Nutcracker, Alpine Chough, Raven, Snow Finch, Citril Finch, Siskin, Redpoll, Crossbill, Rock Bunting.

Autumn: Kingfisher, various passerines on migration such as Woodlark and Skylark, Brambling.

Access
The best way is to travel by SBB (Swiss Federal Railways) via Chur (900) where there's a direct connection to Arosa. The Chur–Arosa line begins on the Bahnhofplatz opposite the main station (930). Trains run every hour and stop at all stations; the journey to Arosa takes an hour. Fast trains run during the winter-sports season (January to March).

Accommodation
Centrally placed in the area is the Naturfreundehaus Medergen on the Tschugger Alp. The restaurant Alpenrose Mädrigen in Langwies is a further good possibility (tel: 081/374 21 57).

In addition, there is plenty of accommodation (all price levels) in Arosa, including a youth hostel in Hubelstrasse (tel: 081/377 13 97) and a campsite (tel: 081/377 17 45). For information, contact: Tourismus Arosa (tel: 081/377 51 51 or 377 51 52).

Site protection
Large parts of the Schanfigg are not under protection, but for the sake of the mountain birds, visitors should still not stray from the paths and trails. Dogs must be kept on the lead throughout the area.

Disabled access
Bacause of its topography and the long distances involved, the site is not suitable for wheelchair-users nor for other disabled visitors.

Nearby sites
A trip to the three Arosa lakes, the various small lakes in the Schanfigg or simply spending some time at a suitable watchpoint on a mountain top or pass can be very rewarding during the migration period.

Early in the morning after very wet nights, you often find Alpine salamanders on the paths. Alpine newt and grass frog are common. Azure hawker and *Cordulegaster bidentatus*, a species having no common English name, as well as other dragonflies and damsel flies, are found at the smaller lakes and pools. Out of the total of 123 species of butterflies recorded in the canton of Graubünden, no fewer than 100 occur in the Schanfigg. Keen botanists will also find the area well worth a visit.

39 RAMOSCH

Canton:	Graubünden (the Grisons)
Grid reference:	818/187
Height a.s.l.:	1000–3410 m
Start:	Scuol
Finish:	Ramosch
Itinerary:	Scuol–Sent–Val Sinistra–Vnà–Ramosch or Scuol–Sent –Ramosch (16 km). Walks can be extended according to taste (for example, up to the alpine zone)
Duration:	allow 1 day (with high-mountain tour 2–3 days); c.17 km
Best time:	June/July
Status:	hunting prohibited, specially protected area for plants; IBA
Map:	LdS 1:25,000; sheet 1199 (Scuol)
Equipment:	telescope, mountain boots, various field guides

Continental climate with dry mesobromion meadows, hedgerows and larch woods: this is the enchanting landscape of the Lower Engadine which is orientated southwest to northeast and which has the upper reaches of the River Inn flowing throughout its length. With an average precipitation level of less than 65 cm per year, the area around Ramosch is one of the driest parts of Switzerland. On the slopes facing southeast there is an ancient landscape of small-scale farming which is not (or no longer) found over large parts of Switzerland. Here, where it has survived, it therefore supports a rich and diverse birdlife of more than 100 breeding species many of which have long since disappeared from other parts of the country. The mountain forests also have some interesting species. The Lower Engadine is well worth a visit, but especially in the early summer. Apart from the rich variety of breeding birds, there are botanical and entomological treasures to be discovered.

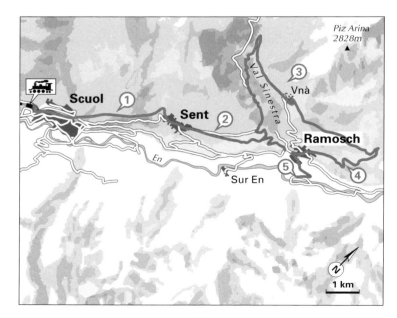

Mixed farmland between Scuol and Sent (photo: P. Rüegg)

Recommended routes

The suggestion that follows is for a ramble which will take you from
Scuol via Sent to Ramosch. There are plenty of opportunities to cut
down the distance if you want, as the villages along the route have a
regular postbus service.

153

The walk begins at at Bogn Engiadin, the health spa of Scuol. Any bus from the railway station will take you there. Follow the road further down and cross the bridge over the small river. Turn right after the bridge and follow the river upstream. Pass underneath the cantonal road then turn right. This will take you directly on the hiking trail. The first part of the walk takes you through the typical, semi-open farmland of Lower Engadine (1) where primarily hedgerow-nesters such as *Sylvia* warblers, Yellowhammer or Red-backed Shrike are common and usually easy to see. In Quail years, the characteristic call of this species is to be heard. The rare Corncrake possibly also breeds, with single calling males occurring sporadically in the spring. After a good hour's walking, you reach the picturesque village of Sent. Here, as in other villages, Crag Martins nest on the houses. In the winter, Alpine Choughs invade these villages, but for breeding they return to alpine habitats high up in the mountains. Behind the village square in Sent, the track branches off from the main road in the direction of Val Sinestra. It is easy to find as all the hiking trails are clearly marked. After 3 km through farmland (2), where similar species (also Tree Pipit) are found to those at point (1), you come to a fork. One track takes you uphill to the road into Val Sinestra, while the other track leads directly to Ramosch. In Val Sinestra, the path turns right at the Kurhaus (assembly rooms), crosses the stream and, after 2 km, reaches Vnà (3) at the foot of Piz Arina. Around Vnà, Bonelli's Warbler, Tree Pipit, Whinchat, Red-backed Shrike and Yellowhammer are common. East of Ramosch, on a south-facing slope (4), the cultivated landscape is especially attractive and supports many bird species that have become rare. Between small field plots grow groups of bushes which mark the border between the fields and meadows. Red-backed Shrike and Yellowhammer are particularly common. Garden Warblers sing, hidden from view. There have been several breeding records of the rare Barred Warbler near Ramosch and Hoopoe has recently started to breed. Many rare species are also found on this dry and warm, south-facing slope. In the woods above Ramosch, the Boscha Grischa, there are Nutcracker, tits, Bonelli's Warbler and finches. If you climb further up towards the tree-line at around 2200 m a.s.l., you may be fortunate enough to see Black Grouse. Another possibility is to climb to the top of Piz Arina, which is one of the best mountains in the region for views over the surrounding countryside. A walk down to the River Inn (En) below Ramosch (5) would also be worth doing. On the open plain below the village, Whinchats and Skylarks nest at high densities. Sot Döss along the Inn and the riverbanks are planted with thick hedges and the small meadows are extremely valuable botanically. Apart from Grey Wagtail and Dipper, you can expect Common Sandpiper (still breeding) on the Inn.

Calendar

Many birds of semi-open, traditional farmland. Over 100 species of birds breed.

Winter: Resident birds winter to some extent in the villages: Alpine Accentor, Alpine Chough, Nutcracker.

Spring: Various ducks and waders (on the new Inn reservoir 'Pradella' below Scuol), a range of small birds.

Breeding season: Honey Buzzard, Sparrowhawk, Golden Eagle, Kestrel, Hazel Grouse, Ptarmigan (only higher up, for example Piz Arina) and Black Grouse (on tree-line), Quail (in Quail years), Corncrake (irregular), Cuckoo, Swift, Hoopoe (breeding near Ramosch), Black and Three-toed Woodpeckers, Crag Martin, Swallow and House Martin, Skylark, Tree and Water Pipits, Dipper, Alpine Accentor (only high up in the mountains), Whinchat, Stonechat (bred near Ramosch in 1996), Rock Thrush, various *Turdus* thrushes, Lesser Whitethroat, Whitethroat and Garden Warbler, Barred Warbler (single pairs, very rare breeder), Bonelli's Warbler, tits, Wallcreeper, Treecreeper, Red-backed Shrike, Nutcracker, Alpine Chough, Raven, Citril Finch, Linnet, Yellowhammer and Rock Bunting.

Access
Take a Rhätische Bahn (RhB) train from St Moritz via Samedan to Scuol (940, 960). There are postbuses serving the surrounding villages (960.70, 960.75, 960.76, 960.80). If you are travelling by car, the best route is through the Prättigau via Davos, the Flüela Pass, Susch and Scuol.

Accommodation
There are plenty of places to stay in the health spa of Scuol and also in Sent. For information on prices and places, apply to the Tourist Information Office (tel: 081/861 22 22). If you want to stay overnight at a central location, i.e. in one of the smaller villages, try Pensiun Arina, 7557 Vnà (tel: 081/866 31 27) or Pensiun Bellavista, 7556 Ramosch (tel: 081/866 31 13).

There are campsites, open all year, near Sent (7554 Sur En (tel: 081/866 35 44)) and Scuol (Camping 'Gurlaina', 7550 Scuol (tel: 081/864 15 01)).

Site protection
In order to preserve the traditional Lower Engadine farming landscape, a conservation plan is being worked out. Entry into the meadows is prohibited to visitors from 1 May. Please obey the law without fail in this respect.

Disabled access
The area around Scuol, Sent and Ramosch is quite easily accessible for disabled visitors (short distances involved). However, the entire route is rather long. The terrain is not suitable for wheelchairs.

Nearby sites
Below Scuol lies the new Inn reservoir 'Pradella' where various ducks can increasingly be seen.

In the Val d'Uina near Sur En on the right bank of the Inn, a steep rocky path leads through two gorges in the direction of the Schlingia Pass. Apart from Crag Martins and a colony of Alpine Choughs, there's a good chance of seeing Wallcreeper here. Hazel Grouse has also been recorded in the general area.

Further up the valley lies Zernez, starting point for a visit to the Swiss National Park. The National Park House is situated here, with an exhibition on the National Park, its fauna and flora (see site 40).

40 THE SWISS NATIONAL PARK

Canton:	Graubünden (the Grisons)
Grid reference:	814/171
Height a.s.l.:	400–2690 m
Start:	*Route A:* P8/P9 (numbered parking spaces along the road over the pass)
	Route B: Buffalora
Finish:	*Route A:* as above. Route B: P4/P6
	Route A: parking space 8 (or 9)–Val Stabelchod–Margunet (2328 m)–Val dal Botsch–P8/P9 (*c.*5 km)
	Route B: Buffalora–Marangun–Fop da Buffalora–Munt la Schera (2587 m)–Alp la Schera–Il Fuorn (P6) or to Punt la Drosa (P4) (*c.*15 km)
Duration:	allow at least 2 days Route A *c.*3 hrs Route B *c.*5 hrs
Best time:	mid-June to mid-July
Status:	National Park; IBA
Map:	LdS 1:50,000; sheet 259 (Ofen Pass)
Equipment:	mountain boots, telescope, picnic lunch

The Swiss National Park in the Lower Engadine is the oldest nature park of its kind in Central Europe. It was founded in 1914 with the visionary aim of leaving a piece of Alpine landscape to go its own way without intervention by man and of uncompromisingly protecting and preserving the characteristic fauna and flora. However, this was only possible after the site had been robbed of its natural riches, timber! The Swiss mountain pine is thus now the dominant tree species, being the first to recolonize areas which were clear-felled earlier. Alpine pastures stretch away above the tree-line. The National Park is nowadays a popular tourist destination and, on fine days in the July holiday season, it is subject to considerable pressure from the sheer numbers of visitors. All the same, it's still worth your while coming if your interest is birds. Various grouse species, raptors and owls, but also various alpine passerines can be seen. The Lammergeiers released regularly in the National Park in 1991 as part of the programme to reintroduce them to the Alps certainly rank as a major attraction.

Recommended routes

The itineraries described here are based on suggestions given in the official National Park Guide for walkers. Two walks are especially suitable for birdwatching.

Route A: the first, three-hour walk starts at point 8 (P8) below Alp Stabelchod (1906 m), goes through the Val Stabelchod round Margunet summit (2,328 m) and through Val dal Botsch back to the starting point (P8) or to Il Fuorn (1794 m). The walk first takes you through mountain-pine forest (1). Nutcrackers are common and observant visitors will perhaps notice the groups of young conifers growing at the base of mountain pines. These are the forgotten larders of Nutcrackers, one of the characteristic birds of the National Park. Other inhabitants of the mountain forest include Crossbill, Citril Finch and other finches, Goldcrest and tits. If you cross the terrain of the Alp Stabelchod, with its large populations of game (roe deer, chamois, ibex, etc.), you soon reach the tree-line. Water Pipits are the commonest birds on the grass-covered slopes. It's certainly worth looking up now and again: Golden Eagle and Lammergeier can appear at any time. A zigzag path will take you rapid-

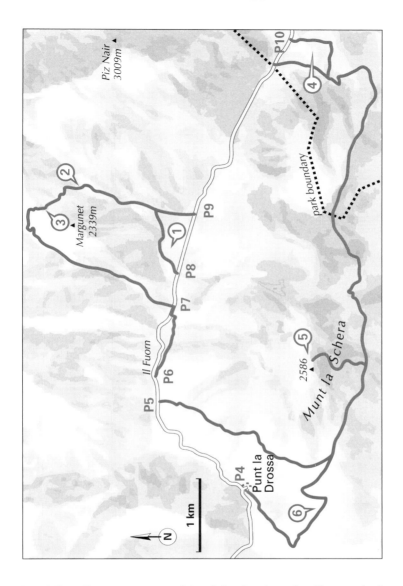

ly uphill until you see some striking dolomite pinnacles. You can look into the Lammergeier release site from this spot and, if you're lucky, you may catch sight of one soaring. Climb further up and you come to a saddle (3) where you are bound to encounter Alpine Choughs or Snow Finches. From there, the only way is downhill. At about 2180 m, there is a fork. Bear left, walk through the Val dal Botsch and, after about 2 km, you'll reach the Ofen Pass road. There, you can either walk back to point 8 (P8) or continue as far as 'Il Fuorn'. The latter route is interesting, as the path again runs through forest and there's another opportunity to see mountain-forest birds. Tits, Nuthatches, finches and

Treecreepers can be expected and Sparrowhawk is also occasionally observed. Golden Eagle, Buzzard, Goshawk and Kestrel soar over the southern slope of Piz dal Fuorn which lies opposite. As the Ofen Pass lies on a bird migration route between the Val Müstair and the Engadine, migrating passerines and raptors can be expected in the appropriate seasons.

Route B: a further interesting walk starts at the postbus-stop Buffalora (1968 m), goes over the alp of the same name to Marangun—Fop da Buffalora and the Munt la Schera summit (2586 m) down to Alp la Schera and Il Fuorn. At the start, the track leads across a small plain to Alp Buffalora (4), then it ascends steadily along the northeast flank of Munt Buffalora. The birds are similar to those at (1). A good hour's walk beyond Alp Buffalora, at around 2370 m, the path divides. The right-hand fork leads to the top of Munt la Schera (5). At this altitude, you will find one of the highest breeding sites for Skylark, but Wheatear, Water Pipit, Black Redstart, Ptarmigan, Alpine Accentor and Snow Finch also occur there. Golden Eagles are not rare. If you stop for something to eat, the Alpine Choughs are not at all shy and can almost become a bit of a nuisance. Dotterel have been recorded on Munt la Schera during the autumn migration period. To descend to Alp la Schera, use the path on the north flank which leads across heavily-eroded slopes. The hut on this alp now serves only as a shelter for the park wardens. Turn north here and a walk of 2.5 km through mixed conifer forest will take you to the pass road at P5; continue to the right and the postbus-stop at 'Il Fuorn' is only a few hundred metres further on. Another possibility from Alp la Schera is to go straight down through the wood (6). Birds typical of mountain woods will be your reward if you choose that detour. Turn off right at the only fork on this stretch and this will take you back to Punt la Drossa and the road over the Ofen Pass.

Calendar

Birds of the subalpine spruce forests and of higher altitudes. Lammergeier release programme since 1991.

Breeding season: Honey Buzzard, Lammergeier, Goshawk, Sparrowhawk, Golden Eagle, Kestrel, Hazel Grouse, Ptarmigan, Black Grouse, Capercaillie and Rock Partridge, Common Sandpiper (rare and irregular), Cuckoo, Eagle Owl, Pygmy and Tengmalm's Owls, Green, Black and Three-toed Woodpeckers, Crag Martin, Tree and Water Pipits, Grey Wagtail, Dipper, Alpine Accentor, Wheatear, Rock Thrush, various *Turdus* thrushes, Lesser Whitethroat, Bonelli's Warbler, tits, Wallcreeper, Treecreeper, Nutcracker, Alpine Chough, Raven, Snow Finch, Citril Finch and various other finches.

Access

To get to the National Park, take the train from Chur via Samedan and Schanf to Zernez (940, 960). Regular postbus services (960.20) operate from Zernez to the starting points on the Ofen Pass. If you are travelling by car, you can come over the Flüela or the Julier Pass. There are a restricted number of signposted parking spaces along the Ofen Pass road. Parking elsewhere is prohibited.

Accommodation

There are only two possibilites in the Park: the hotel 'Il Fuorn' (tel:

081/856 12 26) on the Ofen Pass road and the 'Chamanna Cluozza' (open from the end of June to mid-October (tel: 081/856 12 35)), a mountain hut which can be reached only by a three-hour walk from Zernez. Other possibilities outside the Park: Ofen Pass Hotel in Buffalora and Ova Spin, a park hut near Varusch. Zernez has a large selection of different hotels and hostels. Information from: Kur-und Verkehrsverein (Spa and Tourist Information Office), chasa Fuschina, 7530 Zernez (tel: 081/856 13 00). Campsite: Camping Cul (open from the beginning of May to mid-October (tel: 081/856 14 62)).

Site protection
Many activities which are permitted elsewhere are prohibited in the National Park: lighting fires, picking plants and gathering fungi, the collecting of all living creatures, and camping, including rough camping. Visitors must keep to the marked footpaths. A network of tracks and trails with a total length of 80 km ought to be enough to see all the attractions of the Park.

At present, plans are under discussion to treble the size of the National Park.

Disabled access
The National Park is not wheelchair-accessible and is not suitable for other visitors with walking impairments.

Nearby sites
Very much to be recommended is a visit to the National Park House in Zernez (open June–October), where you can find out about the Park and its fauna and flora (tel: 081/856 13 78). There are, of course, other possible routes than those described above. The best source of information is the *Wanderführer zum Schweizerischen Nationalpark* (*A guide to walks in the Swiss National Park*) by Klaus Robin (obtainable in English bookshops or in the National Park). For further interesting bird-watching sites in the Engadine, see Sites 39 and 41. Particularly worthy of note are the large populations of game animals in the park.

41 MALOJA AND THE UPPER ENGADINE

Canton:	Graubünden (the Grisons)
Grid reference:	770/140 (large region)
Height a.s.l.:	1700 m
Start:	Maloja or St Moritz (excursions into the surrounding area from these places)
Finish:	ditto
Itinerary:	various routes to different sites (Piz Lunghin, delta of the Isola, Stazerwald, Maloja)
Duration:	allow at least 2 days
Best time:	end of March, beginning of April to October
Status:	lakeshore statute of local commune regulating conservation of natural banks
Map:	LdS 1:50,000; special combined sheet 5013 (Upper Engadine)
Equipment:	telescope, warm clothing (especially in spring)

The Upper Engadine is one of the few high valleys in the central Swiss Alps. On a stretch some 22 km long from Maloja to Bever, the valley floor lies at an altitude of between 1815 and 1695 m a. s. l. Precipitation is fairly sparse, the winters extremely cold and dry, with the temperature sometimes falling to -30°C, and summer comes to the mountains fairly late.

The region offers many fascinating habitats and bird species. On the one hand, birds of farmland and of mountains forests which have become rare still breed here, on the other, the Upper Engadine lies on a migration route across the Alps. Unusual species for the Alpine region keep on turning up here. Of particular interest is the chain of lakes which lie between Maloja and St Moritz and also the bends in the River Inn between Samedan and Bever. The conifer forests and the high-mountain regions in the surrounding area are similarly attractive bird-watching sites.

Recommended routes

Maloja, the most southwesterly village in the Upper Engadine, is a good base for a variety of excursions. The first route begins around 200 m west of a gigantic hotel building which you can't possibly miss. A narrow road leads off from the main road in the direction of Pila. You first go through a piece of woodland and, after some 300 m, you come to an open area where a couple of houses form the hamlet of Pila. Immediately after that, you cross the upper reaches of the River Inn and the way then zigzags steeply uphill as far as the Plan di Zoch fork where you bear left. The track climbs evenly up a grassy slope (1), in places densely covered with rocks and stones, where Rock Partridges are relatively easy to find. In the spring, even when the slopes are still under snow, numerous small birds such as hirundines (including Crag Martins), pipits, wagtails and thrushes migrate northeast along the sides of the mountains. If you feel like it, you can climb on up as far as the Lej dal Lunghin lake (2). The special attractions at this altitude are Golden Eagle, Alpine Accentor, Wheatear, Rock Thrush, Alpine Chough and Snow Finch.

Another walk starting in Maloja will take you from the end of the Lej da Segl lake (Silsersee) along the shore to the Isola Delta and on to Sils (or back again). From the postbus-stop on the eastern (i.e. Sils side) of

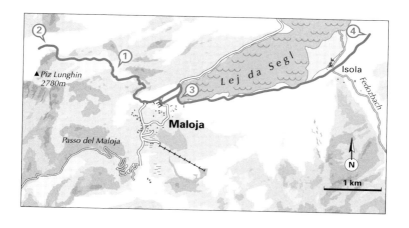

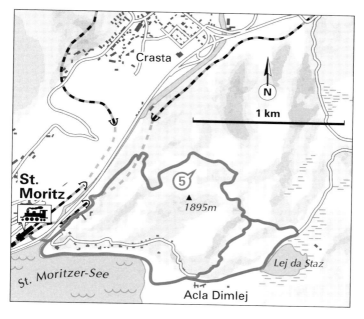

the village, walk a little way along the road to Sils before turning off
onto the track along the lakeshore. The bay of the lake at Maloja (3) is
a very important stopover site for waders and waterbirds in the autumn,
the most numerous being *Tringa* species and a variety of ducks. From
that point, the path runs mostly along the shore towards Isola, with long
stretches taking you through larchwoods where Nutcracker, Crested,
Coal and Willow Tits are your constant companions. Crossbills and
other finches can also be seen there. The Isola Delta (4), which is
formed by the large alluvial plain of the Fedozbach (stream), takes a
good hour's walk to reach. This delta almost divides the lake into two
lake basins. Special attention needs to be paid to the northeast part of

The Fedozbach delta at the Lej da Segl/Silsersee is a regionally-important staging site for waders (photo: P. Rüegg)

the delta. Where the stream empties into the lake there are gravelbanks and islands intersected by numerous water channels and this is very attractive habitat for waders: Little Ringed Plover, Greenshank, Wood and Common Sandpipers are fairly regular visitors; rarities recorded include Knot and Kentish Plover.

A good place for seeing most of the woodland birds and also Pygmy and Tengmalm's Owls is the Stazerwald east of St Moritz (5). This wood is composed of spruce, Arolla pine and larch and has a dense network of hiking trails and other footpaths. The hilltops around 'Fullun' are of particular interest to ornithologists because of the high density of owls recorded there, higher than anywhere else. Another rare breeding bird found there is the Three-toed Woodpecker and there are Nutcrackers, various thrushes, tits, Nuthatches and finches to be seen as well. On leaving the rail station, walk over the footbridge to the St Moritzer-See (Lake St Moritz) and along the lakeshore for 800 m until you branch off left to join a side road. A zigzag path on the other side of the road leads into the wood and on up the slope to La Stretta. If you continue along the side road, this will take you to the Lej da Staz (Stazer See). At the northern end of this lake, a path leads to the left into the forest and this also goes uphill to La Stretta. At the next forks, you can turn left to return to St Moritz or to descend across the northeast slope to Celerina.

Calendar

Many mountain, forest and meadowland bird species; regionally important passage sites for waders and other waterbirds.

Winter: Apart from the resident birds, the following species are able to overwinter in the Upper Engadine: Little Grebe, Teal, sporadically other duck species, Snipe, Great Grey Shrike (irregular near Samedan).

Breeding season: Little Grebe, Tufted Duck, Honey Buzzard, Goshawk, Sparrowhawk, Golden Eagle, Kestrel, Hazel Grouse, Ptarmigan, Black Grouse, Capercaillie and Rock Partridge, Quail (irregular), Moorhen (highest breeding site in Central Europe), Coot, Common Sandpiper, Woodpigeon, Cuckoo, Eagle Owl, Pygmy, Long-eared and Tengmalm's Owls, Wryneck, Green, Black and Three-toed Woodpeckers, Skylark, Crag Martin, Tree and Water Pipits, Yellow Wagtail (irregular breeder near Samedan and Bever), Grey Wagtail, Dipper, Alpine Accentor, Redstart, Whinchat, Wheatear, Rock Thrush, all the *Turdus* thrushes, Lesser Whitethroat, Garden Warbler, Bonelli's and Wood Warblers, Firecrest, Spotted Flycatcher, Long-tailed Tit, various *Parus* tits, Wallcreeper, Treecreeper, Red-backed Shrike, Nutcracker, Alpine Chough, Raven, Snow Finch, Citril Finch, Redpoll and other finches, Reed Bunting.

Spring and Autumn: Many species irregular and rare. In most cases, likely to be found here only after years of birdwatching activity in this region: Black-throated Diver (late autumn), Great Crested and Red-necked Grebes, Black-necked Grebe (irregular), Cormorant, Grey Heron, Wigeon, Gadwall, Teal, Pintail, Garganey (commoner in spring), Shoveler, Pochard, Tufted Duck and Goldeneye; Water Rail and Spotted Crake, Little Ringed Plover, Lapwing, Little Stint, Ruff (mainly in spring), Snipe, Woodcock, *Tringa* species, Black-headed and Common Gulls, Black Tern, Kingfisher, Hoopoe, Wryneck, various larks and hirundines, Tree, Meadow and Water Pipits, wagtails, Nightingale, Bluethroat, Redstart, thrushes, Willow Warbler.

Useful tips
Many of the mountain-forest species are much more active in the spring from March to May than later in the year. The best time to visit the Stazerwald (wood) is early in the morning or at nightfall, because that's when you are most likely to hear owls.

Access
The Engadine is reached by trains of the Rhätische Bahn (RhB) from Chur (940). There is a postbus service from St Moritz into the Bergell region which stops at all the villages on the way (940.75, 940.80). Journey time to Maloja is around 40 minutes. If you are travelling by car, take either the route over the Julier Pass from Thusis via Tiefencastel and Bivio to Silvaplana or that over the Albula Pass from Tiefencastel via Filisur, Bergün and Chamuesch.

Accommodation
The Engadine is a well-developed tourist area. Hotels, hostels and also holiday flats to rent are to be found in all the villages. There are youth hostels in Maloja (tel: 081/824 32 58), on the Via Surpunt 60, 7500 St Moritz (tel: 081/833 39 39) and at Pontresina (tel: 081/842 72 23) and no shortage either of campsites in the Upper Engadine.

   Enquiries to: Verkehrsverein (Tourist Information Office) Maloja (tel: 081/824 31 88), Pontresina (tel: 081/838 83 00) or St Moritz, Via Maistra 12, St Moritz (tel: 081/837 33 33).

Site protection
Most of the wetlands in the Upper Engadine enjoy little or no protection. Any waterbirds present are subject in some cases to considerable disturbance from windsurfers and club anglers. Many mountain slopes, mainly around St Moritz, have suffered massive damage from winter-sports installations. The lakeshore of the Lej da Segl has been protected by a special conservation statute since 1946.

Disabled access
The site is not suitable for visitors with walking impairments and most of the paths are not wheelchair-accessible.

Nearby sites
The magnificent mountain landscape of Graubünden is an invitation to undertake long walks during which other bird species may be added to the list. The Val Roseg near Pontresina is especially lovely.

Riverine (floodplain) habitats along the Inn between Celerina and Samedan, ponds near Samedan (the Golfweiher) and near Bever (the Gravatschaweiher) are all interesting wetland sites. The Gravatschweiher is an important site in the spring and summer for migrant and breeding waterbirds. An extensive area of sedge provides favourable nesting habitat for Little Grebe, Moorhen and Coot. The site lies on the right bank of the river, level with the sharp bend of the Inn at Bever and can be reached on foot from the rail station in about 15 minutes (turn off at the church towards the Inn, continue on farm track, cross river and walk on downstream; circular walk possible).

For the National Park and Lower Engadine, see Sites 40 and 39, respectively.

42 VAL PIORA/LAGO RITOM (PIORA VALLEY/LAKE RITOM)

Canton:	Ticino
Grid reference	695/154
Height a.s.l.:	1850–2200 m
Start:	Piora
Finish:	Piora
Itinerary:	Piora–southern shore of Lago Ritom–Fontanella–Pian Giübin–Alpe Carorescio–Piano dei Porci–Pian Murinascia–Alpe di Piora–Lago Cadagno–Lago di Tom–northern shore of Lago Ritom–Piora
Duration:	allow 1–2 days; distance, depending on route, 17–25 km
Best time:	early summer (end of May to beginning of July); often snow until end of May
Status:	nature reserve, specially protected for plants and as landscape of outstanding natural beauty; IBA
Map:	LdS 1:25,000; sheet 1252 (Ambri–Piotta)
Equipment:	mountain boots, picnic lunch, map 1:25,000

In the midst of the magnificent Ticino Alps lies the Val Piora, a high valley above the Leventina. The area is best known for the artificially dammed Lake Ritom and the special character of the landscape derives from its astonishing variety—the many small lakes, the mountain meadows and pastures with their abundance of colourful flowers, mountain forests, small bogs, boulder scree, precipitous rock faces and majestic towering peaks. With the necessary patience, almost all the typical bird species of the Alps can be found in this stunningly beautiful mountain landscape.

Recommended routes

Your journey into the area around Lake Ritom and the Piora Valley begins with a spectacular ride by funicular railway from Piotta to Piora. This is one of the steepest (87.8% gradient) public railways or cableways in the world. From the top station, follow the narrow mountain road (1) for c. 1 km to the dam wall. There's an Eagle Owl nest-site in the rocks below the road and the owl can occasionally be heard calling late in the evening. By the dam stands the hotel and restaurant 'Lago Ritom'. On the way to the lake, you will already have a chance to see the first mountain birds: Kestrel, Cuckoo, Crag Martins, Grey Wagtail, Lesser Whitethroat, Bonelli's Warbler, tits, Treecreeper, Redpoll, Crossbill and Rock Bunting.

The way now runs along the southern shore of Lake Ritom and through an open conifer wood with many larches where similar species are to be seen. In addition, Mistle Thrush and Nutcracker are relatively common there. Where the wood becomes even more open and gradually changes to meadowland and dwarf-shrub heath, you will find Tree Pipits performing their conspicuous songflights and also Ring Ouzels (2). Green-alder scrub, a favourite habitat of Garden Warblers, often flourishes in cool and shady hollows. On the way to Mottone (3), there's a good chance of coming across Black Grouse in the early morning. It goes without saying that females with broods of young should not be disturbed under any circumstances.

Leave the official hiking trail here and head south towards the slope between the '2115 m' mark (see map 1:25,000) and the Laghetto di

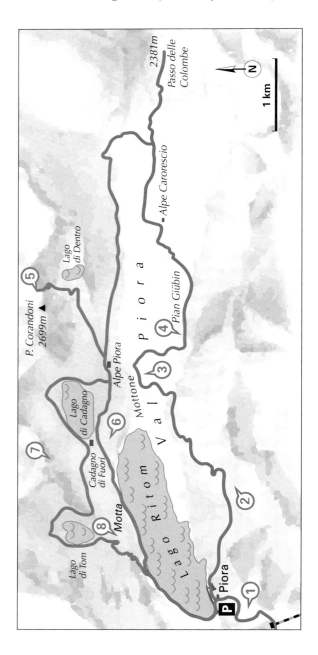

Giübin. If you prefer to stay on the official trail instead of cutting across country for about 2 km, then you can do that without a detour. However, there's a good chance of seeing Alpine Accentor or Ptarmigan along the Costa di Giübin (4). Finally, you cross the Pian

Giübin and pick up the hiking trail again at Sotto l'Uomo. Further bird species likely to be seen along this stretch include Water Pipit, Black Redstart and Wheatear. The walk continues across the Alpe Carorescio and, if you feel like it, you can make the (signposted) detour to the Passo delle Colombe (Alpine Accentor) where you will be rewarded with the wonderful view down into the valley behind you. Back at the turn-off, continue your walk on the other side of the Val Piora via the Pian Murinascia and past the SAT (Societa Alpina Ticinese) hut Capanna di Cadagno (overnight stay possible) in the direction of Lake Ritom to Alpe di Piora. Bluethroats have been regularly observed in this area in recent years. If you have time, you might like to contemplate quite a long trek to the Lago di Dentro lake and as far as 'Miniera' (5). With a measure of luck and some careful scanning, Wallcreepers can be found on some of the many rock faces along the way.

From the Alpe di Piora, there are two possibilities for the return walk to Piora: the first is to walk all round the north side of the picturesque Lago di Cadagno (Lake Cadagno). On the way towards Lago di Tom (Lake Tom), it's worth keeping an eye on the slopes of the Poncione Carioi (7) as they are a favourite site for Rock Partridges. Below the Alpe di Tom, between Motta and the Pian di Lecc, you should spend some time looking for Rock Thrush on the slope (8) before starting along the shore path at the northern end of Lake Ritom.

The other alternative: on the Alpe di Piora, walk past the Centro di Biologia Alpina (Centre for Alpine Biology) and then past Lago di Cadagno on its southern shore. Whinchats are often to be seen at Scopello (6). From there, you reach the track bordering Lake Ritom which will take you along its northern shore and back to Piora. This is also a good path from which to watch Rock Thrushes (8). The track along the north side of Lake Ritom is famous for its lovely meadows with their abundance of exquisite flowers. Honey Buzzard and occasionally Golden Eagle may appear.

Calendar

The Val Piora offers a fantastic Alpine landscape with many birds typical of mountain habitats.

Breeding season: Honey Buzzard, Golden Eagle, Kestrel, Peregrine (probably not breeding), Hazel Grouse, Ptarmigan, Black Grouse and Rock Partridge, Cuckoo, Tengmalm's Owl, Tree and Water Pipits, Alpine Accentor, Red-spotted Bluethroat, Whinchat, Wheatear, Rock Thrush, Ring Ouzel, Lesser Whitethroat, Garden Warbler, Willow Tit ('Alpine Tit'), Treecreeper, Nutcracker, Alpine Chough, Raven, Citril Finch, Linnet, Redpoll, Crossbill, Rock Bunting.

Useful tips

A telescope may indeed be a rather cumbersome object to take on a walk in the mountains, but it really is worth the effort, because with it you can get far better views of shy and distant species.

Access

This site can be very easily reached by public transport. Airolo rail station, to which regional and fast trains run hourly on the Gotthard line (600), serves as the starting point. From Airolo station by postbus to Piotta stop (625.09). From there, it's a mere 10-minute walk to the valley station of the funicular. For timetable information, telephone 091/869 12 22. It's a further 15–20 minutes on foot from the top station of the funicular to Lago Ritom.

If you come by car, you can park at the Lago Ritom hotel, below the wall of the dam.

Accommodation

In Piora, the 'Lago Ritom' hotel (tel: 091/868 14 24) directly by the dam wall of the lake. The Cadagno SAT mountain hut is favourably situated near the Alpe di Piora at 1987 m and has 55 beds available (Capanna Cadagno, M. Guglielmetti, 6776 Piotta (tel: 091/868 13 23 or 091/649 95 76)). You can also stay in the Centro di Biologia Alpina, 6777 Quinto (tel: 091/868 19 70), on the Alpe di Piora.

Site protection

The area around Lake Ritom and the Piora Valley is a nature reserve (the landscape and plants are specially protected too).

Disabled access

The level and well-built path on the northern shore of Lake Ritom is suitable for disabled visitors, but with some reservations. The paths are wheelchair-accessible, relatively flat and well built, but the distances to be covered are considerable (length of the lake: 2.7 km).

Nearby sites

On the way from or into southern Ticino, you pass through the small village of Lodrino, halfway between Biasca and Bellinzona. On the right-hand side of the valley (looking south) and about 1 km outside the village, there's a quarry gouged out of the mountain side—you can't miss it. This is a regular breeding site for Blue Rock Thrush. As work at the quarry creates quite a din during the week, the recommendation is to go there early in the morning (before 07.00 hrs) or at the weekend. In the early morning, the birds are usually to be found on the ground amongst the lumps of rock and boulders.

Blue Rock Thrush (drawing: J. Laesser)

43 MAGGIA DELTA

Canton:	Ticino
Grid reference:	705/112
Height a.s.l.:	200 m
Start:	Locarno
Finish:	Ascona
Itinerary:	Locarno rail station–via lido into the delta as far as Boscaccio–up the Maggia and over the bridge–walk along left of runway–fields both sides of road–to Ascona–bus Nr. 31 from 2nd bridge or from Ascona post office (or on foot) to Locarno
Duration:	allow 2–4 hrs (by bike or on foot)
Best time:	during spring migration
Status:	nature reserve
Map:	LdS 1:25,000; sheet 1312 (Locarno)
Equipment:	telescope, sturdy footwear, perhaps a bicycle

Debris carried by the River Maggia has been deposited over centuries to form an extensive delta. Wide expanses of sand and gravel are the characteristic feature of the outermost point of the river mouth. River deltas are among the most favoured staging sites for passage waders in Switzerland. Most of the wader species recorded in the country can there-

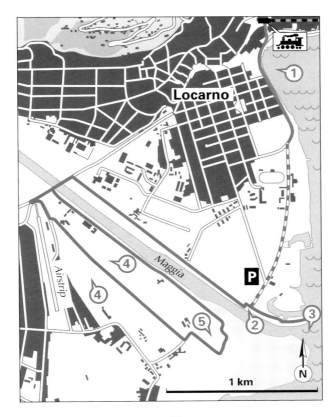

fore also turn up here. On the right-hand side of the delta there is a small remnant of riverine woodland, but this lies within a strict reserve and is inaccessible. Despite the fact that large parts of the area have been built on and other parts are intensively used for agriculture, what is probably the most attractive river delta in Switzerland is still well worth a visit.

Recommended routes

Locarno station is situated very close to Lago Maggiore (Lake Maggiore). As you walk along within the harbour area (1), there are the first opportunities for watching waterbirds and the best place for a quick check to see what grebes, sawbills and other ducks are present is from the jetty. The 2 km along the shore promenade as far as the Maggia Delta are not very interesting from an ornithological point-of-view, but that changes abruptly as soon as you stand on the embankment (2) and gaze out over the wide expanse of gravel- and sandbanks. Check for any waders present before going farther out. Most species stay close to the water's edge. Small plovers in particular often remain motionless on the sand and are therefore difficult to detect. From the outermost tip or toe of the delta (3), you have a further good view out over the sandbanks on the opposite side.

Follow the path along the embankment and cross the Maggia by the first bridge. From here, you pass to the left of the airstrip and, after about 200 m, you immediately turn left again onto a little side road. The latter goes towards the delta between two vast arable fields (4). These fields usually lie fallow in the spring and act as a magnet, drawing down large numbers of migrant passerines to rest and feed. A telescope will be extremely useful. Apart from the problems associated with the identification of pipits and larks, the different races of Yellow Wagtail provide a further challenge for observers. Hoopoe and many Turtle Doves are regular on the fields.

Below the vineyards (5), it's worth looking out for Bluethroat, Whinchat and Stonechat as well as Red-backed Shrike.

Calendar

Important stopover site for waders in Southern Switzerland. Total of 30 wader species recorded to date; often stay for only brief period. Surrounding farmland (often lying fallow during migration periods) important staging site used by many migrant passerines.

Winter: Grebes, Cormorant, ducks (e.g. many Eider), Hen Harrier, Goshawk, Sparrowhawk, Peregrine (regular visitor), Common, Lesser Black-backed and Yellow-legged Gulls.

Spring: All wader species possible; Bittern, Little Bittern, Night Heron, Little Egret, Purple Heron, Osprey, Mediterranean and Little Gulls, Caspian, Common, Little, Whiskered and Black Terns, Turtle Dove, Kingfisher, Hoopoe, Wryneck, Short-toed Lark and Woodlark, Sand and Crag Martins, Tawny and Red-throated Pipits, Yellow Wagtail, Bluethroat, Whinchat and Stonechat, Grasshopper, Sedge and Great Reed Warblers, Lesser Whitethroat, Penduline Tit, Red-backed Shrike, Ortolan Bunting.

Breeding season: Water Rail, Moorhen, Little Ringed Plover, Common Sandpiper, Woodpigeon, Turtle Dove, Kingfisher, Nightingale, Reed,

Great Reed and Garden Warblers, Long-tailed Tit, Golden Oriole, Reed Bunting.

Access
By train to Locarno (600, 620, 630). On foot via the lido into the delta. On the riverside path along the Maggia, a bicycle is more of a hindrance than a help, but one would be useful to cover the large open tracts of farmland. Restricted car parking at the 'Delta' campsite; otherwise rather difficult. If you can't face walking back to Locarno, take bus 31 from Ascona post office. There's another bus-stop on the Ascona side of the second bridge over the River Maggia. Bicycle recommended (bike-hire at Locarno station).

Accommodation
There are many hotels in Ascona and Locarno offering accommodation at all price levels. The 'Delta' campsite is situated on the toe of the delta at Via Respini 7, 6600 Locarno (tel: 091/751 60 81). The youth hostel in Locarno is at Via Varenna 18 (tel: 091/756 15 00).

Site protection
The strict nature reserve on the Ascona side of the Maggia Delta is not accessible. Unfortunately, in the bathing season, the dozens of bathers who reach that part from the other side by swimming or in boats are not easily persuaded of the need to make it a no-entry area.

Disabled access
The area around the river mouth in the Maggia Delta is not suitable for disabled visitors, but the farmland around the runway on the Ascona side is easily accessible.

Nearby sites
Both Pallid Swifts and Swifts breed on the Chiesa di San Antonio church in Locarno (on the side of the road-fork to Monti della Trinità). Not only is this the only Pallid Swift colony in Switzerland, but it is also the north-ernmost point of this species' European range. The colony was discovered as recently as 1987 and fluctuates between 11 and 22 pairs.

The largest wetland in Ticino, the Bolle di Magadino, lies very close by in the mouth of the Ticino river (see Site 44, Bolle di Magadino).

44 BOLLE DI MAGADINO

Canton:	Ticino
Height a.s.l.:	200 m
Grid reference:	709/112
Start:	Tenero
Finish:	Magadino
Itinerary:	Tenero–cross over River Verzasca–Bograsso–Stallone–along Ticino on embankment path–cross over River Ticino–Castellaccio–Bolette–Magadino
Duration:	allow 1 day
Best time:	March–May, at time of spring migration; often interesting in other months (breeding birds, autumn migration, winter visitors)
Status:	nature reserve and Ramsar site; IBA
Map:	LdS 1:25,000; sheet 1313 (Bellinzona)
Equipment:	mosquito repellent, picnic lunch, telescope, possibly wellingtons, possibly bicycle

The Bolle di Magadino are one of a number of alluvial areas of international importance. Situated at the northern end of Lake Maggiore (Lago Maggiore), they comprise the delta zone of the two rivers, the Ticino

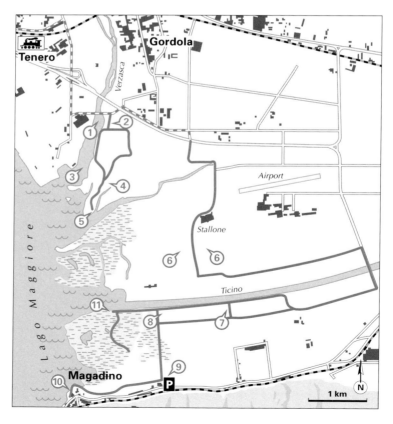

172

and the Verzasca. The Bolle form the last remnant of a natural landscape which formerly extended across the entire Magadino plain. After
the damming of the Ticino in 1890 and the construction of the Verzasca
dam in 1960, the site lost a large part of its natural dynamic.

The special position of the Bolle di Magadino as a transitional zone
between water and land is also reflected in the different types of vegetation which are found here: a belt or zone of floating plants is followed,
as you move landwards, by other vegetation belts—of rushes,
Phragmites reeds and finally one predominantly of sedge. The woodland comprises stands of white willow and grey alder. On the drier
ground there's an oakwood. Extensive agricultural use has also given
rise to various kinds of meadows—wet meadows or those producing
hay used for litter. All these habitats support a special fauna and flora
and together they form the unique alluvial landscape for which the
Bolle are famous.

Recommended routes

Follow the road east for about 500 m from Tenero rail station, branch
off to the right and use the subways to go under the railway track and
the motorway. Then turn left and cross over the Verzasca river (1). It's
worth stopping for a moment on the bridge in order to check for Little
Ringed Plover and Common Sandpiper on the gravelbanks, which will
be more or less exposed depending on the water level. Kingfisher may
also be seen here. Having crossed the bridge, take the first turning right
and you will then enter the riverine woodland (2). Several Nightingales
have territories here which they defend with their loud song, but actually to see these rather nondescript and typically skulking birds will
require a certain amount of patience.

Walk straight on and you come to an information board with a map
of the site. Turn right there and follow the footpath along the Verzasca
river which gets wider and wider just before its mouth (3). Grebes and
ducks, sometimes including sawbills, may be seen as early as this point.
The track now leads through an open oakwood (Goshawk, woodpeckers, tits, *Phylloscopus* warblers) to a small observation tower (4) at the
edge of the wood. From the tower, you can see into the adjoining wet
meadow and an ox-bow lake. First check the meadow, the edge of the
wood and the reedbed before moving on across the wet meadow to a
camouflaged hide (5). The latter enables visitors to watch birds at the
mouth of a canal without disturbing them. This spot is especially attractive to ducks and other waterbirds when the water level is high.

At low water, various wader species are often to be found on the
mudflats which then emerge. It's a good idea to check the edge of the
reeds carefully as this is the favoured haunt of herons, egrets and rails.

As it's not possible to do a circular tour of this site, retrace your steps
(with a slight deviation; see map) as far as the road. Take the underpass
under the motorway, then follow the minor road which branches off right
and runs parallel to the motorway. Take the first turn right and, a little bit
further on, cross the bridge over the motorway. Having passed the airport
(Hen Harrier, Red-footed Falcon, Stonechat), you reach the large farm-
stead called 'Stallone'. You pass to the right of this farm and, about 300 m
further on, come to the embankment path. The large fields and meadows
to the left and right of the track (6) are a favourite staging site used by
many migrating larks, pipits and wagtails. The path to the right is a dead-
end, but it's often worth doing the short walk along it and taking a look.

*Extensive flooding is often a feature of spring in the Bolle di Magadino
(photo: P. Rüegg)*

Following the embankment path will give you the chance of finding
Common Sandpipers. Then cross over the Ticino by the first bridge and
take the first footpath that branches off right, back again towards the
river mouth. In the area around Castellaccio (7), it's worth devoting
some attention to butterflies, as a rare red colour variant of the lesser
purple emperor (a riverine-forest species), is regularly observed there.
There is another information board at point (8). The path straight ahead
to the 'Bolette' takes you directly to the small observation tower (11) by
the Ticino. In spring, the paths are often under water and wellingtons
are recommended. From point (8), the path takes you past a riverine
wood and wet meadows to Magadino. There are further good places for
birding between the entrance to the reserve (9) and the harbour (10)
from where you can get a steamer back to Locarno.

Calendar

Extremely interesting and internationally-important wetland, rich in
birdlife; over 250 species recorded to date (over 70 breeding).
Important staging site used by migrants to feed and rest before and after
crossing the Alps.

Winter: Red-necked Grebe, Bittern, Greylag Goose, Shelduck, Wigeon,
Gadwall, Pintail, Garganey, Shoveler, Pochard, Ferruginous Duck,
Scaup, Long-tailed Duck, Velvet Scoter and Goldeneye, Red-breasted
Merganser and Goosander, Goshawk, Sparrowhawk, Peregrine,
Common and Yellow-legged Gulls, Long-eared Owl, Great Grey Shrike,
Brambling.

Spring and autumn: Night Heron, Little Egret and Purple Heron, Honey
Buzzard, Marsh and Hen Harriers, Osprey, Red-footed Falcon, Hobby,
Spotted Crake, Crane (rare), Ringed Plover, Golden Plover, Lapwing,
Little Stint, Dunlin, Ruff, Jack Snipe (irregular), Snipe, Woodcock,
Black-tailed Godwit, Whimbrel and Curlew, *Tringa* species, Turnstone,
Little Gull, Common, Whiskered, Black and White-winged Black Terns,
Stock Dove, Nightjar, Sand and Crag Martins, Tree, Meadow, Red-throat-
ed and Water Pipits, Bluethroat, Whinchat, Wheatear, Redwing,
Grasshopper, Aquatic, Sedge and Icterine Warblers, Lesser Whitethroat
and Whitethroat, Bonelli's, Wood and Willow Warblers, Pied
Flycatcher, finches, Ortolan and Corn Buntings.

Breeding season: Little and Great Crested Grebes, Black-necked Grebe
(rare), Little Bittern, Teal, Tufted Duck, Black Kite, Quail, Water Rail,
Moorhen, Little Ringed Plover, Common Sandpiper, Woodpigeon,
Turtle Dove, Cuckoo, Scops Owl (rare), Kingfisher, Hoopoe, Wryneck,
Skylark, Yellow Wagtail, Nightingale, Stonechat, Cetti's Warbler (spo-
radic), Marsh, Reed, Great Reed, Melodious and Garden Warblers,
Long-tailed and Marsh Tits, Penduline Tit (exceptional), Golden Oriole,
Red-backed Shrike, Reed Bunting.

Useful tips

If you can't manage a whole day's birding, the advice is to concentrate
on one or other side of the Ticino river.

Access

There is a regular train service to the station in Tenero which is on the Locarno–Bellinzona line (630). The simplest way to get to Magadino is by steamer from Locarno (sailings every hour between 07.00 and 19.00 hrs) or by train or bus (631) from Bellinzona. There is restricted car parking on the Magadino side at the reserve entrance (9) and at the campsite in Tenero.

Accommodation

In Magadino at the Hotel Favini, Via Cantonala (tel: 091/795 15 52). There is the 'Campofelice' campsite at Via alle Brere in Tenero (tel: 091/745 14 17), conveniently located by the mouth of the Verzasca river. Groups planning to stay at least a week will find good-value accommodation in the Sports Centre SZT in Tenero (tel: 091/735 61 11).

Site protection

The core area of the Bolle di Magadino has been a nature reserve since 1974; some of the adjoining land is given over to more environmentally-friendly, extensive forms of agriculture following contracts signed between local farmers and the cantonal government. The Bolle have been a Ramsar site since 1982. However, plans are being discussed to significantly enlarge the nearby airport. This would clearly threaten the reserve.

Disabled access

For visitors with walking impairments, there are many interesting viewing-points within a short distance on the Magadino side. The paths and tracks are flat, but, as in other parts of the Bolle, not necessarily wheelchair-accessible.

Nearby sites

The delta of the River Maggia is very close by and is certainly worth visiting, especially in the spring (see Site 43).

45 MONTE GENEROSO

Canton:	Ticino
Grid reference:	722/870
Height a.s.l.:	1701 m
Start:	Monte Generoso (top station of the rack railway)
Finish:	Bella Vista (intermediate station of the rack railway)
Itinerary:	top station (1601 m)–Monte Generoso (1701 m)–ridgeway to Cima della Piancaccia (1610 m)–along the east flank back to Monte Generoso–just before the top station, left following the ridge (Swiss-Italian border) to Piana–from there along slightly ascending path on the slope back to railway track–path parallel to railway–track to Tiralocchio (possibly loop through the wood)–Bella Vista
Duration:	allow 1 day; distance c.7 km (9 km)
Best time:	spring/early summer
Status:	nature reserve; IBA
Map:	LdS 1:25,000; sheets 1373 (Mendrisio) and 1353 (Lugano)
Equipment:	binoculars, sunscreen (sun-glasses, hat) walking boots, picnic lunch, possibly map

At 1701 metres, the peak of Monte Generoso forms the highest point of the mountain massif between Lake Lugano (Lago di Lugano) and Lake Como (Lago di Como). The mixed broadleaved forests lower down are composed of ash, hornbeam and lime. As you go higher up, those species are finally replaced by sweet (or Spanish) chestnut, birch and beech. Between the alpine pastures, parts of which are no longer cut and are thus becoming overgrown with scrub and trees, there is a scatter of conifer plantations. Rocky terrain is the main characteristic feature of the summit zone and the sheer cliffs on the Lake Lugano side.

Recommended routes

The top station of the rack or cog railway is surrounded by limestone crags with massive and sheer, in some cases overhanging, rock walls. The view from here is truly breathtaking—a fantastic panoramic sweep across South Ticino's mountains and lakes. Rock Thrush, Alpine Swift and Swift, Crag Martin, Alpine Accentor, Wallcreeper, Raven and Rock Bunting are all regular on the sheer rock faces between the top station and Baraghetto (1). With a little luck, you may spot a Peregrine or one of the rare Blue Rock Thrushes.

Follow the ridge north, take the right-hand fork at Cima della Piancaccia (2) and continue along the ridge. Turn right after some 500 m and you come to a hut (3) after about 100 m across country. From here, the path runs at roughly the same height across the slope and back again towards Monte Generoso. Wheatear, Skylark, Water and Tree Pipits are likely to be seen on the way. Quails breed irregularly in the montane grassland and you should listen out for the characteristic call of the species.

Turn off left just before the top station and follow the ridge (Swiss-Italian border) to Piana (4). The track leads up a gentle slope and through lovely mountain meadows with an abundance of flowers and across dry mesobromion grassland back to the railway track. Whinchats and Whitethroats breed below the path.

Back on the ridge, take the wide track parallel to the railway as far as Tiralocchio. Whitethroats also occur there in the broom thickets and the best places for observing this species are on the ridge and on the

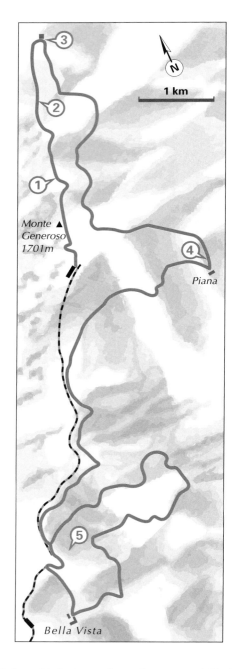

slope of the Italian side between Piana Comune and Tiralocchio.
   Anyone who now feels like watching a few woodland birds (or has
just missed the rack-rail train at Bella Vista) can do a short walk round

the hill (5), Bonelli's Warbler and Wren being the most conspicuous species on the approximately 1-km route.

Calendar

Excellent opportunities for observing many Alpine birds. Total of 131 species recorded to date (canton of Ticino: 304 species). Apart from the typical mountain birds, also species of various other habitats and some passage migrants, within a relatively small area.

Winter: During the cold season, birds are less numerous at Monte Generoso and represented by fewer species. Many of the breeding birds migrate away or descend to lower levels. Alpine Chough and Citril Finches are then often easier to observe. Golden Eagle (regular winter visitor).

Spring and autumn: Monte Generoso acts as a migratory divide between the chain of the Alps and the Po valley. In addition to the 83 species of breeding birds, a further 48 have been observed on migration, including Woodcock, Woodpigeon, Turtle Dove, Meadow Pipit, Yellow Wagtail, Redwing, Ring Ouzel, Grasshopper and Icterine Warblers, Pied Flycatcher and many finch species.

Breeding season: Golden Eagle, Black Kite, Kestrel, Peregrine (occasional), Rock Partridge, Quail, Eagle Owl, Tawny Owl, Nightjar, Alpine Swift and Swift, Hoopoe (irregular), Wryneck, Skylark, Crag Martin, Tree and Water Pipits, Dipper, Dunnock and Alpine Accentor, Nightingale, Whinchat, Stonechat (irregular), Wheatear, Rock Thrush, Blue Rock Thrush (irregular), Melodious Warbler, Lesser Whitethroat, Whitethroat, Garden Warbler, Bonelli's Warbler, Spotted Flycatcher, Willow Tit, Wallcreeper, Golden Oriole, Red-backed Shrike, Nutcracker, Raven, Citril Finch, Redpoll, Yellowhammer, Rock and Cirl Buntings.

Useful tips

Especially at weekends in fine weather and during the summer holidays, Monte Generoso is besieged by large numbers of tourists. A visit during the week or in the early morning is far more enjoyable than being swept along in the tide of visitors. As the first train on the rack railway doesn't leave until 09.45 hrs, we recommend staying overnight at the hotel on the summit.

Access

Regional trains on the Lugano to Mendrisio line (600) operate a regular service to Capolago. Change there to the rack railway which will take you right up to Monte Generoso via the intermediate station of 'Bella Vista'. Anyone with the necessary stamina can hire a bike at Mendrisio rail station and then pedal and sweat their way up the 900-m difference in altitude to 'Bella Vista'.

Accommodation

On the summit, the Hotel Monte Generoso offers both twin-bed rooms and also dormitory accommodation (tel: 091/649 77 22). Various kinds of hotels are available in Capolago and in the nearby Riva-San Vitale. In Melano (2 km north of Capolago), there are two campsites directly by the lake (e.g. Camping Pedemonte (tel: 091/649 83 33)). A conveniently-placed youth hostel is situated in Scudellate, only about 2 km south-east (grid ref.: 724200/86800) of the summit of Monte Generoso in the Valle di Muggio (tel: 091/684 11 36).

Site protection
Monte Generoso is a nature reserve and is included in the Federal Inventory of Landscapes and Natural Monuments of National Importance (BLN).

Disabled access
Monte Generoso is not suitable for visitors with walking impairments. Though some of the rock- and cliff-dwelling birds can be observed from the top station, the site can only be explored really well on foot. It is completely unsuitable for wheelchairs.

Nearby sites
Directly opposite Monte Generoso, on the other side of Lake Lugano, lies Monte San Giorgio. Known internationally among palaeontologists as the site where many rare and spectacular fossils have been discovered, Monte San Giorgio is no less celebrated in entomological and botanical circles. Among the many and, in some cases, rare butterflies, grasshoppers and plants (e.g. black false helleborine) recorded, there are some southern species not found anywhere else in Switzerland. The starting point for a day's walk around Monte San Giorgio is Meride, which can be easily reached by postbus from Mendrisio.

BIBLIOGRAPHY

The following list gives only a brief overview of the most important ornithological publications of recent years and is, of course, not comprehensive. Older works (with the exception of the standard work by Glutz von Blotzheim *Die Brutvögel der Schweiz*, 1962) have been omitted. Regional checklists and handbooks or distribution atlases have appeared for various cantons, but these are not included here either.

Bossert, A. (1988) Die Reservate der Ala [The Ala reserves]. *Orn. Beob.* Beiheft 7.

Glutz von Blotzheim, U.N. (1962) *Die Brutvögel der Schweiz* [*The breeding birds of Switzerland*]. Aarau. 648 pp.

Marti, C. (1987) *Schweizer Wasservogelgebiete von internationaler Bedeutung* [*Waterbird sites of international importance in Switzerland*]. Schweizerische Vogelwarte, Sempach.

Schmid, H. (1999) *Orni-Top-CH*. Schweizerische Vogelwarte, Sempach. [A regularly updated checklist for 22 sites]

Schmid, H., Luder, R., Naef-Daenzer, B., Graf, R., & Zbinden, N. (1998) *Schweizer Brutvogelatlas. Verbreitung der Brutvögel in der Schweiz und im Fürstentum Liechtenstein 1993–1996* [*Swiss Breeding Bird Atlas. Distribution of breeding birds in Switzerland and the Principality of Liechtenstein 1993–1996* with summaries in English]. Schweizerische Vogelwarte, Sempach.

Schmid, H. *et al.* (1992) *Die Limikolenrastplätze in der Schweiz* [*Stopover sites for waders in Switzerland*]. Schweizerische Vogelwarte, Sempach. 159pp.

Winkler, R. (1999) Avifauna der Schweiz [The avifauna of Switzerland]. *Orn. Beob.*, Beiheft 10.

Winkler, R. (1999) Avifaune de Suisse. *Nos Oiseaux*, suppl. 3.

Zbinden, N. (1989) *Beurteilung der Situation der Vogelwelt in der Schweiz in den 1980er Jahren* [*Birds in Switzerland: an assessment of the situation in the 1980s*]. Schweizerische Vogelwarte, Sempach.

Important addresses and contacts

Certain institutions and organizations in Switzerland are actively involved in bird conservation and/or research. Information on topical questions of bird conservation can be obtained from the following addresses:

Schweizer Vogelschutz
SVS—BirdLife Switzerland
PO Box
CH-8036 Zürich
Tel: 01 463 72 71
Fax: 01 461 47 78
E-mail: svs@birdlife.ch
Internet: www.birdlife.ch

Schweizerische Vogelwarte
CH-6204 Sempach
Tel: 041 462 97 00
Fax 041 462 97 10
E-mail: vogelwarte@orninst.ch
Internet: www.vogelwarte.ch

Nos Oiseaux
Musée d'histoire naturelle de La Chaux-de-Fonds
CH-2300 La Chaux-de-Fonds
Tel: 032 913 39 76

Ficedula,
Società pro avifauna della Svizzera Italiana
CH-6835 Morbio-Superiore
Tel: 091 683 33 79

Ala, Schweizerische Gesellschaft für Vogelkunde und Vogelschutz
c/o Schweizer Vogelschutz
PO Box
CH-8036 Zürich

Further national associations concerned with nature-conservation topics:

Pro Natura—Schweizerischer Bund
für Naturschutz
PO Box
CH-4020 Basel
Tel: 061 317 91 91
Fax: 061 317 91 66

WWF Switzerland
PO Box
CH-8010 Zürich
Tel: 01 297 23 23
Fax: 01 297 23 00

International organizations promoting bird and nature conservation throughout the world:

BirdLife International
Wellbrook Court
Girton Road
Cambridge CB3 ONA
UK

For information, apply to the BirdLife Partner for Switzerland: Schweizer Vogelschutz—SVS.

IUCN—The World Conservation Union
Rue de Mauverney 28
CH-1196 Gland
Switzerland
Tel: 022 999 00 01
Fax: 022 999 00 02

Appeal

Please help to conserve important bird areas by playing an active role in nature and bird conservation. Schweizer Vogelschutz SVS—BirdLife Switzerland (see p. 181) will be pleased to answer your queries.

Perhaps you have had some interesting observations during a birding trip which ought not to be allowed just to gather dust in your notebooks? If so, please contact the Information Service of the Schweizerische Vogelwarte. The Information Service (German *Informationsdienst* or ID) has for decades been systematically collecting data on breeding birds, passage migrants and winter visitors throughout Switzerland. Any reports submitted should be on the special record cards and daily recording forms which can be obtained from the Vogelwarte in Sempach (for address, see p. 181).

CHECKLIST OF THE BIRDS OF SWITZERLAND

The following list comprises all species recorded in Switzerland in the 20th century. Species in bold have the status of regular passage migrant, breeding bird or winter visitor in the country. Species not in bold print are those that do not occur regularly or are vagrants (15 records or fewer in the 20th century). With a few exceptions, these require proper documentation for submission to the Avifaunistic Commission (c/o Schweizerische Vogelwarte, 6204 Sempach). Species whose captive origin seems certain or likely are marked with an asterisk (*).

The list contains the scientific (Latin) and English names, and also those in the country's main languages (German, French and Italian).

Red-throated Diver	Sterntaucher	Plongeon catmarin	Strolaga minore	*Gavia stellata*
Black-throated Diver	Prachttaucher	Plongeon arctique	Strolaga mezzana	*Gavia arctica*
Great Northern Diver	Eistaucher	Plongeon imbrin	Strolaga maggiore	*Gavia immer*
White-billed Diver	Gelbschnabeltaucher	Plongeon à bec blanc	Strolaga beccogiallo	*Gavia adamsii*
Little Grebe	Zwergtaucher	Grèbe castagneux	Tuffetto	*Tachybaptus ruficollis*
Great Crested Grebe	Haubentaucher	Grèbe huppé	Svasso maggiore	*Podiceps cristatus*
Red-necked Grebe	Rothalstaucher	Grèbe jougris	Svasso collorosso	*Podiceps grisegena*
Slavonian Grebe	Ohrentaucher	Grèbe esclavon	Svasso cornuto	*Podiceps auritus*
Black-necked Grebe	Schwarzhalstaucher	Grèbe à cou noir	Svasso piccolo	*Podiceps nigricollis*
Cory's Shearwater	Gelbschnabelsturmtaucher	Puffin cendré	Berta maggiore	*Calonectris diomedea*
Manx Shearwater	Schwarzschnabelsturmtaucher	Puffin des Anglais	Berta minore	*Puffinus puffinus*
British Storm-petrel	Sturmschwalbe	Océanite tempête	Uccello delle tempeste	*Hydrobates pelagicus*
Leach's Storm-petrel	Wellenläufer	Océanite culblanc	Uccello delle tempeste codaforcuta	*Oceanodroma leucorhoa*
Cormorant	Kormoran	Grand Cormoran	Cormorano	*Phalacrocorax carbo*
Shag	Krähenscharbe	Cormoran huppé	Marangone dal ciuffo	*Phalacrocorax aristotelis*
White Pelican	Rosapelikan	Pélican blanc	Pellicano	*Pelecanus onocrotalus*
Pink-backed Pelican*	Rötelpelikan	Pélican gris	Pellicano rossiccio	*Pelecanus rufescens*
Bittern	Rohrdommel	Butor étoilé	Tarabuso	*Botaurus stellaris*
Little Bittern	Zwergdommel	Blongios nain	Tarabusino	*Ixobrychus minutus*
Night Heron	Nachtreiher	Bihoreau gris	Nitticora	*Nycticorax nycticorax*
Squacco Heron	Rallenreiher	Crabier chevelu	Sgarza ciuffetto	*Ardeola ralloides*
Cattle Egret	Kuhreiher	Héron garde-boeufs	Airone guardabuoi	*Bubulcus ibis*
Western Reef Heron*	Küstenreiher	Aigrette des récifs	Airone schistaceo	*Egretta gularis*
Little Egret	Seidenreiher	Aigrette garzette	Garzetta	*Egretta garzetta*
Great White Egret	Silberreiher	Grande Aigrette	Airone bianco maggiore	*Egretta alba*
Grey Heron	Graureiher	Héron cendré	Airone cenerino	*Ardea cinerea*
Purple Heron	Purpurreiher	Héron pourpré	Airone rosso	*Ardea purpurea*
Black Stork	Schwarzstorch	Cigogne noire	Cicogna nera	*Ciconia nigra*
White Stork	Weissstorch	Cigogne blanche	Cicogna bianca	*Ciconia ciconia*
Glossy Ibis	Sichler	Ibis falcinelle	Mignattaio	*Plegadis falcinellus*
Spoonbill	Löffler	Spatule blanche	Spatola	*Platalea leucorodia*
Greater Flamingo	Rosaflamingo	Flamant rose	Fenicottero	*Phoenicopterus ruber*
Mute Swan	Höckerschwan	Cygne tuberculé	Cigno reale	*Cygnus olor*
Bewick's Swan	Zwergschwan	Cygne de Bewick	Cigno minore	*Cygnus columbianus*
Whooper Swan	Singschwan	Cygne chanteur	Cigno selvatico	*Cygnus cygnus*
Bean Goose	Saatgans	Oie des moissons	Oca granaiola	*Anser fabalis*
Pink-footed Goose	Kurzschnabelgans	Oie à bec court	Oca zamperosse	*Anser brachyrhynchus*
White-fronted Goose	Blässgans	Oie rieuse	Oca lombardella	*Anser albifrons*
Greylag Goose	Graugans	Oie cendrée	Oca selvatica	*Anser anser*
Snow Goose*	Schneegans	Oie des neiges	Oca delle nevi	*Anser caerulescens*
Canada Goose*	Kanadagans	Bernache du Canada	Oca del Canada	*Branta canadensis*
Barnacle Goose	Weisswangengans	Bernache nonnette	Oca facciabianca	*Branta leucopsis*
Brent Goose	Ringelgans	Bernache cravant	Oca colombaccio	*Branta bernicla*
Red-breasted Goose	Rothalsgans	Bernache à cou roux	Oca collorosso	*Branta ruficollis*

Checklist of the Birds of Switzerland

Ruddy Shelduck*	Rostgans	Tadorne casarca	Casarca	*Tadorna ferruginea*
Shelduck	Brandgans	Tadorne de Belon	Volpoca	*Tadorna tadorna*
Mandarin*	Mandarinente	Canard mandarin	Anatra mandarina	*Aix galericulata*
Baikal Teal*	Gluckente	Sarcelle élégante	Alzavola asiatica	*Anas formosa*
Wood Duck*	Brautente	Canard carolin	Anatra	*Aix sponsa*
Wigeon	Pfeifente	Canard siffleur	Fischione	*Anas penelope*
Gadwall	Schnatterente	Canard chipeau	Canapiglia	*Anas strepera*
Teal	Krickente	Sarcelle d'hiver	Alzavola	*Anas crecca*
Mallard	Stockente	Canard colvert	Germano reale	*Anas platyrhynchos*
Pintail	Spiessente	Canard pilet	Codone	*Anas acuta*
Garganey	Knäkente	Sarcelle d'été	Marzaiola	*Anas querquedula*
Blue-winged Teal	Blauflügelente	Sarcelle à ailes bleues	Marzaiola americana	*Anas discors*
Shoveler	Löffelente	Canard souchet	Mestolone	*Anas clypeata*
Mabled Duck*	Marmelente	Sarcelle marbrée	Carganella marmorizzata	*Marmaronetta angustirostris*
Red-crested Pochard	Kolbenente	Nette rousse	Fistione turco	*Netta rufina*
Pochard	Tafelente	Fuligule milouin	Moriglione	*Aythya ferina*
Ring-necked Duck	Ringschnabelente	Fuligule à bec cerclé	Moretta dal collare	*Aythya collaris*
Ferruginous Duck	Moorente	Fuligule nyroca	Moretta tabaccata	*Aythya nyroca*
Tufted Duck	Reiherente	Fuligule morillon	Moretta	*Aythya fuligula*
Scaup	Bergente	Fuligule milouinan	Moretta grigia	*Aythya marila*
Lesser Scaup*	Kleine Bergente	Fuligule à tête noire		*Aythya affinis*
Eider	Eiderente	Eider à duvet	Edredone	*Somateria mollissima*
Long-tailed Duck	Eisente	Harelde boréale	Moretta codona	*Clangula hyemalis*
Common Scoter	Trauerente	Macreuse noire	Orchetto marino	*Melanitta nigra*
Velvet Scoter	Samtente	Macreuse brune	Orco marino	*Melanitta fusca*
Goldeneye	Schellente	Garrot à oeil d'or	Quattrocchi	*Bucephala clangula*
Smew	Zwergsäger	Harle piette	Pesciaiola	*Mergus albellus*
Red-breasted Merganser	Mittelsäger	Harle huppé	Smergo minore	*Mergus serrator*
Goosander	Gänsesäger	Harle bièvre	Smergo maggiore	*Mergus merganser*
Ruddy Duck*	Schwarzkopfruderente	Erismature rousse	Gobbo della Giamaica	*Oxyura jamaicensis*
White-headed Duck	Weisskopfruderente	Erismature à tête blanche	Gobbo rugginoso	*Oxyura leucocephala*
Honey Buzzard	Wespenbussard	Bondrée apivore	Falco pecchiaiolo	*Pernis apivorus*
Black-shouldered Kite	Gleitaar	Elanion blanc	Nibbio bianco	*Elanus caeruleus*
Black Kite	Schwarzmilan	Milan noir	Nibbio bruno	*Milvus migrans*
Red Kite	Rotmilan	Milan royal	Nibbio reale	*Milvus milvus*
White-tailed Eagle	Seeadler	Pygargue à queue blanche	Aquila di mare	*Haliaeetus albicilla*
Lammergeier	Bartgeier	Gypaète barbu	Gipeto	*Gypaetus barbatus*
Egyptian Vulture	Schmutzgeier	Vautour percnoptère	Capovaccaio	*Neophron percnopterus*
Griffon Vulture	Gänsegeier	Vautour fauve	Grifone	*Gyps fulvus*
Black Vulture	Mönchsgeier	Vautour moine	Avvoltoio monaco	*Aegypius monachus*
Short-toed Eagle	Schlangenadler	Circaète Jean-le-Blanc	Biancone	*Circaetus gallicus*
Marsh Harrier	Rohrweihe	Busard des roseaux	Falco di palude	*Circus aeruginosus*
Hen Harrier	Kornweihe	Busard Saint-Martin	Albanella reale	*Circus cyaneus*
Pallid Harrier	Steppenweihe	Busard pâle	Albanella pallida	*Circus macrourus*
Montagu's Harrier	Wiesenweihe	Busard cendré	Albanella minore	*Circus pygargus*
Goshawk	Habicht	Autour des palombes	Astore	*Accipiter gentilis*
Sparrowhawk	Sperber	Epervier d'Europe	Sparviere	*Accipiter nisus*
Buzzard	Mäusebussard	Buse variable	Poiana	*Buteo buteo*
Long-legged Buzzard	Adlerbussard	Buse féroce	Poiana codabianca	*Buteo rufinus*
Rough-legged Buzzard	Rauhfussbussard	Buse pattue	Poiana calzata	*Buteo lagopus*
Lesser Spotted Eagle	Schreiadler	Aigle pomarin	Aquila anatraia minore	*Aquila pomarina*
Spotted Eagle	Schelladler	Aigle criard	Aquila anatraia maggiore	*Aquila clanga*
Golden Eagle	Steinadler	Aigle royal	Aquila reale	*Aquila chrysaetos*
Booted Eagle	Zwergadler	Aigle botté	Aquila minore	*Hieraaetus pennatus*
Osprey	Fischadler	Balbuzard pêcheur	Falco pescatore	*Pandion haliaetus*
Lesser Kestrel	Rötelfalke	Faucon crécerellette	Grillaio	*Falco naumanni*
Kestrel	Turmfalke	Faucon crécerelle	Gheppio	*Falco tinnunculus*
Red-footed Falcon	Rotfussfalke	Faucon kobez	Falco cuculo	*Falco vespertinus*
Merlin	Merlin	Faucon émerillon	Smeriglio	*Falco columbarius*
Hobby	Baumfalke	Faucon hobereau	Lodolaio	*Falco subbuteo*

Checklist of the Birds of Switzerland

Lanner Falcon*	Lannerfalke	Faucon lanier	Laniario	*Falco biarmicus*
Saker Falcon*	Würgfalke	Faucon sacre	Sacro	*Falco cherrug*
Gyrfalcon	Gerfalke	Faucon gerfaut	Girfalco	*Falco rusticolus*
Peregrine	Wanderfalke	Faucon pèlerin	Pellegrino	*Falco peregrinus*
Hazel Grouse	Haselhuhn	Gélinotte des bois	Francolino di monte	*Bonasa bonasia*
Ptarmigan	Alpenschneehuhn	Lagopède alpin	Pernice bianca	*Lagopus mutus*
Black Grouse	Birkhuhn	Tétras lyre	Fagiano di monte	*Tetrao tetrix*
Capercaillie	Auerhuhn	Grand Tétras	Gallo cedrone	*Tetrao urogallus*
Rock Partridge	Steinhuhn	Perdrix bartavelle	Coturnice	*Alectoris graeca*
Grey Partridge	Rebhuhn	Perdrix grise	Starna	*Perdix perdix*
Quail	Wachtel	Caille des blés	Quaglia	*Coturnix coturnix*
Pheasant	Fasan	Faisan de Colchide	Fagiano comune	*Phasianus colchicus*
Water Rail	Wasserralle	Râle d'eau	Porciglione	*Rallus aquaticus*
Spotted Crake	Tüpfelralle	Marouette ponctuée	Voltolino	*Porzana porzana*
Little Crake	Kleines Sumpfhuhn	Marouette poussin	Schiribilla	*Porzana parva*
Baillon's Crake	Zwersumpfhuhn	Marouette de Baillon	Schiribilla grigiata	*Porzana pusilla*
Corncrake	Wachtelkönig	Râle des genêts	Re di quaglie	*Crex crex*
Moorhen	Teichhuhn	Gallinule poule-d'eau	Gallinella d'acqua	*Gallinula chloropus*
Purple Swamphen*	Zwergsultanshuhn	Talève violacée	Gallinella americana	*Porphyrula martinica*
Purple Gallinule*	Purpurhuhn	Talève sultane	Pollo sultano	*Porphyrio porphyrio*
Coot	Blässhuhn	Foulque macroule	Folaga	*Fulica atra*
Crane	Kranich	Grue cendrée	Gru	*Grus grus*
Little Bustard	Zwergtrappe	Outarde canepetière	Gallinella prataiola	*Tetrax tetrax*
Houbara Bustard	Kragentrappe	Outarde houbara	Ubara	*Chlamydotis undulata*
Great Bustard	Grosstrappe	Outarde barbue	Otarda	*Otis tarda*
Oystercatcher	Austernfischer	Huîtrier pie	Beccaccia di mare	*Haematopus ostralegus*
Black-winged Stilt	Stelzenläufer	Echasse blanche	Cavaliere d'Italia	*Himantopus himantopus*
Avocet	Säbelschnäbler	Avocette élégante	Avocetta	*Recurvirostra avosetta*
Stone Curlew	Triel	Œdicnème criard	Occhione	*Burhinus oedicnemus*
Cream-coloured Courser	Rennvogel	Courvite isabelle	Corrione biondo	*Cursorius cursor*
Collared Pratincole	Rotflügelbrachschwalbe	Glaréole à collier	Pernice di mare	*Glareola pratincola*
Black-winged Pratincole	Schwarzflügelbrachschwalbe	Glaréole à ailes noires	Pernice di mare orientale	*Glareola nordmanni*
Little Ringed Plover	Flussregenpfeifer	Petit Gravelot	Corriere piccolo	*Charadrius dubius*
Ringed Plover	Sandregenpfeifer	Grand Gravelot	Corriere grosso	*Charadrius hiaticula*
Killdeer	Keilschwanzregenpfeifer	Gravelot kildir	Corriere americano	*Charadrius vociferus*
Kentish Plover	Seeregenpfeifer	Gravelot à collier interrompu	Fratino	*Charadrius alexandrinus*
Dotterel	Mornellregenpfeifer	Pluvier guignard	Piviere tortolino	*Charadrius morinellus*
Golden Plover	Goldregenpfeifer	Pluvier doré	Piviere dorato	*Pluvialis apricaria*
Grey Plover	Kiebitzregenpfeifer	Pluvier argenté	Pivieressa	*Pluvialis squatarola*
Red-wattled Plover*	Rotlappenkiebitz	Vanneau indien	Pavoncella indiana	*Hoplopterus indicus*
Sociable Plover	Steppenkiebitz	Pluvier sociable	Pavoncella gregaria	*Chettusia gregaria*
Lapwing	Kiebitz	Vanneau huppé	Pavoncella	*Vanellus vanellus*
Knot	Knutt	Bécasseau maubèche	Piovanello maggiore	*Calidris canutus*
Sanderling	Sanderling	Bécasseau sanderling	Piovanello tridattilo	*Calidris alba*
Little Stint	Zwergstrandläufer	Bécasseau minute	Gambecchio	*Calidris minuta*
Temminck's Stint	Temminckstrandläufer	Bécasseau de Temminck	Gambecchio nano	*Calidris temminckii*
White-rumped Sandpiper	Weissbürzelstrandläufer	Bécasseau de Bonaparte	Piro-piro dorsobianco	*Calidris fuscicollis*
Pectoral Sandpiper	Graubruststrandläufer	Bécasseau tacheté	Piro-piro pettorale	*Calidris melanotos*
Curlew Sandpiper	Sichelstrandläufer	Bécasseau cocorli	Piovanello	*Calidris ferruginea*
Purple Sandpiper	Meerstrandläufer	Bécasseau violet	Piovanello violetto	*Calidris maritima*
Dunlin	Alpenstrandläufer	Bécasseau variable	Piovanello pancia nera	*Calidris alpina*
Broad-billed Sandpiper	Sumpfläufer	Bécasseau falcinelle	Gambecchio frullino	*Limicola falcinellus*
Buff-breasted Sandpiper	Grasläufer	Bécasseau rousset	Piro-piro fulvo	*Tryngites subruficollis*
Ruff	Kampfläufer	Combattant varié	Combattente	*Philomachus pugnax*
Jack Snipe	Zwergschnepfe	Bécassine sourde	Frullino	*Lymnocryptes minimus*
Snipe	*Bekassine*	Bécassine des marais	Beccaccino	*Gallinago gallinago*
Great Snipe	Doppelschnepfe	Bécassine double	Croccolone	*Gallinago media*
Woodcock	Waldschnepfe	Bécasse des bois	Beccaccia	*Scolopax rusticola*
Black-tailed Godwit	Uferschnepfe	Barge à queue noire	Pittima reale	*Limosa limosa*

Checklist of the Birds of Switzerland

	English	German	French	Italian	Latin
—	**Bar-tailed Godwit**	Pfuhlschnepfe	Barge rousse	Pittima minore	*Limosa lapponica*
—	**Whimbrel**	Regenbrachvogel	Courlis corlieu	Chiurlo piccolo	*Numenius phaeopus*
—	Slender-billed Curlew	Dünnschnabelbrachvogel	Courlis à bec grêle	Chiurlottello	*Numenius tenuirostris*
—	**Curlew**	Grosser Brachvogel	Courlis cendré	Chiurlo maggiore	*Numenius arquata*
—	**Spotted Redshank**	Dunkler Wasserläufer	Chevalier arlequin	Totano moro	*Tringa erythropus*
—	**Redshank**	Rotschenkel	Chevalier gambette	Pettegola	*Tringa totanus*
—	**Marsh Sandpiper**	Teichwasserläufer	Chevalier stagnatile	Albastrello	*Tringa stagnatilis*
—	**Greenshank**	Grünschenkel	Chevalier aboyeur	Pantana	*Tringa nebularia*
—	**Green Sanpiper**	Waldwasserläufer	Chevalier culblanc	Piro-piro culbianco	*Tringa ochropus*
—	**Wood Sandpiper**	Bruchwasserläufer	Chevalier sylvain	Piro-piro boschereccio	*Tringa glareola*
—	Terek Sandpiper	Terekwasserläufer	Chevalier bargette	Piro-piro terek	*Xenus cinereus*
—	**Common Sandpiper**	Flussuferläufer	Chevalier guignette	Piro-piro piccolo	*Actitis hypoleucos*
—	Spotted Sandpiper	Drosseluferläufer	Chevalier grivelé	Piro-piro macchiato	*Actitis macularia*
—	**Turnstone**	Steinwälzer	Tournepierre à collier	Voltapietre	*Arenaria interpres*
—	Red-necked Phalarope	Odinshühnchen	Phalarope à bec étroit	Falaropo beccosottile	*Phalaropus lobatus*
—	Grey Phalarope	Thorshühnchen	Phalarope à bec large	Falaropo beccolargo	*Phalaropus fulicarius*
—	Pomarine Skua	Spatelraubmöwe	Labbe pomarin	Stercorario mezzano	*Stercorarius pomarinus*
—	Arctic Skua	Schmarotzerraubmöwe	Labbe parasite	Labbo	*Stercorarius parasiticus*
—	Long-tailed Skua	Falkenraubmöwe	Labbe à longue queue	Labbo codalunga	*Stercorarius longicaudus*
—	Great Skua	Skua	Grand Labbe	Stercorario maggiore	*Stercorarius skua*
—	**Mediterranean Gull**	Schwarzkopfmöwe	Mouette mélanocéphale	Gabbiano corallino	*Larus melanocephalus*
—	**Little Gull**	Zwergmöwe	Mouette pygmée	Gabbianello	*Larus minutus*
—	Sabine's Gull	Schwalbenmöwe	Mouette de Sabine	Gabbiano di Sabine	*Larus sabini*
—	**Black-headed Gull**	Lachmöwe	Mouette rieuse	Gabbiano comune	*Larus ridibundus*
—	Slender-billed Gull	Dünnschnabelmöwe	Goéland railleur	Gabbiano roseo	*Larus genei*
—	Audouin's Gull	Korallenmöwe	Goéland d'Audouin	Gabbiano corso	*Larus audouinii*
—	**Common Gull**	Sturmmöwe	Goéland cendré	Gavina	*Larus canus*
—	Lesser Black-backed Gull	Heringsmöwe	Goéland brun	Zafferano	*Larus fuscus*
—	**Herring Gull**	Silbermöwe	Goéland argenté	Gabbiano reale nordico	*Larus argentatus*
—	**Yellow-legged Gull**	Weisskopfmöwe	Goéland leucophée	Gabbiano reale	*Larus cachinnans*
—	Glaucous Gull	Eismöwe	Goéland bourgmestre	Gabbiano glauco	*Larus hyperboreus*
—	**Great Black-backed Gull**	Mantelmöwe	Goéland marin	Mugnaiaccio	*Larus marinus*
—	Kittiwake	Dreizehenmöwe	Mouette tridactyle	Gabbiano tridattilo	*Rissa tridactyla*
—	Gull-billed Tern	Lachseeschwalbe	Sterne hansel	Sterna zampenere	*Gelochelidon nilotica*
—	**Caspian Tern**	Raubseeschwalbe	Sterne caspienne	Sterna maggiore	*Sterna caspia*
—	Lesser Crested Tern	Rüppellseeschwalbe	Sterne voyageuse	Sterna del Rüppell	*Sterna bengalensis*
—	Sandwich Tern	Brandseeschwalbe	Sterne caugek	Beccapesci	*Sterna sandvicensis*
—	**Common Tern**	Flussseeschwalbe	Sterne pierregarin	Sterna comune	*Sterna hirundo*
—	Arctic Tern	Küstenseeschwalbe	Sterne arctique	Sterna codalunga	*Sterna paradisaea*
—	**Little Tern**	Zwergseeschwalbe	Sterne naine	Fraticello	*Sterna albifrons*
—	**Whiskered Tern**	Weissbartseeschwalbe	Guifette moustac	Mignattino piombato	*Chlidonias hybridus*
—	**Black Tern**	Trauerseeschwalbe	Guifette noire	Mignattino	*Chlidonias niger*
—	**White-winged Black Tern**	Weissflügelseeschwalbe	Guifette leucoptère	Mignattino alibianche	*Chlidonias leucopterus*
—	**Feral Pigeon**	Strassentaube	Pigeon biset domestique	Piccione domestico	*Columba livia domestica*
—	**Stock Dove**	Hohltaube	Pigeon colombin	Colombella	*Columba oenas*
—	**Woodpigeon**	Ringeltaube	Pigeon ramier	Colombaccio	*Columba palumbus*
—	**Collared Dove**	Türkentaube	Tourterelle turque	Tortora dal collare orientale	*Streptopelia decaocto*
—	**Turtle Dove**	Turteltaube	Tourterelle des bois	Tortora	*Streptopelia turtur*
—	Great Spotted Cuckoo	Häherkuckuck	Coucou geai	Cuculo dal ciuffo	*Clamator glandarius*
—	**Cuckoo**	Kuckuck	Coucou gris	Cuculo	*Cuculus canorus*
—	**Barn Owl**	Schleiereule	Effraie des clochers	Barbagianni	*Tyto alba*
—	**Scops Owl**	Zwergohreule	Petit-duc scops	Assiolo	*Otus scops*
—	**Eagle Owl**	Uhu	Grand-duc d'Europe	Gufo reale	*Bubo bubo*
—	Hawk Owl	Sperbereule	Chouette épervière	Ulula	*Surnia ulula*
—	**Pygmy Owl**	Sperlingskauz	Chevêchette d'Europe	Civetta nana	*Glaucidium passerinum*
—	**Little Owl**	Steinkauz	Chevêche d'Athéna	Civetta	*Athene noctua*
—	**Tawny Owl**	Waldkauz	Chouette hulotte	Allocco	*Strix aluco*
—	**Long-eared Owl**	Waldohreule	Hibou moyen-duc	Gufo comune	*Asio otus*
—	**Short-eared Owl**	Sumpfohreule	Hibou des marais	Gufo di palude	*Asio flammeus*
—	**Tengmalm's Owl**	Rauhfusskauz	Chouette de Tengmalm	Civetta capogrosso	*Aegolius funereus*

Checklist of the Birds of Switzerland

Nightjar	Ziegenmelker	Engoulevent d'Europe	Succiacapre	*Caprimulgus europaeus*
Swift	Mauersegler	Martinet noir	Rondone	*Apus apus*
Pallid Swift	Fahlsegler	Martinet pâle	Rondone pallido	*Apus pallidus*
Alpine Swift	Alpensegler	Martinet à ventre blanc	Rondone maggiore	*Apus melba*
Kingfisher	Eisvogel	Martin-pêcheur d'Europe	Martin pescatore	*Alcedo atthis*
Bee-eater	Bienenfresser	Guêpier d'Europe	Gruccione	*Merops apiaster*
Roller	Blauracke	Rollier d'Europe	Ghiandaia marina	*Coracias garrulus*
Hoopoe	Wiedehopf	Huppe fasciée	Upupa	*Upupa epops*
Wryneck	Wendehals	Torcol fourmilier	Torcicollo	*Jynx torquilla*
Grey-headed Woodpecker	Grauspecht	Pic cendré	Picchio cenerino	*Picus canus*
Green Woodpecker	Grünspecht	Pic vert	Picchio verde	*Picus viridis*
Black Woodpecker	Schwarzspecht	Pic noir	Picchio nero	*Dryocopus martius*
Great Spotted Woodpecker	Buntspecht	Pic épeiche	Picchio rosso maggiore	*Dendrocopos major*
Middle Spotted Woodpecker	Mittelspecht	Pic mar	Picchio rosso mezzano	*Dendrocopos medius*
White-backed Woodpecker	Weissrückenspecht	Pic à dos blanc	Picchio dorsobianco	*Dendrocopos leucotos*
Lesser Spotted Woodpecker	Kleinspecht	Pic épeichette	Picchio rosso minore	*Dendrocopos minor*
Three-toed Woodpecker	Dreizehenspecht	Pic tridactyle	Picchio tridattilo	*Picoides tridactylus*
Calandra Lark	Kalanderlerche	Alouette calandre	Calandra	*Melanocorypha calandra*
White-winged Lark	Weissflügellerche	Alouette leucoptère	Calandra siberiana	*Melanocorypha leucoptera*
Short-toed Lark	Kurzzehenlerche	Alouette calandrelle	Calandrella	*Calandrella brachydactyla*
Lesser Short-toed Lark	Stummellerche	Alouette pispolette	Pispoletta	*Calandrella rufescens*
Crested Lark	Haubenlerche	Cochevis huppé	Cappellaccia	*Galerida cristata*
Woodlark	Heidelerche	Alouette lulu	Tottavilla	*Lullula arborea*
Skylark	Feldlerche	Alouette des champs	Allodola	*Alauda arvensis*
Shore Lark	Ohrenlerche	Alouette haussecol	Allodola golagialla	*Eremophila alpestris*
Sand Martin	Uferschwalbe	Hirondelle de rivage	Topino	*Riparia riparia*
Crag Martin	Felsenschwalbe	Hirondelle de rochers	Rondine montana	*Ptyonoprogne rupestris*
Swallow	Rauchschwalbe	Hirondelle rustique	Rondine	*Hirundo rustica*
Red-rumped Swallow	Rötelschwalbe	Hirondelle rousseline	Rondinerossiccia	*Hirundo daurica*
House Martin	Mehlschwalbe	Hirondelle de fenêtre	Balestruccio	*Delichon urbica*
Richard's Pipit	Spornpieper	Pipit de Richard	Calandro maggiore	*Anthus novaeseelandiae*
Tawny Pipit	Brachpieper	Pipit rousseline	Calandro	*Anthus campestris*
Olive-backed Pipit	Waldpieper	Pipit à dos olive	Prispolone indiano	*Anthus hodgsoni*
Tree Pipit	Baumpieper	Pipit des arbres	Prispolone	*Anthus trivialis*
Meadow Pipit	Wiesenpieper	Pipit farlouse	Pispola	*Anthus pratensis*
Red-throated Pipit	Rotkehlpieper	Pipit à gorge rousse	Pispola golarossa	*Anthus cervinus*
Water Pipit	Bergpieper	Pipit spioncelle	Spioncello	*Anthus spinoletta*
Yellow Wagtail	Schafstelze	Bergeronnette printanière	Cutrettola	*Motacilla flava*
Citrine Wagtail	Zitronenstelze	Bergeronnette citrine	Cutrettola testagialla orientale	*Motacilla citreola*
Grey Wagtail	Bergstelze	Bergeronnette des ruisseaux	Ballerina gialla	*Motacilla cinerea*
White Wagtail	Bachstelze	Bergeronnette grise	Ballerina bianca	*Motacilla alba*
Waxwing	Seidenschwanz	Jaseur boréal	Beccofrusone	*Bombycilla garrulus*
Dipper	Wasseramsel	Cincle plongeur	Merlo acquaiolo	*Cinclus cinclus*
Wren	**Zaunkönig**	Troglodyte mignon	Scricciolo	*Troglodytes troglodytes*
Dunnock	Heckenbraunelle	Accenteur mouchet	Passera scopaiola	*Prunella modularis*
Alpine Accentor	Alpenbraunelle	Accenteur alpin	Sordone	*Prunella collaris*
Rufous Bush Robin	Heckensänger	Agrobate roux	Usignolo d'Africa	*Cercotrichas galactotes*
Robin	Rotkehlchen	Rougegorge familier	Pettirosso	*Erithacus rubecula*
Thrush Nightingale	Sprosser	Rossignol progné	Usignolo maggiore	*Luscinia luscinia*
Nightingale	Nachtigall	Rossignol philomèle	Usignolo	*Luscinia megarhynchos*
Bluethroat	Blaukehlchen	Gorgebleue à miroir	Pettazzurro	*Luscinia svecica*
Black Redstart	Hausrotschwanz	Rougequeue noir	Codirosso spazzacamino	*Phoenicurus ochruros*
Redstart	Gartenrotschwanz	Rougequeue à front	Codirosso	*Phoenicurus*

Checklist of the Birds of Switzerland

		blanc		*phoenicurus*
Whinchat	Braunkehlchen	Tarier des prés	Stiaccino	*Saxicola rubetra*
Stonechat	Schwarzkehlchen	Tarier pâtre	Saltimpalo	*Saxicola torquata*
Wheatear	Steinschmätzer	Traquet motteux	Culbianco	*Oenanthe oenanthe*
Desert Wheatear	Wüstensteinschmätzer	Traquet du désert	Culbianco del deserto	*Oenanthe deserti*
Black-eared Wheatear	Mittelmeersteinschmätzer	Traquet oreillard	Monachella	*Oenanthe hispanica*
Rock Thrush	Steinrötel	Monticole de roche	Codirossone	*Monticola saxatilis*
Blue Rock Thrush	Blaumerle	Monticole bleu	Passero solitario	*Monticola solitarius*
Siberian Thrush	Schieferdrossel	Grive de Sibérie	Tordo siberiano	*Zoothera sibirica*
Ring Ouzel	Ringdrossel	Merle à plastron	Merlo dal collare	*Turdus torquatus*
Blackbird	Amsel	Merle noir	Merlo	*Turdus merula*
Fieldfare	Wacholderdrossel	Grive litorne	Cesena	*Turdus pilaris*
Song Thrush	Singdrossel	Grive musicienne	Tordo	*Turdus philomelos*
Redwing	Rotdrossel	Grive mauvis	Tordo sassello	*Turdus iliacus*
Mistle Thrush	Misteldrossel	Grive draine	Tordela	*Turdus viscivorus*
Cetti's Warbler	Seidensänger	Bouscarle de Cetti	Usignolo di fiume	*Cettia cetti*
Fan-tailed Warbler	Cistensänger	Cisticole des joncs	Beccamoschino	*Cisticola juncidis*
Grasshopper Warbler	Feldschwirl	Locustelle tachetée	Forapaglie macchiettato	*Locustella naevia*
River Warbler	Schlagschwirl	Locustelle fluviatile	Salciaiola fluviatile	*Locustella fluviatilis*
Savi's Warbler	Rohrschwirl	Locustelle luscinioïde	Salciaiola	*Locustella luscinioides*
Moustached Warbler	Mariskensänger	Lusciniole à moustaches	Forapaglie castagnolo	*Acrocephalus melanopogon*
Aquatic Warbler	Seggenrohrsänger	Phragmite aquatique	Pagliarolo	*Acrocephalus paludicola*
Blyth's Reed Warbler	Buschrohrsänger	Rousserolle des buissons	Cannaiola di Blyth	*Acrocephalus dumetorum*
Sedge Warbler	Schilfrohrsänger	Phragmite des joncs	Forapaglie	*Acrocephalus schoenobaenus*
Marsh Warbler	Sumpfrohrsänger	Rousserolle verderolle	Cannaiola verdognola	*Acrocephalus palustris*
Reed Warbler	Teichrohrsänger	Rousserolle effarvatte	Cannaiola	*Acrocephalus scirpaceus*
Great Reed Warbler	Drosselrohrsänger	Rousserolle turdoïde	Cannareccione	*Acrocephalus arundinaceus*
Icterine Warbler	Gelbspötter	Hypolaïs ictérine	Canapino maggiore	*Hippolais icterina*
Melodious Warbler	Orpheusspötter	Hypolaïs polyglotte	Canapino	*Hippolais polyglotta*
Dartford Warbler	Provencegrasmücke	Fauvette pitchou	Magnanina	*Sylvia undata*
Spectacled Warbler	Brillengrasmücke	Fauvette à lunettes	Sterpazzola di Sardegna	*Sylvia conspicillata*
Subalpine Warbler	Weissbartgrasmücke	Fauvette passerinette	Sterpazzolina	*Sylvia cantillans*
Sardinian Warbler	Samtkopfgrasmücke	Fauvette mélanocéphale	Occhiocotto	*Sylvia melanocephala*
Orphean Warbler	Orpheusgrasmücke	Fauvette orphée	Bigia grossa	*Sylvia hortensis*
Barred Warbler	Sperbergrasmücke	Fauvette épervière	Bigia padovana	*Sylvia nisoria*
Lesser Whitethroat	Klappergrasmücke	Fauvette babillarde	Bigiarella	*Sylvia curruca*
Whitethroat	Dorngrasmücke	Fauvette grisette	Sterpazzola	*Sylvia communis*
Garden Warbler	Gartengrasmücke	Fauvette des jardins	Beccafino	*Sylvia borin*
Blackcap	Mönchsgrasmücke	Fauvette à tête noire	Capinera	*Sylvia atricapilla*
Yellow-browed Warbler	Gelbbrauenlaubsänger	Pouillot à grands sourcils	Luì forestiero	*Phylloscopus inornatus*
Bonelli's Warbler	Berglaubsänger	Pouillot de Bonelli	Luì bianco	*Phylloscopus bonelli*
Wood Warbler	Waldlaubsänger	Pouillot siffleur	Luì verde	*Phylloscopus sibilatrix*
Chiffchaff	Zilpzalp	Pouillot véloce	Luì piccolo	*Phylloscopus collybita*
Willow Warbler	Fitis	Pouillot fitis	Luì grosso	*Phylloscopus trochilus*
Dusky Warbler	Dunkellaubsänger	Pouillot brun	Luì fuscato	*Phylloscopus fuscatus*
Goldcrest	Wintergoldhähnchen	Roitelet huppé	Regolo	*Regulus regulus*
Firecrest	Sommergoldhähnchen	Roitelet à triple bandeau	Fiorrancino	*Regulus ignicapillus*
Spotted Flycatcher	Grauschnäpper	Gobemouche gris	Pigliamosche	*Muscicapa striata*
Red-breasted Flycatcher	Zwergschnäpper	Gobemouche nain	Pigliamosche pettirosso	*Ficedula parva*
Collared Flycatcher	Halsbandschnäpper	Gobemouche à collier	Balia dal collare	*Ficedula albicollis*
Pied Flycatcher	Trauerschnäpper	Gobemouche noir	Balia nera	*Ficedula hypoleuca*
Bearded Tit	Bartmeise	Panure à moustaches	Basettino	*Panurus biarmicus*
Long-tailed Tit	Schwanzmeise	Mésange à longue queue	Codibugnolo	*Aegithalos caudatus*
Marsh Tit	Sumpfmeise	Mésange nonnette	Cincia bigia	*Parus palustris*
Willow Tit	Mönchsmeise	Mésange boréale	Cincia bigia alpestre	*Parus montanus*
Crested Tit	Haubenmeise	Mésange huppée	Cincia dal ciuffo	*Parus cristatus*
Coal Tit	Tannenmeise	Mésange noire	Cincia mora	*Parus ater*
Blue Tit	Blaumeise	Mésange bleue	Cinciarella	*Parus caeruleus*
Great Tit	*Kohlmeise*	Mésange charbonnière	Cinciallegra	*Parus major*

Checklist of the Birds of Switzerland

Nuthatch	Kleiber	Sittelle torchepot	Picchio muratore	*Sitta europaea*
Wallcreeper	Mauerläufer	Tichodrome échelette	Picchio muraiolo	*Tichodroma muraria*
Treecreeper	Waldbaumläufer	Grimpereau des bois	Rampichino alpestre	*Certhia familiaris*
Short-toed Treecreeper	Gartenbaumläufer	Grimpereau des jardins	Rampichino	*Certhia brachydactyla*
Penduline Tit	Beutelmeise	Rémiz penduline	Pendolino	*Remiz pendulinus*
Golden Oriole	Pirol	Loriot d'Europe	Rigogolo	*Oriolus oriolus*
Red-backed Shrike	Neuntöter	Pie-grièche écorcheur	Averla piccola	*Lanius collurio*
Lesser Grey Shrike	Schwarzstirnwürger	Pie-grièche à poitrine rose	Averla cenerina	*Lanius minor*
Great Grey Shrike	Raubwürger	Pie-grièche grise	Averla maggiore	*Lanius excubitor*
Woodchat Shrike	Rotkopfwürger	Pie-grièche à tête rousse	Averla capirossa	*Lanius senator*
Jay	Eichelhäher	Geai des chênes	Ghiandaia	*Garrulus glandarius*
Magpie	Elster	Pie bavarde	Gazza	*Pica pica*
Nutcracker	Tannenhäher	Cassenoix moucheté	Nocciolaia	*Nucifraga caryocatactes*
Alpine Chough	Alpendohle	Chocard à bec jaune	Gracchio	*Pyrrhocorax graculus*
Chough	Alpenkrähe	Crave à bec rouge	Gracchio corallino	*Pyrrhocorax pyrrhocorax*
Jackdaw	Dohle	Choucas des tours	Taccola	*Corvus monedula*
Rook	Saatkrähe	Corbeau freux	Corvo	*Corvus frugilegus*
Carrion/Hooded Crow	Raben-/Nebelkrähe	Corneille noire/mantelée	Cornacchia nera/grigia	*Corvus corone corone/cornix*
Raven	Kolkrabe	Grand Corbeau	Corvo imperiale	*Corvus corax*
Starling	Star	Etourneau sansonnet	Storno	*Sturnus vulgaris*
Rose-coloured Starling	Rosenstar	Etourneau roselin	Storno roseo	*Sturnus roseus*
House Sparrow	Haussperling	Moineau domestique	Passera europea	*Passer domesticus*
Spanish Sparrow	Italiensperling	Moineau cisalpin	Passera d'Italia	*Passer hispaniolensis italiae*
Tree Sparrow	Feldsperling	Moineau friquet	Passera mattugia	*Passer montanus*
Rock Sparrow	Steinsperling	Moineau soulcie	Passera lagia	*Petronia petronia*
Snow Finch	Schneefink	Niverolle des Alpes	Fringuello alpino	*Montifringilla nivalis*
Chaffinch	Buchfink	Pinson des arbres	Fringuello	*Fringilla coelebs*
Brambling	Bergfink	Pinson du Nord	Peppola	*Fringilla montifringilla*
Serin	Girlitz	Serin cini	Verzellino	*Serinus serinus*
Citril Finch	Zitronengirlitz	Venturon montagnard	Venturone	*Serinus citrinella*
Greenfinch	Grünfink	Verdier d'Europe	Verdone	*Carduelis chloris*
Goldfinch	Distelfink	Chardonneret élégant	Cardellino	*Carduelis carduelis*
Siskin	Erlenzeisig	Tarin des aulnes	Lucherino	*Carduelis spinus*
Linnet	Hänfling	Linotte mélodieuse	Fanello	*Carduelis cannabina*
Twite	Berghänfling	Linotte à bec jaune	Fanello nordico	*Carduelis flavirostris*
Redpoll	Birkenzeisig	Sizerin flammé	Organetto	*Carduelis flammea*
Crossbill	Fichtenkreuzschnabel	Beccroisé des sapins	Crociere	*Loxia curvirostra*
Scarlet Rosefinch	Karmingimpel	Roselin cramoisi	Ciuffolotto scarlatto	*Carpodacus erythrinus*
Pine Grosbeak	Hakengimpel	Durbec des sapins	Ciuffolotto delle pinete	*Pinicola enucleator*
Bullfinch	Gimpel	Bouvreuil pivoine	Ciuffolotto	*Pyrrhula pyrrhula*
Hawfinch	Kernbeisser	Grosbec casse-noyaux	Frosone	*Coccothraustes coccothraustes*
Lapland Bunting	Spornammer	Bruant lapon	Zigolo di Lapponia	*Calcarius lapponicus*
Snow Bunting	Schneeammer	Bruant des neiges	Zigolo delle nevi	*Plectrophenax nivalis*
Pine Bunting	Fichtenammer	Bruant à calotte blanche	Zigolo golarossa	*Emberiza leucocephalos*
Yellowhammer	Goldammer	Bruant jaune	Zigolo giallo	*Emberiza citrinella*
Cirl Bunting	Zaunammer	Bruant zizi	Zigolo nero	*Emberiza cirlus*
Rock Bunting	Zippammer	Bruant fou	Zigolo muciatto	*Emberiza cia*
Ortolan Bunting	Ortolan	Bruant ortolan	Ortolano	*Emberiza hortulana*
Rustic Bunting	Waldammer	Bruant rustique	Zigolo boschereccio	*Emberiza rustica*
Little Bunting	Zwergammer	Bruant nain	Zigolo minore	*Emberiza pusilla*
Reed Bunting	Rohrammer	Bruant des roseaux	Zigolo di palude	*Emberiza schoeniclus*
Red-headed Bunting*	Braunkopfammer	Bruant à tête rousse	Zigolo testa aranciata	*Emberiza bruniceps*
Black-headed Bunting	Kappenammer	Bruant mélanocéphale	Zigolo capinero	*Emberiza melanocephala*
Corn Bunting	Grauammer	Bruant proyer	Strillozzo	*Miliaria calandra*

INDEX OF SPECIES BY SITE NUMBER

Song 5, 6, 11, 20, 29, 37, 41
Tit, Bearded 8, 14, 25, 27, 32
Coal 1, 18, 20, 41
Crested 1, 18, 20, 35, 36, 38, 41
Long-tailed 7, 12, 14, 25, 29, 31, 36, 41, 43, 44
Marsh 44
Penduline 2–4, 7, 8, 14–16, 21, 23–25, 28, 30, 32, 43, 44
Willow 1, 18, 20, 35, 36, 38, 41, 42, 45
Treecreeper 18, 29, 35, 37–42
Short-toed 25, 29, 31
Turnstone 2, 4, 14, 44

Wagtail, Grey 1, 2, 6, 7, 12, 14, 25, 26, 31–33, 35–42
White 6, 25, 31–33
Yellow 2, 4–7, 10, 11, 14, 15, 17, 21, 23, 25, 28, 29, 31, 34, 41, 43–45
Wallcreeper 5, 6, 11, 12, 17, 20, 35–42, 45
Warbler, Aquatic 7, 8, 30, 44
Barred 17, 39
Bonelli's 11–13, 17, 22, 34–42, 44, 45
Cetti's 44
Garden 1, 7, 8, 13, 15, 19, 22, 25, 29, 30, 35, 36, 39, 41–45

Grasshopper 7, 8, 12, 14, 15, 22, 27, 28, 30, 32, 34, 43–45
Great Reed 2, 4, 7, 8, 14, 15, 22, 23, 27, 28, 30, 32, 34, 43, 44
Icterine 15, 22, 23, 32, 34, 36, 44, 45
Marsh 1, 4, 7, 10, 15, 16, 22, 25–30, 32, 34, 44
Melodious 2, 17, 44, 45
Orphean 17
Reed 1–4, 7–9, 14–16, 22, 25–30, 32, 34, 43, 44
Savi's 4, 7, 8, 14, 15, 21, 27, 28, 30, 32
Sedge 7, 8, 15, 22, 25, 28, 30, 43, 44
Subalpine 17, 34
Willow 1, 2, 5, 8, 10, 14, 15, 22, 25, 27, 28, 30, 32, 34, 41, 44
Wood 11, 29, 34, 41, 44
Waxwing 9
Wheatear 2, 4–7, 10, 11, 14, 16–18, 20, 21, 23, 34–38, 40–42, 44, 45
Whimbrel 2, 3, 7, 9, 14, 21, 44
Whinchat 1, 4, 5, 7, 10–12, 14, 15–17, 18, 21–23, 25, 27, 28, 30, 32, 34–39, 41–45
Whitethroat 7, 14, 15, 17, 34, 39, 44, 45
Lesser 6, 14, 15, 17, 20,

25, 28, 32, 35–45
Wigeon 7, 9, 14, 25, 26, 28, 33, 41, 44
Woodcock 1, 11, 14, 17, 20, 24, 29, 35, 41, 44, 45
Woodlark 5, 6, 8, 10, 11, 14, 17, 19, 20, 22, 23, 28, 43
Woodpecker, Black 1, 5, 10–13, 15, 18, 20, 24, 29, 35–41
Great Spotted 10–13, 15, 18, 29, 35
Green 10–13, 15, 16, 18, 25, 29, 31, 33, 35, 36, 38, 40, 41
Grey-headed 12–14, 25, 27, 29
Lesser Spotted 3, 4, 8, 9, 13–17, 25–27, 29, 32, 34, 36, 38
Middle Spotted 13, 25, 28, 29
Three-toed 5, 18, 20, 35–41
Woodpigeon 5, 10, 12–14, 19, 20, 24, 25, 29, 41, 43–45
Wren 45
Wryneck 7, 8, 14–17, 22, 34, 36, 41, 43–45

Yellowhammer 1, 7, 8, 15, 17, 28, 29, 31, 34, 36, 39, 45